To Hokies fans everywhere

CONTENTS

chapter 1
HOKIES TRADITIONS

WHAT IS A HOKIE?

College football fans have been asking that question for more than a century. The origin of the word *hokie* actually has nothing to do with a turkey. The term was first coined by Virginia Tech student O.M. Stull (class of 1896), who used "Hokie" in a spirit yell he composed for a campus-wide contest.

Virginia Tech was founded in 1872 as a land-grant institution in Blacksburg, Virginia, and was originally known as Virginia Agricultural and Mechanical College. In 1896 the Virginia General Assembly changed the school's name to Virginia Agricultural and Mechanical College and Polytechnic Institute. Of course, the revised name was something of a tongue-twister, so Virginia Tech's fans and alumni fondly referred to their school as "V.P.I."

With a new name came a new fight song. V.P.I. held a contest with a $5 prize going to the writer of the best cheer. Stull entered his song, now known as "Old Hokie":

Hokie, Hokie, Hokie, Hy
Techs, Techs, V.P.I.
Sola-Rex, Sola-Rah.
Polytechs-Vir-gin-ia.
Rae, Ri, V.P.I
Team! Team! Team!

After selecting Stull's fight song, V.P.I. formed a committee to adopt new school colors, which would replace the originals hues of black and gray (some V.P.I. fans even thought the black and gray stripes resembled prison uniforms!). The committee selected burnt orange and Chicago maroon because no other college utilized that combination of colors. Burnt orange and Chicago maroon debuted on V.P.I.'s football uniforms against Roanoke College on October 26, 1896.

LANE STADIUM

With a capacity of 66,233, Virginia Tech's Lane Stadium isn't nearly as big as many of the cathedral-like college football stadiums around the country.

But with a rabid and devoted fan base and stands that sit right on top of the action, Lane Stadium provides the Hokies with one of the best home-field advantages in college football. In fact, Rivals.com in 2005 named Lane Stadium the most difficult venue for road teams in the country, saying:

> Lane Stadium in Blacksburg, Virginia, doesn't blow people away by the brute strength of a massive stadium, but with knowledgeable fans that always reach a frenzied pitch at the right time, the Hokies make the most of their numbers. Every good stadium has at least one end zone designed for deafening noise levels, and the enclosed south end zone at Lane Stadium fits the bill perfectly. Holding more than 11,000 screaming Virginia Tech fans, the section amplifies noise and renders audibles useless. That's not to mention the isolation factor. With the nearest major airport nearly 45 minutes away, opponents' fans are never out in force at Lane Stadium.

Virginia Tech cadets fire a cannon on the field prior to the start of a game against Maryland at Lane Stadium. *Photo courtesy of AP Images*

Original construction of Lane Stadium began in April 1964 and was completed four years later. The Hokies didn't even wait for their stadium to be completed; they played their first game there on October 2, 1965. The Hokies defeated William and Mary by a 9–7 score with fans sitting only in the west stands and center section of the east bleachers. Lane Stadium was officially dedicated before Virginia Tech's 22–14 victory over rival Virginia on October 23, 1965.

The first televised game was played at Lane Stadium the next year, when a regional TV audience watched Virginia Tech defeat Florida State 23–21 on October 29, 1966. Lights were added to Lane Stadium in 1982 and were first used in the Hokies' nationally televised 21–14 Thanksgiving Day victory over Virginia on November 25, 1982.

Prior to the 2002 season, Virginia Tech added 11,120 seats in the south end zone to enclose that end of the stadium. The double-deck stadium resembles the Cleveland Browns' "Dawg Pound" section, which gets fans closer to the playing field. Virginia Tech officials replaced the press box in 2004 and also added additional luxury suites, a president's area, private club seating, and new concessions stands.

In 2005 Lane Stadium was given a distinct Virginia Tech touch, with Hokie Stone added to the walls in each of the end zones. When football fans across the country watch the Hokies play on TV, there's no longer a question as to where the game is being played.

Hokies in Their Own Words

BILL ROTH

BROADCASTER, 1988–PRESENT

I remember the first time Mike Tirico, who was a classmate and close friend of mine at Syracuse, and I came to Blacksburg to broadcast a Syracuse–Virginia Tech game. It was 1985.

I bought a hat because I loved the streamlined logo. I really thought Tech was a cool place, even when I was a junior at SU. I wore that hat. I really thought, *This is a cool hat. I know it's not my school. I'm going to Syracuse and wearing a Virginia Tech hat.* There's some irony to it. It's like going to the Eagles concert, and three years later you're playing the drums with Don Henley on stage. It was kind of like that for me getting hired at Tech a couple years later right out of college.

Being from the Pittsburgh area, a lot of my friends came to Tech, and a lot of Pittsburgh-area guys played football at Tech. Dave Braine, who was Tech's athletics director, was from Grove City, Pennsylvania. Dave had gone to North Carolina and played football there, but he was a western Pennsylvania guy.

Tech was the kind of the place I'd always dreamed of. I had the chance to be the voice of one team, which was also my dream after growing up listening to Myron Cope and Jack Fleming and Harry Kalas and Bob Prince and Mike Lange. The fans were really, really passionate. There was an opportunity to be statewide with it. It wasn't about just one town.

Tech reminded me so much of Penn State, where I'd been many times as a kid. The geographic makeup of the alumni base—you know, they're far away—the mission of the university, the academic standing of the school. In talking with [Braine], and later with coach [Frank] Beamer, it was obvious that this could be a Penn State. This could be a school that wins a ton of games, and we could get great affiliates throughout the state and not just a local following, but more of a regional following. Fans were really passionate, and I was 22 years old thinking this was unbelievable.

I was so honored at that point when I came in and met our coaches and our fan base. I went to several Hokie Club meetings and met the people that I still know today. I went on dozens and dozens of those tours and saw how important Tech was to them. They were hungry for a winner because they were so passionate about their school and loud and proud. I got that within the first 10 minutes of my first Hokie Club meeting in Pulaski.

My first game as a Tech employee was that 1988 game at Clemson [Tech lost 40–7]. I remember driving in to Clemson on Route 76, and there were Tigers paws on the asphalt. I was driving by the Tigers car wash, the Tigers diner, and Tigers bank and trust.

I pulled up in front of that stadium, and I remember thinking, *I am doing exactly what I always wanted to do.*

Clemson had an excellent team with Terry Allen, who ended up with the Washington Redskins. He had a big game that day against Tech. It was Will Furrer at quarterback [for Tech]. It was his very first game. That's a tough place to start as a rookie.

I was so blessed to have [Tech network analyst and former Tech football player] Mike [Burnop] with me that day. I'm still blessed to have Mike. He is the perfect analyst. We've become such great friends over the years, but back then, it was our first game together. My thought then was, *Just don't screw it up. Give the time and score. Give the down and distance. Don't mess it up.* I was really lucky to have the job. *Don't screw it up.* That was my only thought.

Over the years, I've really been lucky to have great relationships with our coaches. I've had the opportunity to ask, "Hey, what do you call in this formation?" I still do that today. I'll go to practice, see something new, and ask [offensive coordinator Bryan] Stinespring or Coach Beamer, "What is that?" Or I'll ask one of our basketball coaches, "Hey, why are you all calling that?" A lot of times, I don't know, and I don't want to make it up.

I've worked for great coaches, two awesome athletics directors, and three tremendous presidents who've been very supportive and who like me. That's helpful.

Back in the early days, they let me out during the summer to do Richmond Braves baseball, which was good because I was able to do some stuff during the day throughout the state, and then at night do some games. Richmond, to be quite honest, was a more central location. It worked out fine. I got to do some baseball, which was great. With baseball going to the playoffs and football going to bowl games and basketball going to postseason play then, there was just no downtime.

Once the Big East membership happened, there was more to do in the off-season from a Hokie Club standpoint and with affiliates, so there really wasn't time to do baseball. The Virginia Tech franchise really took off after we got into the Big East and were winning. All of a sudden, after Virginia Tech won the Sugar Bowl [in '95], so many other things popped up. There's videos and there's books and there's twice as many speaking engagements for clients.

As far as my favorite memories are concerned, I remember in '95 we were trailing Virginia in the fourth quarter and had to come back to win that game, and Virginia Tech eventually won the Big East. Back in that day, Tech had to beat Virginia to go to the Sugar Bowl.

[Jim] Druckenmiller led Tech back, and the Hokies scored three touchdowns late in the fourth quarter to win. The Jim Druckenmiller–to–Jermaine Holmes touchdown call is one that's up there for me. It was ad-libbed, not planned—none of them are—but sometimes you feel like you do it justice. It was such a great play. You'd hate to have one of the greatest plays in school history and you blow it. The Nebraska call [in '09 in Tech's 16–15 win; "It's a miracle in Blacksburg! He did it, Mikey! Tyrod did it!"] was also pretty neat for me.

I thought Mike and I were having a great call the night of the national championship game [against Florida State on January 4, 2000] at the Sugar Bowl. That was a very special night. There were going to be some calls from that game, too, because Michael [Vick] was unbelievable. You don't know those calls because we didn't win the game. The Florida State guy got the legendary calls from that game. You've got to win the national championship.

As the years have gone by, it has become apparent that the crowds at Lane Stadium and inside Cassell Coliseum have become the third members of our broadcast team. There's nothing we can say when "Enter Sandman" is blaring and the crowd is roaring, other than maybe a, "Here they come," and stop talking for 30 seconds. For the listener at home, or for a viewer, there's nothing an announcer can say in that moment. You've got to let it go. It's the same in basketball—less is more. That's the big thing I've learned.

Mike and I have never missed a game, but we've had some pretty crazy schedules. I remember two years ago [for basketball] we went back and forth to Puerto Rico twice. It was Friday night before Tech was about to play Duke at Lane Stadium. I was in Blacksburg, but my toothbrush was in a hotel in Puerto Rico. We never checked out of the hotel. On Thanksgiving Day 2010, we broadcast the Oklahoma State–Virginia Tech basketball game in Anaheim. After we did the game, we grabbed a soda, took the red eye to Dulles, drove to Blacksburg overnight, and did the UVA football game.

I still get the sense of just how unique it is to do this job. This is an unbelievable time to be at Virginia Tech. They ask to speak to the students the night before classes start. They bring all the freshmen into Lane Stadium. There's always 4,000 or 5,000 kids in the south end zone, and it's a night with a picnic out there and everything.

One of the things I tell all these kids is, "You're at Virginia Tech, which is a great, great school, and some of the most amazing moments of your life are going to happen here because of when you're here." It's not just that they're here at Tech, it's *when* they're here. The legendary, iconic coach is here right now. The greatest athletic events are happening now. The people you see on campus and around town are going to have streets and buildings and statues in their honor. This is the golden era, and that's what neat about it.

What makes Virginia Tech so unique and so special is the relationship between the students and the alumni of the school. It is unique to other schools, and I think the reason is because for so many Hokies, the greatest moment of your life occurred while you were in school here—your greatest academic success, you met your husband or wife here, you made your greatest friends here, you developed emotionally and academically here. The most fun and the greatest moments of success and achievement happened here with all your friends.

The worst day of your life happened here, too—April 16 [the campus shootings that took the lives of 32 students in 2007]—and it was with those same people. That same closeness and cohesiveness was present. We saw how the university reacted and the way the students got together and how the alumni reacted to that event.

It was brutal to go through that, but the Hokie Nation was so strong. It was like a model of how to handle something like that. I think now you look back on it, and the tightness remains. When the highest highs and the lowest lows are with the same group or the same family, there's a tremendous bond there. The sum of all that is what makes us Hokies.

Bill Roth graduated from Syracuse University in 1987 with a degree in broadcast journalism. Now in his 23rd season as the lead play-by-play announcer of Virginia Tech football and basketball, he also serves as the host of the weekly radio shows featuring Tech head coaches Frank Beamer and Seth Greenberg. Roth was inducted into the Richmond Hokie Club Hall of Fame in 2008.

"ENTER SANDMAN"

Ohio State's marching band dots the *i*. Tennessee's football team runs through the *T*. Clemson's football players touch Howard's Rock before running into Death Valley.

Many college football teams have pregame traditions, and Virginia Tech is no different. With Metallica's "Enter Sandman" blaring over Lane Stadium's speakers, Virginia Tech fans start bouncing up and down before the Hokies run onto the field. If that doesn't get fans' goose bumps rising, they might want to check themselves for a pulse.

Virginia Tech's pregame tradition is relatively new; it started after the school erected a new scoreboard with a giant video screen before the 2000 season. The marketing department wanted to produce an entrance video for the Hokies. A handful of songs were considered, including Guns N' Roses' "Welcome to the Jungle" and the Alan Parsons Project's "Sirius." But Virginia Tech officials settled on Metallica's eclectic hit.

"Enter Sandman" made its debut at Lane Stadium before the 2000 opener against Georgia Tech, which was canceled shortly after kickoff because of thunderstorms. Before a particularly chilly night game in 2001, members of Virginia Tech's marching band, the Marching Virginians, started jumping up and down during the song. Soon, everyone in the stadium copied them. A Virginia Tech tradition was born.

Before the Hokies upset No. 23 Maryland 23–13 at Lane Stadium on November 6, 2008, ESPN analyst Chris Fowler aptly summarized Virginia Tech's "Enter Sandman" entrance. "Enter night. Enter Hokies," Fowler said. "One of the most dramatic and frenzied entrances in college football. This is Thursday night, where the Hokies excel. This is an entrance unlike any other in college football."

LUNCH PAIL

Virginia Tech's famed "Lunch Pail" was a concept designed by longtime Hokies defensive coordinator Bud Foster. The battered coal miner's lunch pail became a trademark for the Hokies' black-and-blue defense.

Pulling from his roots in the coal-mining region of Illinois, Foster wanted to instill a blue-collar work ethic in his players. The battered lunch pail features the word "WIN" on the front, which symbolizes Foster's strategy for succeeding on defense and in life.

"W-I-N: What's Important Now," Foster says. "To make change; to influence; to use this moment to be better than the last; to achieve greatness in all aspects of your life. Win at home. Win at school. Win at business. Win at life."

In the past, the lunch pail was filled with the defense's mission statement, keys to success and season goals. Over time, players began adding pieces of turf from road victories.

Foster has traditionally awarded the lunch pail to the team's defensive MVP from the previous week's game. During his junior season in 2004, defensive end Darryl Tapp staked claim to the pail and never gave it back. Tapp wasn't going to surrender the pail until someone else outworked him for it. No one ever did. Tapp even kept the pail with him after he was drafted by the Seattle Seahawks.

"What the lunch pail is about is going out and earning success and deserving victory, whatever it is, whether it's on the field or off the field," said Foster, who was named Virginia Tech's defensive coordinator in 1995.

Following the horrific April 16, 2007, shooting on the Virginia Tech campus, the lunch pail carried the names of 32 victims into Lane Stadium. The names were listed on a laminated card, with a maroon ribbon in the middle. Underneath the victims' names was the motto the Hokie Nation embraced as it tried to recover from the worst school shooting spree in U.S. history: "We will remember. We will prevail. We are Virginia Tech."

HOKIE STONE

The stone exterior of buildings on the Virginia Tech campus might look like ordinary limestone to visitors, but anyone who has attended the school or cheered for the Hokies knows its official name is "Hokie Stone."

Originally known as "our native stone," Hokie Stone is a dolomite limestone named for the school's Hokie mascot. While Hokie Stone is actually limestone, the color of the stones varies from building to building, depending on the rock's content and color variations caused by environmental changes.

Virginia Tech's campus buildings were originally finished with bricks, but university officials worried they too closely resembled cotton mills and shoe factories of the late 19th and early 20th centuries. Virginia Tech's fifth president, Joseph D. Eggleston (1913–1919), ordered every new building on campus to be finished with limestone blocks.

On older buildings on the Virginia Tech campus, such as Holden Hall, the Hokie Stone is completely gray. Newer buildings feature Hokie Stone with a variety of colors due to impurities. The older pinkish Hokie Stone was formed during an era when the region faced a desert-like climate that had a bleaching effect on rocks. Darker gray and black colors were formed during wetter conditions.

Nearly 80 percent of the Hokie Stone included in campus construction is obtained from a 40-acre quarry owned by Virginia Tech, which has been in operation since the 1950s. The school

Quarterback Tyrod Taylor throws a pass in a 2010 game with Lane Stadium's Hokie Stone in the background. *Photo courtesy of AP Images*

purchases the remaining 20 percent of stone used in construction from a nearby farm to ensure variations in color. University employees use black powder to dislodge the stone into block sizes required for construction projects and finish the blocks by hand using chisels and hammers. Virginia Tech's quarry operation produces about 55 tons of Hokie Stone per week. A single ton will cover about 35 square feet of a building.

Virginia Tech's football players touch a block of Hokie Stone while leaving the tunnel to run into Lane Stadium before every game.

TWO BANDS

Virginia Tech is one of a handful of schools in the country with two marching bands. The Highty Tighties are the regimental band of the Virginia Tech Corps of Cadets, which has sounded its horns and beat its drums for more than a century. The Marching Virginians came along much later and draw from the school's general student body.

Known as "the Spirit of Tech," the Marching Virginians were formed in 1974 and include students from all walks of campus life. The band was formed at the behest of Virginia Tech president T. Marshall Hahn Jr., who wanted an all-university marching band representing the Hokies at football games and other events. None of the students who participate in the marching band are awarded scholarships; competitive auditions are open to all students. The Marching Virginians are considerably larger, with about 300 or more members each season.

The Marching Virginians are far less formal than the Highty Tighties. Entering Lane Stadium before football games, band members fall out of rank and touch their hands to the Hokie Stone at the entrance of the field. Between the third and fourth quarters of football games, the band's tuba section leads fans through their own version of "Hokie Pokie."

The Highty Tighties were first formed during the 1892–1893 school session, with some members of the band having served in the Spanish-American War. The Highty Tighties have marched in presidential inaugural parades 11 times, first for President Woodrow Wilson in 1917 and most recently for President George W. Bush in 2005.

Formally known as the Virginia Tech Regimental Band or V.P.I. Cadet Band, the band earned the moniker "Highty Tighties" in one of two ways, according to legend. One legend claims it was

Members of the Virginia Tech Corps of Cadets Highty Tighties band perform prior to the start of the 2010 Virginia–Virginia Tech game. *Photo courtesy of AP Images*

coined while cadets were marching in a parade honoring Field Marshall Ferdinand Foch of France in 1921. During the parade, a drum major attempted a mace toss as he marched past the reviewing stand. Wind blew the mace, and it fell to the ground. Undisturbed, the drum major caught the mace off one bounce, while still rendering a proper salute to the reviewing officer. According to legend, Foch allegedly yelled, "hoity-toity," which was his way of describing a show off.

Another local legend claims the name Highty Tighties is derived from a cheer the band cried while it was housed in Lane Hall. While waiting for meals, each unit would give the following cheer while waiting in the stairwell:

Highty tighty, Christ Almighty, who the hell are we?
Riff ramm, goddamn, we're from Division E!

chapter 2

GREATEST HOKIES TEAMS

1905

Hunter Carpenter was Virginia Tech's first great player, and he wasn't even known to opposing coaches and fans by his real name. Carpenter first played for the Hokies under the alias "Walter Brown" because his father had forbidden him to play the rugged sport of football. Not until Carpenter's father saw him play against VMI in 1900 did he give his son permission to play the sport.

In 1903 Carpenter helped defeat Navy 11–0, kicking a 46-yard field goal. According to published reports, he played most of the game without a jersey or stockings because they had been ripped from his body. Carpenter played at North Carolina in 1904, before returning to Blacksburg for the 1905 season.

In 1905 Carpenter helped Virginia Polytechnic Institute finish the season with a 9–1 record, including impressive victories over Army, North Carolina, South Carolina, and Virginia. Carpenter scored 82 points, including five touchdowns in the South Carolina game, and helped his team outscore its opponents by a combined total of 305–24. VPI's only loss came against Navy by a 12–6 score.

Carpenter was never named to an All-America team because Walter Camp vowed he would never name a player he hadn't seen play to the team. Carpenter was inducted into the College Football Hall of Fame in 1957.

1916

The 1916 Hokies were led by Monk Younger, who grew up in Lynchburg, Virginia, and played his freshman season at Davidson College in North Carolina. After transferring to Virginia Tech in 1916, Younger helped guide the Hokies to a 7–2 record and the school's first South Atlantic Conference championship under coach Jack Ingersoll.

After the Hokies lost to Yale 19–0 in the fourth game of the 1916 season, Younger was personally congratulated by legendary Yale coach Walter Camp for his play against the Bulldogs. Camp later referred to Younger as the "Southern Panther." The Hokies' only other loss in 1916 came against West Virginia by a 20–0 score. Virginia Tech's defense posted shutouts in five of nine games, including a 40–0 rout of N.C. State and 52–0 shutout of Wake Forest.

1918

Virginia Tech's first undefeated season came in 1918, when America's attention was focused on World War I. Coach Charlie Bernier led the Hokies to a 7–0 finish and Southern Atlantic Conference championship. VPI outscored its seven opponents by a combined score of 152–13 (the Belmont Athletic Club and Camp Humphreys were among the opponents, and a scheduled game against 1917 national champion Georgia Tech was canceled because of war considerations).

VPI played a limited schedule because the War Department prohibited teams from traveling during certain times. A flu outbreak in Blacksburg also drastically reduced the size of the Hokies' roster.

The Hokies' best player was Henry L. Crisp, a North Carolina native who lost his right hand in a farming accident at age 12. He still managed to do most of VPI's running and kicking in 1918. Crisp was perhaps best known for bloodying opponent's faces with his leather-covered stump of a right arm, according to news reports.

1932

The 1932 Hokies finished 8–1 under coach Henry Redd and came within one game of winning the school's first Southern Conference championship. The Gobblers, another nickname used at the time, upset Georgia in Athens, Georgia, by a 7–6 score, after team captain Bill Grinus blocked the Bulldogs' point-after kick that would have tied the score. Virginia Tech also defeated Kentucky by a 7–0 score in Blacksburg.

After starting with a 6–0 record, Virginia Tech had a chance to win the Southern Conference championship. But the Gobblers had to travel to Alabama to play the Crimson Tide for their homecoming game. More than 11,000 fans, the second-largest crowd to ever watch a game at Alabama's Denny Stadium, saw Tech take a 6–0 lead on the Crimson Tide. But Alabama eventually wore down the Hokies and walked out with a 9–6 victory.

Tech defeated Virginia and Virginia Military Institute in its final two games to finish 8–1.

1954

Led by halfback Dickie Beard, who earned the moniker the "Cumberland Flash" because of his quickness, the 1954 Virginia Tech team finished 8–0–1 under coach Frank Moseley. The Hokies narrowly missed out on winning the school's first Southern Conference championship, which was claimed by West Virginia and All-America linebacker Sam Huff.

Beard wasn't the Hokies' only fast running back. Halfbacks Billy Anderson, Leo Burke, and Howie Wright were each capable runners. Beard led the Southern Conference in rushing with 647 yards in 1954 and was named the Associated Press Athlete of the Year in Virginia.

Senior Johnny Dean and sophomore Billy Cranwell were the team's quarterbacks, and Don Divers was a two-way star. Divers intercepted two passes and returned them for touchdowns in Virginia Tech's 46–9 victory over Virginia Military Institute, a feat that wouldn't be duplicated by another Hokies player until Ashley Lee did it against Vanderbilt in 1983.

Virginia Tech upset Clemson 18–7 on the road and also defeated N.C. State 30–21 and Virginia 6–0. Tech's only blemish was a 7–7 tie against William and Mary in the Hokies' homecoming game. Virginia Tech had 366 yards of offense in the game, but was undone by miscues and mistakes.

Hokies in Their Own Words

LEO BURKE

RUNNING BACK, 1952–1955

I was born and raised in Hagerstown, Maryland, and was fortunate enough to play for a high school football coach named Mel Henry, who had played and coached at Virginia Tech. Early in my career, when I was a sophomore in high school, he invited me to go along on a recruiting trip to Virginia Tech with some older boys from our team. I went along and fell in love with the campus.

Not long after that, I met a gal from a nearby town and we fell deeply in love. We had plans to get married when she graduated from high school, but there were several schools recruiting me at the time that had rules against their student-athletes being married, such as the U.S. Military Academy at West Point, the University of Maryland, and Notre Dame. Those schools discouraged you from getting married. However, the athletics director and football coach at Virginia Tech had no such rules. So that was one of the leading reasons that I decided to go to Virginia Tech.

I went to Virginia Tech as a three-sport athlete in football, baseball, and basketball. I only played two years of basketball, during my freshman and sophomore seasons, because, as you can realize, the burden on the academics was so great that I just couldn't keep up with things. I had to give up one sport. I was on a football scholarship and, at the time, had aspirations of pursuing a career in professional baseball, so basketball was the odd sport out.

The year before I went to Virginia Tech in 1952, there was a rule in place that prohibited freshmen from playing on the varsity teams. But before the 1952 season, they changed that rule, and I was fortunate enough to play varsity football, baseball, and basketball as a freshman at Virginia Tech.

I played quite a bit as a freshman on the football team, and what I remember most was the difference of the caliber of football players at the college level. A very big thing was the adjustment to college life. We had an awful lot of boys whom Coach Frank Moseley and his staff had recruited who were outstanding athletes. But they just couldn't cope with the military regiment and demands that he put on his football players. So every day, in the middle of the night, there would be one or two players who would decide that they just weren't cut out for it, so they packed their bags and off they went. A lot of them were a lot better athletes than I was.

I don't think there was anyone, including the wives at the time, who questioned who was in charge at Virginia Tech. Coach Moseley was in complete control of our lives, really, and we didn't mind because we bought into the system. We knew if we wanted to develop as athletes and people that he had a good philosophy. I was one year older than my wife, so I went to Virginia Tech in 1952 while she was completing her senior year in high school. Then, upon her graduation, she and I got married that summer, and she moved to Blacksburg with me. Judy and I have been together for 51 years now. She deserves the recognition.

In 1954 I was playing fullback when I sustained a back injury and was out for four or five games, missing a good part of the season. Our quarterback, Johnny Dean, broke his leg that season. Billy Cranwell replaced him at quarterback, and Don Divers came in and took my position at fullback. I came back near the end of the 1954 season.

I know it was a great bunch of individuals. We had great togetherness, and I think that was fostered by Coach Moseley and his philosophy. I had the utmost respect for Coach Moseley. I think he instilled a little bit of fear in anybody who played for him. He was a strict disciplinarian and he demanded a lot from you, but I got along very well with him. I understood what it was all about. My high school coach coached similarly, and I just think he was a wonderful coach and a wonderful guy. He was hard, and there were several times that we said and did things behind his back that we didn't have the nerve to do in front of him. But after we were finished, when the season was over, we realized what had to be done to be successful, and he sure did it.

Back in 1953 there were some great athletes here prior to us. They didn't have the success, but they had the ability and apparently didn't have the leadership or determination to go on. But when Moseley came here, those things started changing. I would have liked to have seen what would have happened if the boys prior to us had the opportunity to play for him. Coach Moseley deserves all the credit, in my estimation, in turning the program around.

When I graduated in 1956, I took a job with the telephone company in Virginia. I wanted to play baseball, but at the time they had a rule in professional baseball that if a team signed an individual to a major league contract, they had to carry him on the major league roster for two years. I had talked to Paul Richards, who was the manager and general manager of the Baltimore Orioles, and I told him, "I want desperately to play, but I want a bonus to play." If the bonus exceeded $4,000, they had to sign you to a major league contract and retain you on the big-league roster.

But Richards told me that they had something like seven players they were required to carry on the major league roster. He said, "We'd like to give you whatever you want as far as a bonus, but we just can't afford to do that because we have no room. We already have too many guys sitting on the bench and watching and learning." They were playing occasionally but weren't starting and taking up room on the roster. So I told Richards I was going to get into the business world, so I took a job with the telephone company and worked for them that year.

Finally, when it got close to spring training the following year, the more I thought about it, the more I realized this opportunity comes once in a lifetime. I went and talked to my wife and decided that we would go ahead and sign with the Orioles the next year in 1957. I was awed by the opportunity to play major league baseball. I wasn't sure I had the ability to play on the major league level, but apparently someone thought I did. To watch and be with and play with players during that era, probably the greatest players to ever play major league baseball, was absolutely astounding. I can sit down and name players who are Hall of Famers whom I either played with or played against, and it was just awesome.

Running back Leo Burke also played basketball and baseball for the Hokies. He played professional baseball until retiring in 1965.

I played with Bob Gibson, Stan Musial, Lou Brock, and Curt Flood when I played with the Cardinals. I'll always remember

Musial's funny stance. Back in those days, snuff was not popular, but a lot of major league players chewed tobacco. I started dipping snuff, and I remember the day when Musial gave me the nickname "Snuffy" because I was doing snuff. When I finished my career, I was fortunate to play with guys like Ernie Banks, Ron Santo, and Billy Williams.

I played with Jim Fregosi and Chuck Tanner, who later became major league managers, when I was with the Los Angeles Angels for two seasons. Jim and I played in the minor leagues together, and Chuck and I were roommates. We were in Denver playing one day, and after the game, we had gone to get something to eat and were standing on the corner to catch a taxi. I very vividly remember Chuck telling me, "Roomie, we're at the end of our careers now, and if you get a job in the major leagues as a manager, you call me to be your coach and I'll do the same." Well, he was the fortunate one, and I was the one left holding the bag. Years later, my daughter was married in a small town in Pennsylvania where Chuck lives, and we had the reception at his restaurant.

I did play professional baseball for nine years, but only three seasons in the major leagues. They weren't full seasons. I started at the beginning of the season, and was optioned out. I was called up at the end of the season on several occasions, and then was optioned out. I played outfield at Virginia Tech and was signed as an outfielder, but then I was optioned to Miami of the International League during the second season I played professionally. Pepper Martin was the manager of the Miami team, and our second baseman there sustained a season-ending knee injury. So Pepper converted me to the infield and made an infielder out of me. In the majors, I played every position but pitcher. I even caught a couple of games in emergency situations.

The closest I ever got to a pennant chase was when I was with the Angels. They optioned me out at the beginning of the 1962 season to Dallas–Fort Worth, Texas. I had a great season there, and they called me up at the end of the season. That was the year after the league had expanded, and two new teams were added. I was drafted with a bunch of other players from the Orioles organization by the Angels. The Angels called me up at the end of the 1962 season, and we were involved in a title chase there. We blew it at the end. We were only four or five games behind the New York Yankees and had a series at New York with a chance to cut into it, but we gave a few games away. We finished third in the standings.

I did play most of the season in 1964 and part of the following year with the Chicago Cubs. When they decided to option me out, I decided to retire.

I lived in Hagerstown for most of my life, but two years ago, I relocated to Blacksburg, primarily because of my close association with a lot of the people in the area. I still have a lot of friends here and still have teammates here whom I travel with regularly: Dickie Beard, Jack Prater, Terry Strock, and George Preas, just to name a few. I think that emphasizes the fact that to be a team, you really have to have respect and understanding and a close association with your teammates. We've maintained that over the years. It was so great back then that it continued throughout our lives. I think every one of us breathes Virginia Tech and probably bleeds maroon and orange.

It just makes me so proud to be a Hokie. Of course, the success we've had in recent years in our athletics program, especially with the football program, really emphasizes that. I don't take any credit for the success we've had, but it makes me proud to know I was a part of it.

Leo Burke was a standout running back and fullback for the Hokies from 1952 to 1955. He also played on Virginia Tech's basketball team in 1952 and 1953, and played four seasons on the school's baseball team, leading the Hokies to the 1954 NCAA tournament. Burke signed a professional baseball contract with the Baltimore Orioles in 1957 and played parts of seven seasons in the major leagues before retiring in 1965. He is retired and lives with his wife, Judy, near Blacksburg, Virginia.

Hokies in Their Own Words
JACK PRATER
CENTER/LINEBACKER, 1950–1951, 1954–1955

I was born in Atlanta and lived in Georgia until my family moved to Miami, so my older brother could become a jockey. My brother, David, weighed about 109 pounds. He got a job exercising horses and, because of his size, he was a perfect specimen to become a jockey. He rode in the Kentucky Derby and also was a leading rider in Canada.

I grew up in Miami and attended Edison High School. They hired my coach, Lee McKinney, to coach the defensive line at Virginia Tech. I stayed in Miami for my senior season, and he sent for me the next year. He was my boss, so there wasn't much recruiting involved. I had a hard time finding Blacksburg. My sister was the secretary to the president of National Airlines, so she got me a plane ticket to go to Virginia Tech. I flew to Charlotte and caught a Greyhound bus to Blacksburg.

I got to Virginia Tech in the middle of the night, and there wasn't a human being in sight. The next thing I knew, a car came driving up the hill, and it was my coach. He took me down to the gym and had a room for me there. I had no idea where I was or what the place looked like because it was dark. I thought it was such a small town that there couldn't be a college around there anywhere. But it was an experience, I'll tell you that.

I got to Virginia Tech in the fall of 1950, and Robert McNeish was the coach of the varsity team. He quit midway through the season, and they moved the coach of my freshman team, Allan Learned, up to the varsity as interim coach. The freshman team was undefeated in 1950, and the varsity team didn't win a game. It was a right difficult time. I was playing center and linebacker, and we played both ways all the way through my senior year.

When they hired Coach Frank Moseley that winter, it was quite an experience because a lot of people left. They couldn't adjust to the change and just left. A lot of the players were veterans who had been in the military, and they weren't willing to pay that price. We had some guys from Georgia and Florida and quite a few Virginia boys. We probably had 32 freshmen who came in with me and about eight or nine of them quit when Moseley got there.

We went 2–8 during my sophomore season in 1951. They went 0–10 during my freshman year, so we got a little bit better and better. Moseley had a couple of good recruiting years and brought some good football players in there. I played for Coach Moseley and coached for him and raised money for him. He was a real strong man. He was a Bear Bryant figure. When he made up his mind, there was no changing it. He was just a really strong person. He was respected and feared at the same time. He was a good man, don't get me wrong—if you needed help, he would help you. But when you were on the football field, it was strictly business. He's probably the best disciplinarian Virginia Tech ever had.

After the 1951 season, my father had a stroke and I had to drop out of school and went home to be with him. Of course, that made me eligible for the military draft. Sure enough, I got a letter from the president and was called into the Army about a month later. I had qualified to go to Officer Candidates School, so when I got to Fort Jackson, South Carolina, I had to take 16 weeks of heavy infantry training. I got there in June 1952, and football season came along in August. I had just finished basic training and got permission to go out for the post football team. I lucked out and made the team. They had had a world championship football team the year before, but most of those guys had gotten out of the Army by the time I got there.

They put together another good football team. Our first game was against the Philadelphia Eagles in Philadelphia, and I lined up as a defensive end. I was a sophomore in college going up against a professional football team. But most all of the guys I played with in the Army were from the Southeastern Conference. There weren't many Southern Conference players who were on our football team. The next year, we had a civilian coach, Beattie Feathers, who had just left North Carolina State, and he put together an undefeated team. We were national service champions. I played my regular positions, center and linebacker, on that team. It was a great experience for me and a growing-up period, too. Everybody on that Army football team tried to recruit me to their schools: Tennessee, Miami, and Florida State.

Alf Satterfield, one of the Virginia Tech coaches, found out I was getting out of the service. Coach Feathers had run into him and told him he had a Virginia Tech football player on the Army team. Alf called me and asked me to come up to Blacksburg to visit, he wanted to talk to me about coming back to school. I had a weekend off from the Army, so I just hitchhiked up to Blacksburg.

Jack Prater was a starting center and linebacker for Virginia Tech during three seasons and later became an assistant under Hokies coaches Frank Moseley and Jerry Claiborne.

I thought the world of Alf Satterfield and thought he was my real coach. He held everything together at Virginia Tech, he really did, because it was tough times. We talked a long time, and he told me it was different than what it was before. I believed him and had a lot of friends on the football team, so I wasn't coming into a strange place. I agreed to come back and went home and told my folks. I went back up to Tech and watched the spring game in 1954 and made my commitment then.

That 1954 team was probably the most unified bunch of guys that has ever been around. We were more like brothers than any other bunch of guys I've ever been associated with. Winning was everything to all of them and it meant that practice was going to be hard and we were going to get better. Moseley taught us that winning was everything, and not many coaches can do that, even today. He did a good job. Everybody who played for him respected him and liked him, and he was probably the toughest coach I've ever been around.

We went 8–0–1 during the 1954 season and should have won the Southern Conference, but we didn't play West Virginia. We were going to the Sun Bowl, but the Virginia Tech faculty voted not to go because they had lost some money the last time they'd gone and didn't want to lose money again. We were the second choice of the Gator Bowl in Jacksonville, Florida, but they ended up taking Auburn instead and had two Southeastern Conference teams in the game. It was a strange thing. Most of the players looked at each other and thought they were crazy. It was really disappointing.

We were a little bit disappointed by our senior season in 1955 because we really felt we were going to have a great season. We lost to Wake Forest in the first game and finished 6–3–1. We'd graduated a lot of players from the year before and didn't have the same unity. Back then, Richmond and Virginia Military Institute had good football teams. We beat Florida State 24–20, and I intercepted a pass and returned it 73 yards. We scored a touchdown right after that, and Dickie Beard ran it in. He had the easy route.

As soon as I finished school, I went back to Florida and was an assistant coach at my high school for a couple of years. I was a teacher at the school and really enjoyed it. I had married a girl from Blacksburg, and we were living in Miami at the time, but we went up to Virginia Tech during the summer to see her family. I went over to see Moseley, and he talked me into coming back as an assistant coach at Virginia Tech.

I worked at William and Mary, and we had some good years there. I worked for Jerry Claiborne at Virginia Tech and then was hired by the University of Miami as the offensive line coach. I had a really exceptional time recruiting at Miami because I was a Florida boy and knew a lot of people in the area. I recruited one of the greatest football players of all-time, Ted Hendricks, who was a sensational defensive end at Miami. That sort of put me on the map because he was one of the finest players I had seen in my life. He could do more things than anybody I'd ever seen. I recruited Tommy Francisco, who was a running back at Virginia Tech under Claiborne, and I thought he was the best high school football player to ever come out of Virginia.

It's been a fun life all the way around, and I've enjoyed it. I've had pretty good tours as a coach, but Blacksburg became my home, and we've really enjoyed living there. I really respect the principles Virginia Tech people have and the system that they have. They always strive to be ahead and they always strive to be the best. That's the feeling all over campus.

Jack Prater, 75, was a starting center and linebacker for Virginia Tech during three seasons: 1951, 1954, and 1955. He later became an assistant under Virginia Tech coaches Frank Moseley and Jerry Claiborne and was a longtime fund-raiser for the Virginia Tech athletics department. He is retired and lives in Blacksburg, Virginia.

1963

Led by bruising fullback Sonny Lutz and speedy quarterback Bob Schweickert, who were affectionately known as "Mr. Inside" and "Mr. Outside," respectively, Virginia Tech won its first Southern Conference championship by finishing 8–2 in 1963 under coach Jerry Claiborne.

After losing to Kentucky 33–14 in the opener, Virginia Tech won its next six games, including a 31–23 upset of nationally ranked Florida State in Tallahassee, Florida. Newt Green blocked an FSU punt in the game, and Jake Adams caught the ball in the air and returned it 38 yards for a touchdown to help Tech seal its victory.

The Hokies shut out rival Virginia by a 10–0 score and defeated West Virginia 28–3 on the road. Virginia Tech's only other defeat was a 13–7 loss at North Carolina State.

Schweickert was named Southern Conference Player of the Year after running for 839 yards and setting a conference record with 1,526 yards of offense. Lutz scored 10 touchdowns and was named All–Southern Conference.

Hokies in Their Own Words

BOB SCHWEICKERT

QUARTERBACK, 1961–1964

I had about 24 colleges that had offered me scholarships. Jerry Claiborne, of course, was the head coach at the time, and John Shelton had been assigned to me to see if they could get me to come to Tech. It was a unique way that it finally transpired. They came to my home after I visited Virginia Tech, which I loved. My brother was two years ahead of me and had gone to Tech, so I knew a little bit about it. I also knew there was an opportunity in my sophomore year, when they would be looking for a quarterback. My freshman year, there would be a senior quarterback, but Terry Strock would be leaving, and they'd be looking for someone.

They came to my home, and my father had left home when I was 12, so my mother was there with Coach Claiborne and Coach Shelton. They pulled a very unique move on me as an 18-year-old. They put a contract out on the table, put a pen on top of it, and then left. They were gone for a while so that I could make my decision as to what I was going to do: either sign it or not sign it. You can imagine, you're sitting there with this major decision of your life, and there's no one to talk to. Probably the easiest thing to do was to sign it rather than not sign it. I thought it was a very classic move that they pulled. So I signed it, and they were back in probably 45 minutes or so, and of course, they were very happy to see the signature there. It was a bit of a relief to me also because, during that time, I had a lot of people pulling and pushing at me. It was good to finally have the decision made and to finally know where I was going to be.

I had other scholarship offers from North Carolina, South Carolina, and Maryland. But as far as considering other schools, I guess my heart was in Virginia. I really didn't want to leave Virginia. I felt that if we were raised there and went to school at Midlothian High School, I wanted to play at a Virginia college. The University of Virginia was not part of the equation. Virginia Military Institute said I was too small. Most of the interest was from out-of-state colleges: Cincinnati, Wake Forest, and a lot of different schools. But my heart was really in Virginia, so that made it simpler for me that I would want to stay and play for my own state.

I never threw a drop-back pass in my life. We didn't have pee wee football when I was a kid because the community I grew up in was much too small. So I started playing in the eighth grade. Of course, on the playground I was always running and throwing the football. So it was kind of a natural for me. My coaches probably saw I could run, so they designed offenses around the run, then with the option of the pass. In high school, I never threw a drop-back pass. Of course, with Jerry Claiborne, we never had a drop-back pass, even in our game plan. I was always a roll-out, running, throwing quarterback.

I started my college career on the freshman team in 1961. It was interesting because Virginia Tech had a quarterback named Darrell "Peaches" Page from Georgia, who was a [high school] All-American. When I got there, they had pretty much assigned the freshman quarterback job to him, and I guess I was going to be sitting on the bench, which was not something exciting. I had played quarterback as a freshman in high school on the varsity team because we had just started football at my high school the year before. Before I got to Virginia Tech, I had always played, and had always played 60 minutes, because I was also a free safety on defense, was our punter, kicked the extra points, and did the kicking off.

But Darrell was the starting quarterback on the freshman team, and what we did in those days was let the freshmen be the guinea pigs for the varsity. What I did was prepare the varsity for the team they were going to play. I was the quarterback in practices running the other team's offenses for our defense to look at. Darrell was the quarterback, so I didn't even know if I was going to get an opportunity in the games. Finally, during our freshman season, we had lost a couple of games where they gave me the job, and we won the next three games. That's when they had a feeling,

I guess, that I might be able to play quarterback for the varsity team during my sophomore season.

During the preseason before my sophomore year in 1962, we were having a scrimmage game, and I rolled out and was running with the football. Somebody grabbed me and had me standing straight up, and two of my players came from opposite directions and absolutely crushed me in the middle. My left shoulder socket split, which was unique. I've never heard of that. I've heard of broken collarbones, but the socket actually split. So I had to wait it out, and there is nothing you can do for a broken socket. You can't cast it; you can only put it in a sling and hope that it will heal. Every time the ball moved inside the socket, it was a very, very painful thing. But what I did was I went in the shower every night and just about scorched my skin with the hot water. I'd lift my arm and move my arm around, and they said that really kept calcium from forming on the joint where it was split. Today, I still don't have pain in my left shoulder.

I came back for the Florida State game, the seventh game in the 1962 season, and played the last four games. I guess Tulane was the breakout game. We'd lost to Florida State 20–7 in Tallahassee, and with an injured shoulder like that, it's going to take a number of hits to determine whether you're going to be able to take a blow. So the first time out was a bit nerve-racking for me, but I was fine after that. I think today I would have been redshirted, but they needed a quarterback so badly that they just kept me around until I was ready. I should have been redshirted and come back the next year and played 10 games. But that's the way they did it, and that's the way the Good Lord had it planned.

When I go back over my career and remember certain things, I'll just never forget the Tulane game in 1962. Here I was, 19 years old and playing at Tulane, which was a big stadium in New

Orleans. We were kind of underdogs everywhere we went, and those thoughts do go through your mind—*If I can score a touchdown here, we can win the game and beat Tulane.* I can remember the play right now.

It was late in the game, and we were trailing. I was running down the sideline. My muscles started to burn, and I felt like I wasn't going anywhere. I thought I was going to get run down by the defenders coming to tackle me. It was so exciting that, as I was running down the field, tears were just streaming down my face. It sounds strange, but it's true. It was an emotional time for a young fellow who was finally getting his opportunity and was running 74 yards for a touchdown. So when I finally got to the end zone, I leaped up in the air because I was so happy to cross the goal line. But when I came down, I missed my feet. You can imagine what that looked like. I went down on my face, basically. But I was excited about it, and we did win the game.

Some people have said that that was kind of the start of the two-and-a-half years of success. The next season we won eight games and won the Southern Conference championship. I remember that we had a unique team. When you look at some of the teams today and the caliber of talent they have, I think we didn't have as much talent as some people, but we had a bigger heart than anybody we played. I think Coach Claiborne was a coach we believed in, and when you believe in one another and believe in your coach, good things seem to happen.

Jerry Claiborne was wonderful at giving us a mental edge when we were going to play someone. I'll never forget when we played at West Virginia late in my junior season in 1963, and Jerry Claiborne decided to open the game with an onside kick. We saw a defect in their coverage and we knew that the tackle off to the left was going to turn and run as he was going to block and was going to leave a hole. We rolled up and kicked the football right to the spot that he ran out of, and Tommy Marvin caught it on the run and we ended up scoring a touchdown on our first drive, even though we had to kick off.

There were things like that we just believed in. I really think that, as a team, we were people who pulled for one another. Between you and me, when I got to the New York Jets, I found a bunch of individuals who played for themselves—but we played as a team. The only reason we won at Virginia Tech is because we covered for one another and everybody gave 100 percent. That, of course, is the way Jerry wanted it; that's the way he trained us; and that's the way we played.

We had lost to Florida State during my sophomore season, in 1962. They had done the "gobble, gobble" at the end of the game. We were in Tallahassee, and they knew they had the game won, so they started this "gobble, gobble" cheer. All of their players were making fun of us. Well, you're not supposed to do that kind of stuff because eventually it comes back to haunt you.

We came back and beat them 31–23 in Tallahassee in 1963. The next season in 1964, they came into Blacksburg ranked 10th in the nation and undefeated. They left with their tails between their legs after we beat them 20–11. We gave them the old Seminole chant, "Wooh! Wooh! Wooh! Wooh! Wooh!" as they walked off the field. We had to get back at them, which we did, and that was probably the highlight of the season.

After that game, the coach from Florida State at the time, Bill Peterson, said he had never had a quarterback beat him with his foot. That's what he believed. As a punter, I never believed in lining up and punting the football to the receiver. In our huddle, I would always try to tell the guys where I was going to punt the football, either left, right, or straight, depending on the situation. I think in

In 1963 Bob Schweickert led the Hokies to their only outright Southern Conference championship and was named third-team All-America by the Associated Press.

that game, they were not able to return any punts and we had a lot of punts and got lots of distance. That was the key to those punts, I believe, because they were not able to get any yardage.

Late during my senior season, we went to Syracuse as four-touchdown underdogs. We were outweighed 40 pounds per man and had 50 players to their 120. We were outmanned in all categories. Interestingly, we went to the stadium, and I had a slight separation in my right shoulder, which, of course, was my throwing arm. We went through the warm-ups without the quarterback throwing a pass. I don't think I've ever seen a team during the pregame go without its quarterback throwing a pass. But I couldn't throw, and we were trying to not let them know that.

They shot up my arm with novocaine to kill the pain, and what did Claiborne do? He called a pass on the first play of the game, and I threw the funniest looking, end-over-end pass you've ever seen to Tommy Marvin. But he caught it, and we gained 44 yards on the first play. We had Syracuse down 15–0 in the first half. I had rushed for over 100 yards in the first half, and I was actually running for my life.

I never believed in running out of bounds. I never did that to keep from taking a hit. On one play in the Syracuse game, I got to the sideline and lowered my shoulder to take a hit, and this guy came with his fist and went right through my face mask and broke the mask on my helmet. He hit my right eyeball and knocked it into my head. He did not hit any of the bone around my eye, just the eyeball. He didn't try to do that, but in those days, you wanted to get a quarterback out of the game anyway you could. Of course, my eyesight was messed up severely. I couldn't see straight. One eye was looking up and the other one was looking straight.

I didn't get to play anymore after I was hurt. They wanted me to punt, and I was on the sideline trying to catch the snap. There were two balls coming at me, and I knew which one I had to catch, but my depth perception wasn't good. While I was practicing, I dropped two out of the five, and it wasn't worth it for me to go in and punt.

I'll never forget that we called a tackle-eligible play against Syracuse, because in those days you had to warn the officials if you were going to run a funny-looking play. We called it and ran a tackle-eligible play and scored a touchdown, but they called it back because of an ineligible official. As I was standing on the sideline, a Syracuse police officer came over to me, put his arm around me, and said, "Son, don't get your hopes up. The officials will take this game from you before you leave." Sure enough, we lost that touchdown to the officials. Their quarterback rolled out five yards beyond the line of scrimmage and, of course, our defensive backs pulled up, and they threw a touchdown pass off of it to beat us 20–15.

After the game, you had to go up through the stands, and their fans were just trying to bang on us. I had my helmet on, I couldn't see anything and thought my eye was destroyed. I thought I wasn't going to be able to see anymore. They took me to the hospital in Syracuse, and there was supposed to be a specialist to come see me. But nobody ever came. When my eye went up into my head, it broke the shield area around my sinuses. All of the air was going up into my head, which was very painful when you tried to breathe.

I went home and spent the next week in the hospital in Roanoke. I just kept working with my eye. There were a bunch of kids in the hospital because it was an ear, nose, and throat hospital for children. The little kids were sitting around doing puzzles, so I took the bandages off my head and started putting the puzzles together. Each day, my eyes started getting closer and closer and closer together until, finally, they both focused together.

After the Syracuse game, we had a week off because we were playing Virginia Military Institute the following Thursday. Once my eyes became focused again, they put added protection in my helmet, and I played against VMI in the last game of the season. We beat VMI 35–13 and finished the season with six wins.

I remember Sonny Utz, an unselfish man who gave himself to me to block and clear the path for me, that's what I remember about him. Sonny Utz was not a big man compared to runners today, but he had a big heart. Of course, we didn't know he had a weak heart at the time, and we lost him when he was very young. Sonny was unselfish and he was a great teammate. He was one of the finest blockers there ever was. We called him "Mr. Inside" because we knew if we needed a yard or two or three, we'd give it to Sonny up the middle, and he would get it. Of course, the advantage I had was if I faked to him, the defense would collapse on him, and guess where I was going? I was going on the outside, so they started calling us "Mr. Inside" and "Mr. Outside." I'll always remember the way Sonny Utz gave himself up for me.

After I graduated from Virginia Tech, I got drafted by the New York Jets and the San Francisco 49ers [because of the NFL and AFL situation]. The AFL was trying to survive and make a name for itself, so it actually had a secret draft. I don't think it had ever been done before or after. But they met all day on a Thursday and had the entire draft in a room with the owners and the men who were going to be doing the drafting. They picked their entire draft in one day.

Then they got on the telephone. I was over at the home of the young lady I ended up marrying, and it was 12:00 at night when the phone rang. It was the New York Jets. They called my mother and said, "We've got to get in touch with him," so she gave them the phone number. This was a Friday night and Saturday morning was the NFL Draft. The Jets called me and said, "Bob, we want you to know the Jets are going draft Joe Namath of Alabama, John Huarte of Notre Dame, and you as their top three draft choices. The only thing we ask is that you don't sign any contracts with the

NFL until we have an opportunity to talk to you." They picked three quarterbacks.

So Saturday morning, the NFL and AFL drafts began, even though the AFL had really already had its draft. I had planned that, if the Dallas Cowboys drafted me in the NFL, I was going to the Cowboys. Tom Landry had been my coach at the Senior Bowl, and the Cowboys had showed me so much interest, I decided that's what I was going to do. Well, the phone rang and it was the San Francisco 49ers. They said, "Bob, we want you to know we're going to pick you in the first round, and we've got two draft picks." They said they were going to choose Ken Willard, a running back from North Carolina, with their first choice, and then they were going to draft me. They said they would give me the same contract they gave to Ken Willard, so I wouldn't have to negotiate a contract.

There I was sitting in the kitchen of the house where we'd had nothing our whole life. I was 22 years old and a man of my word, and the 49ers told me I had to promise I'd sign a contract with them before they'd draft me because they could not waste a first-round pick. I told the 49ers I could not make a promise to them, but I would promise that I wouldn't sign anywhere else without coming to San Francisco and seeing what they had to offer me. We talked for an hour and they had one hour to conclude a draft pick. At the end of the hour, they said, "We pass." There I was with egg on my face, and it probably cost me $25,000.

Later that day, the phone rang again in the second round, and it was the San Francisco 49ers. They said, "We can't pay you what we would have paid you, but we would like to draft you. We just need your word that you will sign our contract." I said I couldn't sign, and they said, "We pass." They passed one more time and eventually chose me with their fourth pick. But money was not the thing, and they weren't going to buy me with money.

During the draft, there were representatives from the New York Jets, the NFL, and the Dallas Cowboys, where I thought I was going to play, sitting in my mother's house. Walt Michaels from the Jets, said, "Let's get dressed and fly to New York." I told my mother, "Come on, Mom, let's get dressed and go to New York." We went up to New York and got to Shea Stadium on Sunday, and I was greeted by the owner of the Jets, his wife, and his son. They took me to their home. During the game, I sat in a VIP suite, and after the game, I went down to the locker room and met with Jets coach Weeb Eubank. This was right after their final game of the season, and he asked the press to leave his office because he wanted to talk to me.

Eubank looked at me and said, "Bob, here's how we plan to use your talents. We know you can run with the football. We're going to let Joe Namath take us down the field. When we get down to the 5-yard line and Joe can't run, you're going in to take us into the end zone. How does that sound to you?" It sounded like the right kind of plan because I couldn't throw the ball 65 yards. My game was to roll out and run with the football, and that tears up a defense. I was like a kid in a candy shop. He just offered me what I wanted, and I said, "I can come to New York and help your football team. It's not that far from Virginia, it sounds great." Afterward, we couldn't get a plane back to Virginia, so the Jets chartered an airplane for my mother and me to fly home because I had to be in school on Monday. I was impressed.

But I couldn't commit to the Jets because I told the 49ers I would visit with them and talk with them. I took my girlfriend and mother to San Francisco. I was greeted by a representative of the owner and was driven around San Francisco for a few minutes. I was taken to where they have their training camp and Jack Christiansen, who was the head coach of the team, was there. He said, "Hi, Bob. We're glad to have you out here. I hope you sign your contract with the 49ers." Then he left. I never met the owner and had two minutes with the coach. Their stadium was absolutely falling apart, and the 49ers were drawing about 25,000 fans. I had just left Shea Stadium, where the Jets had 65,000 screaming fans. The 49ers had John Brodie, who was a drop-back passer, and George Mira, who was a scrambling, running quarterback. What are you going to do? My choice was made.

There seemed to be more of an opportunity with the Jets, even with Joe Namath there, so my choice was made. But Weeb Eubank never let me do what he said he was going to do one time in three years. I sat on the bench behind Namath and was the backup punter, a running back, a flanker back, and a split end. Part of my job there was to read defenses and record our offenses for film sessions. One of the things that really bothered me during that time was Weeb was not a man of his word. When you promise someone something, you should do what you're going to do. Yet he never did it.

Finally, in my fourth year, I had a contract signed to go back to the Jets, and I was called up to the Army. I had joined the Green Berets because there was a reserve unit that had some vacancies and it was during Vietnam. I had been in ROTC at Virginia Tech and was a company commander. I joined a reserve unit in White Plains, New York, and they were trying to send me to six months' basic training. I got a deferment during football season during my first three years with the Jets, but then the Army said they couldn't give my any more deferments, and I went into the Army before my fourth year with the team. Of course, that's the year the Jets won the Super Bowl [beating the Baltimore Colts 16–7 in Super Bowl III on January 12, 1969].

Earlier that season, I was stationed in Missouri, and the Jets had lost six games and won four. Weeb Eubank got on the phone to me in Missouri and my wife in Chicago. He said, "Bob, we need you to come back. There are four games left and you'll play as soon as you get here." I was listening to him and thinking to myself, *The man lies*. I didn't believe I'd get to play, that I'd just sit on the bench. So I made the decision not to go back. The Jets won all four, beat Oakland in the AFL championship game, and I sat in Chicago watching the Jets win the Super Bowl on television. I could have been there, but we had a coach I couldn't believe.

So I never played football again and went to work with Mr. Edward Lane, whom Virginia Tech named its stadium for, and went to work in one of his factories. After several months, they sent me on the road to see if I could become a salesman, and I liked it so much, I stayed with it.

Bob Schweickert was Virginia Tech's starting quarterback during the 1962, 1963, and 1964 seasons. In 1963 the scrambling quarterback led the Hokies to their only outright Southern Conference championship and was named third-team All-America by the Associated Press. Schweickert overcame injuries during his senior season and was named All-America by the Football Writers Association. Schweickert is now an ordained minister and lives in Grayslake, Illinois.

1975

With running coach Jimmy Sharpe's wishbone offense, the 1975 Virginia Tech team upset SEC power Auburn on the road and also stunned Florida State in one of the most dramatic finishes in school history. After losing their first two games against Kentucky and Kent State, the Hokies won eight of their next nine contests to finish with an 8–3 record, the school's best finish since 1966.

Virginia Tech stunned Auburn 23–16 at Jordan-Hare Stadium in Auburn, Alabama. Running back Roscoe Coles had an 89-yard touchdown run, and quarterback Phil Rogers threw for one touchdown and ran for another score. With the Hokies holding a seven-point lead in the final minutes, Auburn drove to Tech's 5-yard line, but couldn't score on four straight plays.

Against Florida State, senior Wayne Latimer kicked a 61-yard field goal, the longest in school history, to knock off the Seminoles by a 13–10 score. Florida State drove inside Tech's 15-yard line in the final minutes, but Tech's defense again stood tall.

Hokies in Their Own Words

ROSCOE COLES

TAILBACK, 1974–1977

I was being recruited by most of the schools on the East Coast, and by schools from as far away as Arizona and Colorado. I visited quite a few of them: Michigan State, South Carolina, North Carolina, Temple, and Kentucky. The biggest issue was my size. People saw me play on film and thought I played big, but when they saw me in person, I was just a little guy.

I didn't understand that process, and it didn't make a lot of sense to me. I was about 5'10" and 156 pounds, but I knew I could play at that level. One of the things I remember most is that my equipment never fit. I was so little compared to most of the other guys on the team, my pants didn't even fit right. My pants were always sliding to the side. In every picture that Virginia Tech has of me, my pants are crooked.

Charley Pell was recruiting me for Virginia Tech. I grew up in Virginia Beach and went to Bayside High School. I flew to Blacksburg in a private Leer jet, and it was a gloomy day. It was raining and it was cold. It looked pretty darn gloomy, to be honest. The place looked like a prison with all that stone and dark buildings. It just reminded me of ancient times. Coach Jimmy Sharpe had just taken over after Charlie Coffey was fired by Virginia Tech. I guess they had gotten a late start on recruiting and were behind everyone else. I remember talking to the coaches and thinking, *New coaches mean an opportunity for me to play.* I remember visiting Michigan State, and the coaches there were pretty much set on the guys they already had.

There were two other players from the Tidewater area who were being highly recruited, Larry Bethea and Tommy Graves, and we went to all of these places together on the weekends. Both of them ended up signing with Michigan State and played there. [Bethea was drafted in the first round of the 1978 NFL Draft by the Dallas Cowboys, and Graves was an eighth-round selection by the Pittsburgh Steelers the following year.]

I got to Virginia Tech in the fall of 1974, and Phil Rogers and George Heath were the tailbacks. We ran the wishbone, so you had to have two backs because there was contact every play. We ran a physical, brutal offense. I didn't play that much during the first three games of my freshman season, and I thought about transferring. I ran back kickoffs the first three games but didn't play that much on offense. I thought I was just as good as the rest of those guys. I'm a football player; I wanted to play football and wasn't playing. I wasn't accustomed to not playing. I'd never sat on the bench in my life. I didn't talk to Coach Sharpe, but I talked to other guys at other schools about transferring.

I guess I proved myself on the practice field, however. They started putting me in games, and I almost ran for 700 yards during my freshman season. It was a new coaching staff, so it was an adjustment for everybody. One of the reasons I had gone to Virginia Tech was that I thought I would have an opportunity to play because everybody was new. When new coaches come into a school, chances are they're going to play the kids they bring in. I thought that was going to be an advantage for me, and it was. But we struggled that first season and finished with a 4–7 record.

We opened the 1975 season losing to Kentucky and Kent State. But then we won eight of our last nine games and really had it going pretty well. We beat Auburn and Houston on the road. I had an 89-yard run against Auburn for a touchdown, and we won 23–16. Then we beat Florida State and Virginia at home but lost a tough one at West Virginia, 10–7. We won our last four games of the season after that and finished with an 8–3 record.

We were pretty good in 1976 and finished 6–5. We played at Texas A&M in our second game and lost 19–0. It was about 120 degrees on that artificial turf, and it was miserable. The whole time the fans were swaying back and forth in the stadium and, man, they were loud. So the heat was killing us and the fans were killing us. It was the 12th man and the 13th man. Near the end of the game, I was getting ready to receive a kickoff, and Ellis Savage jumped in front of me and snatched the football. Before he could even take a step, a Texas A&M player hit him so hard that it about broke him in half. He crumbled when he was hit and broke a couple of his ribs. We had a long flight back to Virginia, and he was in so much pain. They showed that play about 100 times on the highlight show, and we just cringed every time we saw it. Every

Although he was somewhat small for a Division I running back, Roscoe Coles was Virginia Tech's leading rusher for three straight seasons, from 1975 to 1977.

time I see him, that's the thing he talks about: stealing that kickoff return from me.

But during my senior season in 1977, it appeared to me that things started to change. Teams were doing a better job of defending the wishbone, and we didn't have a lot of success on offense. Football is a team sport, and you've got to have 11 guys on the same page to be successful day-in and day-out. I broke my hand during my senior season and played with a cast. I don't know how I played at all during my senior season.

We went 3–7–1 that season, and Coach Sharpe got fired after the last game of the season, a 27–7 win over Virginia Military Institute. I thought Coach Sharpe was a pretty good coach. He was a good leader, and I liked him. Coach Sharpe was a little guy. There were a lot of things we probably didn't know about Coach Sharpe, but the things I knew were good things. We went to work out one day, and Coach Sharpe wasn't there. They told us he'd been fired. We didn't get to say good-bye or anything. It kind of messed me up because I didn't get much direction as far as preparing for the NFL Draft and didn't get drafted.

Danny Ford was one of his assistant coaches, and he was one of those coaches who was always challenging his players. Sometimes, we'd end practice by boxing. You'd box for four or five minutes, and it would really wear you out because everybody was throwing punches like crazy. One day, Coach Ford put on the boxing gloves and decided to box against Paul Adams because he thought he could take anybody out there. Paul was about 6'2" and 240 pounds. Coach Ford was a lanky guy and maybe weighed 185 pounds, but he liked to think he was a big, tough guy. Paul knocked him out. That was a treat. It knocked the tobacco right out of Coach Ford's mouth.

Coach Ford always had tobacco in his mouth. He always left the cups and bottles lying around after he had spit in them. One day, his sons came into the locker room and started drinking out of one of the Pepsi bottles. The kid took a swallow, and his face turned green, and he said, "Eeeeew!"

I was getting ready to get out of school and, not knowing how the draft worked and what the protocol was, I depended on the coaches for direction. I had about five NFL teams that contacted me about signing as a free agent. I was disappointed and it was pretty discouraging. I thought I was a pretty good back. In fact, I knew I was the best back in the country.

In the end, I thought I proved a lot of people wrong. I'm sure a lot of the teams I played against thought I was too small. Virginia Tech was the only place where I felt like I was really wanted. But I really never had anything to prove because there's never been a doubt in my mind that I could play football. I always knew I could play with the best of them.

I stayed at Hillcrest Dormitory, which was up near the duck pond. We had a ton of fun in that dorm. One day it snowed. It seemed like the whole campus came over to challenge the jocks to a snowball fight. There were probably two or three thousand people standing outside the dorm. They were all yelling into the dorm, "Snowball fight! Snowball fight!" We probably had about 150 people in the dorm. We all busted out of the doors, and that whole crowd made a U-turn and started running the other way. We were all throwing snowballs, and Adams was throwing punches instead of snowballs. He was knocking people out! It was unbelievable. It was just a sight to see. There were only a few of us who came out of the dorm, but they were all running the other way.

I remember Tom Beasley and Curt Lowery shared a dorm room. The window was always open. They were avid hunters and would kill animals and bring them back to the room. That room was always cold, and it was always gross. It was the nastiest room

I ever saw. There were just all kinds of things in there: deer, possums, skunks, raccoons. They were real country boys. They would hang those animals over other people's beds and doors. They were always pulling practical jokes. I was a city kid. I'd never seen stuff like that.

My mom and dad came to every game I played at Virginia Tech. They saw all of my runs. Sometimes the crowd would stand up and start shouting, "Let's go, Roscoe!" To hear forty or fifty thousand people chant your son's name, I'm sure that's something they were very proud of. To be honest, I don't remember hearing it because I was so focused when I played. I think my mom and dad enjoyed it more than I did.

I've got so many great memories of playing at Virginia Tech. One of the things I'm most proud of is that I graduated in four years. I was part of the Core Cadets, pledged a fraternity, and was president of the Monogram Club. I accomplished a lot of things I wasn't supposed to. I feel like we paved the way for a lot of kids who came to Virginia Tech after us. They didn't have to put up with a lot of the things we went through.

Roscoe Coles was Virginia Tech's leading rusher for three straight seasons, from 1975 to 1977. The Virginia Beach, Virginia, native ranks third in school history with 3,459 career rushing yards, and his 89-yard touchdown run in a victory at Auburn in 1975 is the second longest in Hokies history. Coles ran for 214 yards in a 35–31 loss to Tulsa in 1976, third most in a game by a Hokies player. Coles is an assistant principal at E.E. Smith High School in Fayetteville, North Carolina.

Hokies in Their Own Words
BILLY HARDEE
CORNERBACK, 1972–1975

I grew up in Mulberry, Florida, and my high school coach, Carl Ellis, became one of the assistant coaches at Virginia Tech. He recruited me, Phil Rogers, and a bunch of guys. There were only four black guys on the football team at Virginia Tech when we got there, and they brought in about 12 before my freshman season.

I visited Virginia Tech and watched a basketball game in January 1972. The mountains were pretty and there was snow on them. It was beautiful country. Plus, it was something different and a chance to start over. I didn't want to go to Miami or Florida State because that would have been like high school all over again. I knew a bunch of the guys at Miami, a bunch of guys at Florida State, and a bunch at the University of Florida. Minnesota was recruiting me, and the University of Florida offered me a scholarship after the high school all-star game. They were recruiting some guys who they thought were better than me, but after that all-star game, they were all recruiting me.

I wanted to try something different. I had never been anywhere before. I was born and raised in Mulberry, Florida, and when the opportunity came to play football at Virginia Tech, I took advantage of it. I played on the freshman team in 1972 and was the leading receiver.

During my sophomore season in 1973, I played opposite Ricky Scales and started after the second or third game. My breakout game came at South Carolina in the fifth game that season, which was one of the better offensive games of my career. I had a 96-yard kickoff return for a touchdown and a 74-yard touchdown catch.

I caught the touchdown on about the second play of the game. I ran a fly route, Rick Popp threw me the ball, and I made a couple of guys miss. The kickoff return for the touchdown came on the opening kickoff of the second half. [The Hokies lost to South Carolina 27–24.]

We had the worst defense in the country during my sophomore season. It was terrible. We played at Alabama late in the season and they were ranked No. 2 in the nation at the time. Scales and I were saying, "Man, we can beat these guys." Offensively, we only got one touchdown. Every time we kicked off to them, they scored really quickly. One time we punted the ball to them, and before we got to the sideline, Wilbur Jackson had run for an 80-yard touchdown. I'm telling you, man, we had the worst defense in the country. We beat Virginia and Florida State only because they were worse. That was the blind leading the blind. Florida State wasn't very good, either.

Coach Charley Coffey got fired after we finished 2–9 in 1973. They brought in Jimmy Sharpe as our new coach, and one of the first things he did was move me from wide receiver to defensive back. I was playing baseball and wasn't even in town. I didn't even know the guy. He called me into his office and said, "Are you a football player or a baseball player?" I said, "Hey, man, I can be either one. I'm starting on the football team and I'm starting on the baseball team." He said, "Well, you're on football scholarship, so I want you at spring practice." I went out to practice the next day, and all the receivers were lined up. The receivers coach looked at me and said, "Who are you?" I told him I was Billy Hardee. He said, "You're over there with the defensive backs."

So I went over to practice with the defensive backs, and we started beating each other to death. My arms were black and blue for days. I was killing myself. After lunch, I went in and called my mom first and called Florida State second. They said they couldn't talk to me until I was released from my scholarship. So during lunch the next day, Charley Pell came up to me and said, "Do you want to be released from your scholarship?" I said, "Yes, Coach, I came here to be a wide receiver. If I'm going to be miserable, I'm going to be miserable closer to home."

They told me if I went through spring practice at defensive back and it didn't work out, they'd move me back to wide receiver before the season. They said we only needed one receiver, and Ricky Scales was starting. I told them I'd be a backup because Scales couldn't play the whole game. But I ended up coming back to school that fall anyway.

I ended up starting at cornerback for the entire 1974 season. They took kickoff returns from me and gave them to Roscoe Coles because he was a little bit faster. They tried to take punt returns from me, but nobody else could catch the punts. Plus, Roscoe and those other guys who were faster than me didn't want any part of punt returns because they'd get hit too much.

Sharpe took all the good athletes and put them on defense, so we were a little bit better during my junior season. During my sophomore season, we had a pretty good offense but a terrible defense. By my senior season, we had a suspect offense and a defense that was ranked among the best in the nation. I think we gave up one touchdown pass my entire senior season and had a really good secondary. We didn't have any big stars, but we had four really good players. I was definitely the most cocky. We had Tom Beasley on the defensive line and Rick Razzano at linebacker.

We got beat pretty badly by Kentucky in the first game of the 1975 season, then went to Kent State and lost that game. We were down 17–0 at halftime in that game, but we shut them out in the second half and lost 17–11. The offense couldn't get anything

Billy Hardee was recruited from Florida to play wide receiver at Virginia Tech but was moved to cornerback. Reluctant to play defense at first, he became one of the country's top defensive backs.

going. But then we won our next four games, beating Richmond, Auburn, Florida State, and Virginia. The Auburn win was a really big win for us because they'd been predicted to finish No. 1 or No. 2 in the nation that season. My buddy, Mitzi Jackson, was Auburn's star running back, and we had played in the Florida North-South All-Star game together. We had lost our first couple of games, but Auburn had all these All-Americans and they had started reading their press clippings. If they hadn't had a place-kicker who made three field goals of 40 yards or more, we would have beat them worse than we did. They only scored one touchdown, and we upset them 23–16.

We played Florida State the next week and won 13–10. Those games were always like homecoming games to me. We'd lost to Miami 14–7 during my junior season. Beating Florida State was always good because I had a lot of friends who played there. Florida State always had coaching problems until Bobby Bowden got there.

We were tied with West Virginia, 7–7, at halftime, and I thought Beasley, Bill Houseright, Razzano, and those guys were going to start a fight in the locker room with the offensive guys because the offense wasn't doing anything. They were telling the offense, "You guys just don't fumble the football, and we'll win the game." They went out and fumbled the ball in the second half, and West Virginia kicked a field goal to beat us 10–7. That was it.

That was the worst feeling I ever had flying back to Blacksburg. It was like there were two teams on the plane because there was such division between the offense and defense. The offense was sitting on one side and the defense on the other. There were a lot of cold stares on that plane. We couldn't wait to get to practice on Monday and beat their butts.

But we came back and won our last four games that season, beating William and Mary, Houston, VMI, and Wake Forest. We went 8–3 that year, and with our defense, we should have been 10–1.

After my senior season at Virginia Tech, I didn't get drafted by an NFL team. I got picked up as a free agent by the Seattle Seahawks. The Tampa Bay Buccaneers wanted to move me back to wide receiver, but I hadn't played that position for a couple of years, so I wasn't comfortable with it. So I went to Seattle instead and got cut near the end of training camp. The Denver Broncos called me late in the 1976 season after a couple of their guys got hurt, and they paid me $4,000 to play two games. I played the entire 1977 season for the New York Jets the following season and then went to Canada.

My brother, Ron Hardee, was supposed to come to Virginia Tech two years later, but there was a coaching change and he ended up going to the University of Texas–Arlington. My other brother, Ray Hardee, went to Iowa State. My son, Billy Hardee III, played football at Virginia Tech, too. He had gone to Florida Southern University to play soccer, but I hadn't wanted him to go there. The guy down there wasn't playing him, so he decided to leave. My wife was on an airplane flying back to Virginia to see her mother, and Frank Beamer was sitting across the aisle from her. He asked how Billy was doing, and she said, "Oh, I wish he would have gone to Virginia Tech." Frank said, "Tell him to give me a call." Billy wasn't on scholarship the first year, but he ended up starting as a senior in 2002, and Frank put him on scholarship. He had a good career there. He was a good student. He went to medical school after graduation.

I've got great memories of Virginia Tech. I go back and see how big it is and how pretty it is. I'm so proud of Coach Beamer and what he's done. I've got to listen to all these Florida State and Miami fans down here, but I'm proud of the place. What I miss the most are the old guard from Virginia Tech. That's a great place to go to school. I wish I could have stayed there forever.

Billy Hardee started at wide receiver for the Hokies in 1973 and started at cornerback in 1974 and 1975. He still owns Virginia Tech records for kickoff returns when he returned 33 for 758 yards in 1973. His 96-yard kickoff return for a touchdown against South Carolina still ranks as the fifth-longest in school history. Hardee had three interceptions as a junior and seven as a senior, and his 10 career interceptions ranks 11th in school history. Hardee played in the NFL, Canadian Football League, and USFL. He returned to Virginia Tech in 1978 to earn a master's degree in sports management and was a graduate assistant for two years under Coach Frank Beamer. He is an assistant principal and lives in Winter Haven, Florida.

Hokies in Their Own Words
TOM BEASLEY
Defensive Tackle, 1973–1976

I didn't have a lot of options coming out of high school. I went to a very small high school in southern West Virginia and basically had two scholarship offers: Marshall University and Virginia Tech. It was a couple of years after Marshall had the plane crash that killed the football players and coaches, so their program was still in a lot of disarray. So my only real option was Virginia Tech.

I knew a little about Virginia Tech, though I certainly didn't know anything at all about Virginia Tech's history having grown up in West Virginia. But I can tell you very clearly that, during my first visit to Virginia Tech's campus, I just fell in love with the place. I think if I had 15 scholarship offers, Virginia Tech would have been my choice after visiting the campus. That part of the country is just gorgeous.

West Virginia never sent me a letter and never made a phone call to me. I got nothing from West Virginia. It wasn't disappointing because I don't know that I would have been called anything close to a blue-chipper coming out of high school. I went to a really small high school—my graduating class at Northfork High School had 108 students. As a senior in high school, I was 6'4" and weighed about 190 pounds. I had never touched a weight before I went to Blacksburg.

I think there was some raw potential there, but I also think you had to look pretty close to pick up on it. I think I had lineman's speed, but at that size, I needed to put on a significant amount of weight, which was a problem I had the entire time I played football. The most I weighed at Virginia Tech was 235 pounds, and it wasn't until my last two years in the pros that I was able to get up to the 270 to 275 range.

I graduated from high school in 1973 and played as a true freshman at Virginia Tech that fall. What I remember most about my freshman season was that I went down there initially as an offensive lineman and absolutely got my butt handed to me the first two or three weeks. We used to have what we called—excuse my language—"turd bowls." Every Wednesday, the players that were third-, fourth-, fifth-, sixth-team, or worse would have a scrimmage after practice on Wednesday afternoons. I was so far down the depth chart that I didn't even get to play in the "turd bowls."

I was, like, fifth-, sixth-, or seventh-team. I think there were 63 scholarships given out before my freshman season, and we just had a ton of kids there. I just didn't have a lot going on playing on the offensive side of the ball. I played guard, and they moved me to center, and that clearly wasn't my position, so they bumped me out to tackle and back to guard. At this time, I probably weighed about 210 pounds, and that was a pretty light offensive lineman even back in that era.

But we had a scrimmage one Wednesday, and toward the end of the practice we had a number of defensive tackles get hurt. Carl Ellis was the defensive tackles coach, and when another tackle went down, Coach Charlie Coffey yelled at Coach Ellis, "Carl, get somebody else out there! You're holding up the scrimmage!" Coach Ellis looked at him and said, "Charlie, that's it. We don't have any more defensive tackles." I was standing right next to Coach Coffey, and he looked at me, trying to remember my name, but he didn't know it. The freshman had their names written on the backs of their helmets, but I had my face turned toward him, so he couldn't see my name. You could just see the wheels turning in his head, and finally he grabbed my jersey and said, "You, get in there!"

I went into the scrimmage, and there were probably 10 plays left. I got to the ball eight or nine times in those 10 plays. The scrimmage was over, and I was walking off the field. I heard Coach Coffey yell at Coach Ellis, and I saw them talking for a few minutes. Coach Ellis came to me and said, "Tom, you're going to be working with the varsity defensive tackles starting tomorrow." About two games later, I had worked my way into a starting position. I was grossly undersized but just had a knack for finding the ball, and some good things happened. But at one time, we had nine freshmen starting on defense. We were extremely, extremely light on defense.

That first season was really kind of odd. We had gone 2–9, and Coach Coffey was taking a lot of heat, but he had weathered the storm. I think everybody had agreed to give him another year, and

I thought he was going to be there for the next year. Then out of the blue, he resigned on his own—at least that was my take on it. They had not even begun the process of trying to find a replacement. We went a couple of months without any coaches being there before Jimmy Sharpe came on board.

Coach Sharpe came to Virginia Tech from an incredible program after spending 12 years with Bear Bryant at Alabama, four as a player and eight as a coach. He came there meaning business. He got all the scholarship players and walk-ons together, and the first thing he told us was that half of us in that room would not be there in a month. He said, "The reason you're not going to be here is because I'm going to run you off. A lot of you are here for the wrong reasons." He said, "I can assure you, the ones who will be here in a month are here to play football. The rest of you are going to pack it up and get out."

And that was the case. I don't know how many kids walked away from full rides, but they just came in and worked us to death. We had gone a couple of months without any supervision, without any structured off-season program as far as lifting and conditioning, so a lot of guys had fallen out of shape and put on some weight. These guys came in and worked us harder than we'd ever been worked. It was pretty tough. It was a pretty tough spring that year.

We were extremely young again on defense during my sophomore season in 1974. The year before I got there in 1973 was Don Strock's senior season, and their whole scheme was to outscore folks. Most of the talent and skill players were on the offensive side of the ball. We had a lot of guys leave, some guys who were good athletes and could play, but they left the program. We were light in numbers because of that tough spring we had gone through. It was the first year the new coaches were there, and they

had a very limited time in recruiting. Most of the high school players had already signed before Sharpe and his staff got to Virginia
Tech. It was a tough first year and obviously a transition year.

But the core group of guys who weathered the storm that first
spring were there to play football. I think that any time a group
of people go through a tough situation like that, I don't care if it's
sports, the military, or whatever, there's a bonding that occurs.
We just came together as a unit, and there was kind of synergistic
effect. We were excited about the caliber of coaches we had on
board and fully believed in them. Jimmy Sharpe and most of his
staff were player's coaches. Players were just highly motivated to
do anything and everything they had to do to win. I think that was
the biggest factor for us turning it around. We just had to weather
that first spring, mature, and learn the new systems, new defense,
and new techniques. It takes time to learn those new things and
master them.

We opened the 1975 season and lost to Kentucky and Kent
State right off the bat. We beat Richmond and went to play at
Auburn. I'm a jokester and a prankster, and I don't get too nervous
or worked up. It was third or fourth down at the goal line, and
we were up 23–16 late in the game. They had called a timeout
and we had called a timeout. I distinctly remember Rick Razzano
and about three or four other guys were really worked up, and I
thought they were all going to have a stroke before the next snap.
The blood vessels in their foreheads and necks were just about
ready to pop. Bill Houseright had gotten married during his freshman season, and his wife had a twin sister. So I tried to lighten
up the huddle a little bit and said, "Hey, Billy, you seen Margie
lately?" I was just trying to ease things up.

We played Florida State the next week, and there were a couple
of big goal-line stands in that game, too. In the Virginia game

that season, it was late in the game and their quarterback, Scott Gardner, was driving them down the field. I was able to penetrate and beat my man, and I sacked the quarterback and caused him to fumble. Mike Stollings, who grew up about 12 miles from where I grew up in West Virginia, recovered the fumble. In all these games, you just had a number of people making big plays. That game was my opportunity and my time, but we had a number of folks who had that potential. We just did whatever it took. It was, *Who was going to make the big play?*

Short yardage and goal-line situations are all about penetration. We had some players who were cutters and slicers, guys who could get great penetration. I think that was the key to all of those. We were just playing sound football. Everybody was taking care of their responsibilities, and you just knew you could count on the guy next to you and the guy behind you. We just fed off each other and complemented each other. We were still grossly undersized at a lot of positions—I was light, Bill was light, Keith McCarter, one of the defensive ends, was light—so we were smaller, quicker, and lighter, and were better able to penetrate. That's what you've got to have to stop people.

We finished 6–5 during my senior season in 1976, but we beat West Virginia, and obviously, that was pretty big. I always took a lot of heat in the summers when I worked in the coal mines in West Virginia. A lot of the engineers and a lot of the upper management were West Virginia graduates, and a lot of the guys I worked with in the mines were Mountaineers fans. I just took a tremendous amount of heat being a player at Virginia Tech and having lost to them in each of my first three seasons. So it was great to finally beat them as a senior, 24–7, in Blacksburg. Obviously, every dog has its day, and I made up for some lost time.

Tom Beasley was buried on the depth chart as an offensive lineman before being moved to defensive tackle, where he started four consecutive seasons.

My father had worked his way through school in the coal mines, and my father was in banking. He was the president of a small bank down in southern West Virginia. In that area in those days, there just weren't a lot of options. If you didn't work in the mines, you either pumped gas or bagged groceries. It was a rural area. Most of the mines had great summer programs for college students, and they paid great. You had ample amounts of overtime, and the pay was probably three or four times what you would get from jobs outside the mines. When you lived in coal-mining communities, it just wasn't a big deal. My grandfather worked his way through school in the coal mines, my dad did, and I did. It's just what you did in that area.

I was just general labor in the coal mines. The first year, I was on the shovel belt and things like that. My second year, I worked laying track. My third year, I worked on a blasting crew where we drilled and set off charges. It's really kind of funny. Working in the mines was a tremendous benefit for me athletically. When you're working in coal, being 6'5", you have to develop great flexibility in your knees, hips, and ankles, and you also have to learn leverage. Because I was always so grossly undersized, leverage was critical for me. One of the best ways to learn leverage was working in the mines. We had one section of the mine where the coal was about 28 inches. When you're lifting, pulling, carrying, and dragging heavy equipment or belt structure or whatever, you learn leverage.

I got drafted by the Pittsburgh Steelers in the third round of the 1977 draft. I didn't watch a lot of pro football, and Pittsburgh clearly was not one of my favorite teams. I remember getting a call from the Steelers' personnel director to inform me that they had just selected me in the draft. The very next call I got was from a reporter from the Pittsburgh area, and his first question was, "Whose place are you going to take on the Steel Curtain?" The

Steel Curtain, of course, was L.C. Greenwood and Joe Greene on the left side, and Ernie Holmes and Dwight White on the right side. It was just one of those situations where you go from being a big fish in a small pond to a very small fish in a very large pond. But I truly learned more football from Joe Greene than I did from all those coaches throughout my entire playing career. I was drafted to replace Joe, and he was just a tremendous teacher. I learned so much about football.

Obviously, it was a great privilege to win two Super Bowls. When you look over the years at the incredible players who played their entire careers and never had the opportunity to play in a Super Bowl, it was very fortunate for me to be in the position during my second and third years in the league to do that. I'm not into diamonds and gold—and, yes, I have two Super Bowl rings—but the thing I cherish most about those two seasons was being a part of a group of people who put aside their individual interests and just focused on the common goal of being the best in the business. We had an attitude of doing whatever it took to make it happen.

I could have never imagined Virginia Tech getting to where it is today. Obviously, we struggled most of the time I was there. I felt like Jimmy Sharpe would do some wonderful things at Tech, and he did. I wish he had been there longer. But Frank Beamer has really taken the program to being a high-profile contender every year. Beamer and his staff are doing a sensational job there.

My son, Chad Beasley, was being very highly recruited coming out of high school, but he very quickly narrowed it down to Virginia Tech and Tennessee. Living in Gate City, Virginia, there are probably more Tennessee fans than Tech fans. But when we were up there on our visits and had our conversations with Coach Beamer, we quickly realized that he's a better man than he is a coach. And he's a great coach. Obviously, they had a great program, great facilities, and great environment. But Coach Beamer and his staff were just a cut above other places.

As a father, it's neat to see your kids develop from the stands, to see them learn some of the critical lessons of playing team sports and grow and develop. Obviously, Chad has incredibly fond memories of Tech, and I was happy that he was able to go there and stay healthy, and that things worked out. I'm very, very proud of that, more than anything I did at Tech.

What does it mean to be a Hokie? As a player, there was a commitment to the school and the program and an equally deep commitment to your fellow players. There was a tremendous amount of respect we had for each other, and a willingness to do anything and everything we possibly could to win each game we played. We had some big wins at Virginia Tech, but to me it's just a group of individuals who were committed to each other.

Tom Beasley was a starting defensive tackle for the Hokies for four seasons, from 1973 to 1976. He was a third-round draft choice of the Pittsburgh Steelers in the 1977 NFL Draft and played on Super Bowl championship teams during the 1978 and 1979 seasons. Beasley is a wellness consultant for Nikken, a Japanese-based company, and lives in Gate City, Virginia.

Hokies in Their Own Words
BILL HOUSERIGHT
NOSE TACKLE, 1973–1977

I was fortunate to be recruited by several schools, and at the time, it just seemed like Virginia Tech was the best place for me. I knew several people in the area where I grew up who had attended Virginia Tech, so it was no big deal. You make these decisions as a youngster, and that's where you end up. I was very fortunate to have been selected to the *Parade Magazine* All-America team, and I may have been the only player from Virginia who received that honor.

Back in the 1970s, schools were signing 60 or 70 players every year. Some schools' third teams were as good as other schools' first teams because there just wasn't a lot of parity in college football back then. Schools were recruiting me from all over the country, but I was looking to stay close to home, and it was either going to be the University of Tennessee or Virginia Tech. Carl Ellis recruited me for Virginia Tech, and he was an old Tennessee boy. Charlie Coffey was the coach at Virginia Tech, and Phil Battle was the coach at Tennessee. I just felt more comfortable at Virginia Tech, so that's where I signed.

I played as a freshman at Virginia Tech in the fall of 1973 and started six games at defensive end. I guess I was one of the first freshmen to start. We lost our first six games that season. I was coming off an ultra-successful high school career, but we fell on some hard times at Virginia Tech. Of course, we were playing a lot of young people. At the time, I was so green and dumb that I didn't know what was going on. I wasn't a really smart football player. As far as the things that were happening on the field, they were kind of hard to deal with at the time. When we went down to play Alabama, we had a bunch of freshman on the field and took a beating, 77–6.

But we hung around, everybody grew up and matured a little bit, and the whole group became a pretty close-knit bunch. We got a lot better as time went on. Coach Coffey left after my freshman season in 1973. I don't know if he got fired or resigned.

I know there was a lot of pressure on him, but I know he didn't have to coach to make a living because he owned a trucking company down in Tennessee. I always thought a lot of Coach Coffey. I thought he was a good man and a man of integrity. Unfortunately, I didn't get to know him that long, probably less than a year.

Coach Jimmy Sharpe came in before my sophomore season in 1974. He was a Bear Bryant disciple and told us off the bat, "If you want to be here, you're going to have to work to be here." That's what we did. It was one of those deals where only the strong survived. You could bring in as many freshmen as you wanted back then, so it really didn't matter how many players left. It was like a meat grinder during that spring and fall. We ended up developing a close-knit bunch because of how hard it was. I think Jimmy was really a player's coach.

I took a leave of absence during the 1974 season. I got married right before I enrolled at Virginia Tech. I was an 18-year-old young man with a family. Back in those days, there weren't any time limits on how long we could practice, how long we could meet, and all those things. We basically lived over at the football facility. You went to class in the morning, to practice in the afternoon, and watched film during the evening. You got home when you got home, then got up the next morning and did it again. That's just the way it was. Changes took place after we left.

I came back to Virginia Tech in 1975 and rejoined the football team as a sophomore. That was our best season under Coach Sharpe, and we finished 8–3. We started awfully slow that season and lost to Kentucky and Kent State. We went to Kentucky and couldn't run an offense. We went to Kent State, and I think they had one first down in the last 43 minutes of play—but we still got beat. But then we got our motor running and were pretty darn good. We were playing great defense, got our offense going, and came back and beat Richmond at home.

I'll never forget during the Auburn game, sitting down near the goal line late in the game. I was a whole lot more intense than Tom Beasley ever was. He was always playing loose. Auburn had the ball, first-and-goal on our 5-yard line, and he looked at me and said, "Hey, Bill, you seen Margie lately?" I don't know what I said to him, but I can't say it again. Tom ended up marrying Margie, my wife's twin sister. We went on to hold them and won the game 23–16. It was a big win for Virginia Tech at the time. Coach Sharpe was from Alabama, so they were always one of our archrivals.

The next week against Florida State, Wayne Latimer kicked a 61-yard field goal. There was about a 40 mph wind behind his back. The wind was really blowing that hard, but he kicked it dead center, and we won 13–10. That was a big win for us. We had a couple of goal-line stands near the end of the game. Even back then, Florida State was doing all of these double reverses and reverse passes and other trick plays. We didn't have much substitution back then, and when we were playing against all that stuff, the misdirection stuff really hampered us.

We were 4–2 going into the West Virginia game, and they beat us 10–7 after we fumbled a kickoff inside our 5-yard line and they ran a punt back inside our 20. That loss knocked us out of a bowl game. We thought we were going to the Peach Bowl. Being an independent, we didn't have a lot of choices as far as bowl games back then.

Charley Pell was the defensive coordinator at the time, and Buddy Bennett was just a wild man. The misdirection was really hard on us because everybody was running so hard. We ran so much and were in such good shape, with the attention level we had to play with, I don't know if some of the kids today could have played back then. Of course, we wouldn't be nearly as big as them, and they'd probably mash us. I remember one spring I was down to 205 pounds playing nose tackle in college. It was a different time and a different era.

We went 6–5 during my junior season in 1976, and I was really banged up that entire season. I played with a steel plate in my shoe. I'd take a little medication, get loosened up, play a little bit, then get some more medication at halftime, and play again. I just played when I had to. We beat West Virginia that season and should have beaten Florida State in the last game, but they threw about four or five bombs against us, and we lost 28–21.

I was pretty healthy during my senior season, but it was a really tough year for us. We had a lot of young kids playing and a lot of players we had to replace. We lost some games that were unbelievably close. We could have very easily had a winning record and maybe been 8–3 with some of the close games we lost. I can remember playing left defensive end, nose tackle, left defensive tackle, and right defensive end—I played wherever I was needed on the defensive front because we had so many young kids out there. If we had gotten some breaks here or there, our record would have been a lot better. But I think the circumstances led to people looking at some things off the field, but we never saw those as players. I always thought a lot of Coach Sharpe and really liked his staff. But that's part of the game.

I went into coaching right after my football career was over. I could have stayed on at Virginia Tech and been a graduate assistant. In hindsight, that might have been the best thing to do, but back then they were on the road all the time. I wanted to spend some time with my family. I moved back to my hometown of Gate

Bill Houseright was a very active nose tackle for the Hokies during the 1970s and, along with his future brother-in-law, Tom Beasley, led Tech to an 8–3 record in 1975. Three of Houseright's sons later played at Virginia Tech.

City, Virginia, and coached there for 15 years. I got out of coaching in 1997 when I had both my knees replaced. I went and got my master's degree and took another job as a football coach and assistant principal.

I've had three sons play at Virginia Tech. My last son, Jonas, was a walk-on there. My first son, Bill Jr., was on the 1995 Sugar Bowl team. Then he got a neck injury, and they told him he'd better stop playing. Jake was heavily recruited by a lot of schools and was a pretty good player at Tech. He had some knee issues as well, and I think that hurt him, but he was a good player when he was there. Jeremy, my third son, didn't go to Tech because he suffered a brain injury playing high school football and had to have surgery. He's doing great now, but they never would release him to play football again. He played college basketball at the University of Virginia–Wise. They all got football in their systems and want to do it until someone tells them they can't do it anymore.

I'm just tickled to death that all my sons have had the opportunity to go to Virginia Tech and play football and be a part of that atmosphere. I think Frank Beamer and his staff are really classy people, and it's a good place to have your sons go. You know they'll be well taken care of and there's enough discipline. It's just a great situation to be in.

There were many times when I looked at Virginia Tech and thought to myself, "Why not?" You had all these teams playing in these conferences, and for Virginia Tech to finally get into a conference and succeed on the level that they have, I think it's great. I am totally amazed every time I go to Virginia Tech and see how it has grown, and the extravagance of it all. They're really big-time now, and they're where they need to be.

What does it mean to be a Hokie? I would say it is to know that you belong to a fraternity that is ever-growing and ever-proud to be a member of that institution. Just to be a part of that family is a fantastic feeling. Once you're there and you've been a part of it, the friends and the people you've been around mold you into who you are and what you believe. You can never go back there and not run into someone who brings those memories back. It's a special place.

Bill Houseright was a starting nose tackle for the Hokies during four seasons, from 1973 to 1977. Along with his future brother-in-law, Tom Beasley, Houseright helped lead Virginia Tech to an 8–3 record during the 1975 season, the high mark of Coach Jimmy Sharpe's tenure. Three of Houseright's sons became football players at Virginia Tech. He lives in Twin Springs, Virginia, and is an assistant principal and athletics director at Twin Springs High School.

1980

After opponents started breaking Sharpe's wishbone offense on a steady basis, Virginia Tech lured North Carolina coach Bill Dooley to Blacksburg. Dooley struggled in his first two seasons but transformed Tech's fortunes in 1980, leading the Hokies to an 8–4 record and the school's first bowl game since 1968.

Bruising tailback Cyrus Lawrence was a big reason for Virginia Tech's success in the early 1980s. On the second carry of his college career, Lawrence ran 59 yards for a touchdown. He ran for 1,221 yards in 10 games in 1980 to set a school single-season record, and left school as Tech's all-time leading rusher after his senior season in 1982.

The 1980 Hokies blasted rival Virginia 30–0 and defeated West Virginia 34–11. After beating VMI 21–6 in the regular season finale, Virginia Tech was invited to play the University of Miami (Florida) in the Peach Bowl in Atlanta. The Hurricanes won the game by a 20–10 score.

Hokies in Their Own Words
CYRUS LAWRENCE
TAILBACK, 1979–1982

The recruiting process was a very grueling situation, and I'll never forget how I ended up playing at Virginia Tech. You have mega schools recruiting you, and as a young man, you've got to decide where you are going to be a student-athlete. Being a Virginian myself, born and raised in Virginia, I wanted to play at a Virginia college. At the time, Virginia Tech had a growing program, and I was being recruited by more than 100 schools. We had some players from my high school who carried the torch onto Virginia and Virginia Tech, and I wanted to stay in Virginia, so those were the schools I narrowed my choices down to.

I went up to North Carolina and North Carolina State, and had visits to Virginia and Virginia Tech. I had other chances to go out West to Southern California and could have visited Penn State, but I didn't want to play football for a school that far away from home. I wanted to stay in the surrounding area and play at a Virginia school.

Coach Billy Dooley had come to Virginia Tech from North Carolina in 1979 and had a strong program at North Carolina with Amos Lawrence, Lawrence Taylor, and those guys. Like

Coach Frank Beamer now, he was definitely a drawing point to Virginia Tech because he recruited heavily in Virginia, had a reputable name, and of course, he ran an offense I really liked.

Knowing Coach Dooley and the type of offense he regimented, it was a running offense. It was a lot like the high school offense we ran. I was a running back who liked to carry the football, and I wanted to go to a school where I had an opportunity to do that. Coach Dooley's offense was an I formation with a tailback, much like the offense we ran at South Hampton High School in Hampton, Virginia. Coach Dooley's offense fit my running style because I was a durable running back, and he really liked to hand the football off to his running backs. So Virginia Tech is where I decided to go to college.

My freshman season, I shared playing time with Kenny Lewis and Mickey Fitzgerald. Mostly, Kenny was in the tailback position and Mickey was in the fullback position. It was Kenny's senior season, so I knew I wouldn't have to wait long to get into the starting lineup. Also, it was good for me, because anytime you can come into a program and have experienced players in front of you on the depth chart, you can learn a lot from them.

Kenny was a very knowledgeable running back. He definitely had a lot of patience and taught me a lot of things about the game. Going from high school to college, it's a big transition, and to have a person like that in front of me was a blessing. We got along fine, and there was no animosity between us in reference to our splitting playing time. Being that he was a senior and I was a freshman, it was a great learning experience. It was great to come into a system where you have experienced running backs willing to work with you.

Mickey was like a Larry Csonka, a big, strong fullback. Man, he would run right over you. But off the field, Mickey was a very

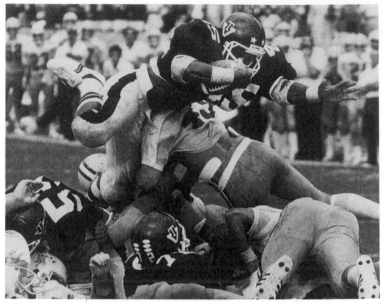

Cyrus Lawrence was a durable, bruising running back who led the team in rushing for three straight seasons.

gentle guy. He was very athletic, and of course, I was always looking to run behind him. It was a pleasure to come in and play with a fullback of that caliber.

Every running back has a different style. Throughout my football career, I was always geared to carry the football 30 or 35 times a game, and I enjoyed that. It may sound crazy, but as the game went on, my game got better. That was a strong point in my running game; I would get stronger as the game wore on. With some running backs, as the game went on, they might get tired or fatigued in the third or fourth quarter. But I always seemed to hit my peak during the third and fourth quarter.

I ran for 59 yards the second time I touched the ball in a game against Appalachian State during my freshman season. But to be honest with you, I wasn't a flashy runner and never had been. I could take it to the house or leave it. I think that was probably one of my greatest assets. I didn't have to have the 50- or 60-yard runs, like a scatback always seems to do. I was used to carrying the ball 30 or 35 times a game. I think I was a better runner inside the tackles because of my stature, and I was strong. It was hard for defenses to find me. I could get the four or five yards, which is critical, and you can't always bust that long run. If you can get one, that's great, but the coaches always said, "It's a game of inches."

I always looked forward to the Virginia game. Virginia and Virginia Tech have always been big rivals. It was a state school rivalry and everybody was pumped and ready to play in 1980, my sophomore year. It was just one of those games where everything worked right—I got good blocks, and the offense was running on all six cylinders. [The Hokies beat Virginia 30–0.] It was a very exciting time. It's something you can't really put into words, but it was great to do that against your big state rival.

We had a very good season going, we ended up 8–3 that year; but as a team, we were looking ahead instead of concentrating on each game. I think we probably just took Richmond for granted. You have to take one game at a time. I can't take anything away from Richmond. They came ready to play and we didn't. I think if we had to do it all over again, it probably would have been a different story. But you live and learn, and those are some of the heartaches of being an athlete. When you make mistakes, you try not to go and make the same mistake again. That's part of playing sports.

In 1980 we had some very good players who worked hard and were dedicated. We'd had a very good off-season program. We came into the season and had a goal to get a bowl game. As a whole, we focused and had a good game plan. With the exception of losing to Clemson and Florida State, we could have easily been undefeated.

I'll never forget going down to Atlanta to play in the Peach Bowl against Miami. They had Jim Kelly and Jim Burke and a lot of players who went on to play in the NFL. Of course, they beat us, but it was a very good game. I ran for about 134 yards in that game, but I think I had 126 of them at halftime. I think they made some changes at halftime, and I think we made some changes. I think we came out flat in the second half and let them get the upper hand. We beat them in the first half, and they beat us in the second half. But it was still exciting. It was good to be down in Atlanta playing in a bowl game on national television and getting national recognition. It was fun, and despite the 20–10 loss, it was a good learning experience.

I hurt my knee the fourth game of my senior season against Wake Forest. I was running an inside-tackle play, made a divert cut, and injured my knee. I missed six games. I came back for the Virginia game and was able to play in the last game of my senior year. I was able to go on and play in a Senior Bowl that was played in Japan in 1983. I played with Eric Dickerson and Babe Laufenberg. That was a great experience. I was drafted by Seattle in 1983, but because of the knee injury, my football career pretty much dissipated.

Not to philosophize too much, but I believe I was very blessed to have an opportunity to do the things I did. I always enjoyed playing sports, and I was a great competitor. But I knew in my heart that one day all great things must come to an end. It was a disappointment not to be able to carry on all the hard work that I had put into something. But football had always been a learning experience in my life, and I went on in life and got an education and earned my degree in marketing.

The NFL is not for everybody. Having one foot in and one foot out, it wasn't the fact that I wasn't good enough to play in the NFL. Opportunities did just not render at the time. But it was all a great experience. If I had to do it all over again, I'd do it again. I think sports are a great thing for young people. Even as an adult, I can take the lessons I learned playing football at Virginia Tech—hard work and dedication and work ethic—and use them in raising my children. They know if you want something badly enough, you can achieve it, and they know not to give up. I know things aren't always going to go the way I want them to go, but you can't be a quitter, and I've never been a quitter.

I've never been a person who looks in the past because life goes on, and you've got to be prepared for that.

Cyrus Lawrence is Virginia Tech's all-time leading rusher with 3,767 yards. He ran 843 times in four seasons, from 1979 to 1982, also a career record. Lawrence's 1,403 rushing yards in 1981 are the second-most in school history. Lawrence also holds school records for carries in a game (42 against Memphis State in 1981) and carries in a season (325 in 1981). He lives in the Tidewater area of southeast Virginia and works as a regional sales director. He and his wife have three sons.

1986

The 1986 season was full of surprises for Virginia Tech. After finishing 6–5 the previous season, the Hokies weren't expected to do much in 1986.

Virginia Tech opened the season by losing to Cincinnati 24–20 after a tipped pass helped keep alive the Bearcats' winning drive. The Hokies won their next four games, including road upsets of Clemson and Syracuse, before tying South Carolina 27–27.

Virginia Tech lost to Temple 29–13 in Norfolk, Virginia, but it was later revealed that the Owls used an ineligible player. Temple had to forfeit the game, and the Hokies were awarded a victory.

Virginia Tech won its last four games, including a 42–10 rout of rival Virginia, and finished the regular season with a 9–1–1 record. The Hokies were invited to play North Carolina State in the Peach Bowl in Atlanta. Virginia Tech kicker Chris Kinzer kicked a 40-yard field goal as time expired, giving the Hokies a 25–24 victory, their first victory in a bowl game.

1995

The 1995 Hokies took their fans on a memorable ride no one would soon forget, and probably did more to help transform Virginia Tech from a regional program to a national powerhouse than any other team in school history.

The 1995 season didn't start well. The Hokies dropped consecutive home games against Boston College and Cincinnati out of the gates and were staring at a potential 0–3 record with Miami (Florida) coming to town. The Hokies had never beaten the Hurricanes in 12 tries. But behind a bruising running game and stingy defense, Virginia Tech stunned the 'Canes 13–7 at Lane Stadium. Virginia Tech ran for 300 yards—the first team to do it against Miami since 1979—and had six sacks on defense.

After stunning the Hurricanes, Virginia Tech won its next eight games. The Hokies' 36–29 victory over rival Virginia in Charlottesville in the regular season finale was one of the most memorable games in school history. Trailing the No. 13 Cavaliers 29–14 going into the fourth quarter, the Hokies scored 22 straight points to win the game. Quarterback Jim Druckenmiller threw a 32-yard touchdown to Jermaine Holmes with 47 seconds left for the winning score.

The Hokies finished as cochampions of the Big East Conference and represented the league in the Bowl Alliance. Virginia Tech was invited to play mighty Texas in the Sugar Bowl in New Orleans. On New Year's Eve 1995, more than 25,000 Virginia Tech fans watched their team upset the Longhorns 28–10 in the Louisiana Superdome to cap an unforgettable 10–2 season.

Hokies in Their Own Words

JIM DRUCKENMILLER

QUARTERBACK, 1992–1996

My college decision was an easy choice. Virginia Tech was the only Division I school to offer me a scholarship. It was kind of a weird situation. I got hurt the first six games of the season when I was at Fork Union Military Academy. At the end of the season I was throwing some passes with Tyrone Davis, a wide receiver who went to the University of Virginia, and rehabbing with him. Rickey Bustle and Steve Marshall, two of the Virginia Tech assistants, came through looking for players at Fork Union, and John Shuman, who was the coach at Fork Union, told them about me. Well, they came out and watched me workout, and I never even knew it. I never even met them. About two weeks later, they called me and asked me if I wanted to visit Virginia Tech. I said, "Sure." The rest is history.

I had never heard of Virginia Tech before I went there. I grew up a Penn State fan. Both my uncles went to Penn State, but it didn't work out that way for me. Instead, it worked out for the best, but I didn't know that when I first got to Tech. I was one of 11 quarterbacks walking into the film room at Tech as a freshman.

Jim Druckenmiller led the Hokies to a 20–4 record during his two seasons as the team's starting quarterback and guided Virginia Tech to appearances in the Sugar Bowl and Orange Bowl.

I was, like, the third- or fourth-to-last one on the depth chart. At one point, I was the 11th quarterback. I'm sure of it. I remember the only way I moved up the depth chart at all early on was because one of those quarterbacks turned into a tight end and another one flunked out of school.

It was my redshirt sophomore year before I really felt like I fit in. Luckily, I went to school with a few guys at Fork Union who also went to Tech, so I had a support system. I was wondering if I'd ever get an opportunity at Tech. I think I fit in as a member of a team, but I wondered if I'd ever get to play. I didn't feel like I was getting any reps. I even considered transferring to a little college called East Stroudsburg in Pennsylvania, which is about an hour east from where I grew up in Northampton, Pennsylvania. Luckily, I got hooked up with a guidance counselor who helped me mature, get me on the right path at Tech, and kept me there. But I did think about transferring. I thought, *Wow, I could drop down to Division II. Maybe play a few years and see what happens.*

I remember backing up my redshirt sophomore year. Then, Maurice DeShazo got hurt and I stepped in and had a little bit of success. I remember sitting there in the Gator Bowl, too, at the end of my redshirt sophomore year and watching Maurice throw five or six interceptions, and I thought, *Are you ever going to put me in?* But it's funny how things work out. Now, I don't think there's any place more beautiful than Tech. It's a beautiful area and just a great place to go to school.

Of course, it's always intriguing to watch a program turn the corner. There's something to be said about actually being a part of it. There are many, many of us who made it happen. Even in the 2–8–1 season in 1992, you've got to say some of those guys contributed to it because a lot of players in the future wouldn't have come there if they didn't get that feeling that things were turning around. You don't appreciate it at the time because you get caught up in the moment.

I've got a lot of great memories from those years, but none was greater than the Virginia game in 1995. My roommate was Chris Malone, who was a guard. I remember calling a play where I was going to throw a wide screen pass to Cornelius White, and he was going to throw it back to me. I called the play in the huddle, and Chris looked at me and said, "That ain't gonna work." Well, I threw the pass to Cornelius, who got it to me, and I ran for a first down. I just got up and winked at Chris. That was a crazy game. I remember Virginia got the ball back pretty late in the fourth quarter. I was down a little bit, and my running mate and one of my best friends, George DelRicco, grabbed my face mask as I was running off the field and said, "You'll get it one more time." Sure enough, we got the ball back and wound up winning the game 36–29 with that big catch by Jermaine Holmes.

That whole season was crazy. It was my junior year, and we lost to Boston College and Cincinnati at the start of the year. Then, Miami came to town. I was probably off-key a little that week, very moody and probably yelling a whole lot. The only thing I remember about the rest of that week was hugging Billy Conaty, my center, after we won that game and telling him, "We're going to win 10 straight." And that's what we did.

I mean, they weren't all good memories. I remember Syracuse in my senior year and we lost up there in the Carrier Dome 52–21. That was a bad game. I didn't feel good about that loss. I also remember, in our spring game of 1994 or 1995, Waverly Jackson came through the line and nearly broke my ankle. I'm still trying to remember why I wasn't wearing a yellow jersey in that game. I remember playing against Boston College in my junior year, there was a defensive lineman who would later play in the NFL up in

Minnesota and horse-collared me. My head bounced off the turf, and I didn't know the answer to two plus two for a while.

But I wouldn't trade any of those experiences. I made some really good friendships there. George and I lived across from each other in the apartment complex at Terrace View in Blacksburg. That's how we got to be so close. Our families got really close, too. I still talk to one of George's uncles. He calls me whenever he's wondering what's going on. Ken Landrum, another one of my teammates, was the best man in my wedding. Treg Koel was another one of my closest friends. Tally Hair was too. He was from Allentown, Pennsylvania, which was like 20 minutes from where I grew up.

Then, there's Coach Bustle. I still talk to him to this day. It's the same with Mike Gentry. I'd do anything for those guys. Coach Gentry is just a guy you respect. He always treated me fairly. As long as you followed through with the work he was asking you to do, he'd still put his arm around you, even if you failed. Coach Bustle and I had some friction early on. I kept bugging him about getting reps in practice. He told me going into my junior year that if I didn't win the starting job that year, the job would probably go to Al Clark and stay that way.

I asked Coach Bustle what I needed to do to win the job and what I needed to do beyond that. One of the images I have in my memory is walking off the Orange Bowl field at the end of my career and both of us crying. That was probably one of my toughest memories at Tech. The picture of us crying was on the cover of the *Miami Herald* the next day.

I went through a lot of things at Tech. No matter what I think about some of the things that happened off the field, we'll never know what some people thought about me. I know some individuals liked me and some individuals didn't like me. Whatever anybody says, I was always a happy-go-lucky guy and never wanted to hurt anybody. I always wanted to make life fun.

I try to get back to Tech once a year. If I move back to the area with my job [as regional manager for Choice Point, a company that provides security services, such as workplace drug testing and background checks], I'd like to make it back to Tech a whole lot more. I've still got friends there. It's an amazing place. I won't deny it. I'd definitely have to say those were the best years of my life.

Jim Druckenmiller was Virginia Tech's starting quarterback in 1995 and 1996, leading the Hokies to a 20–4 record and appearances in the Sugar Bowl and Orange Bowl. In the 1995 Sugar Bowl in New Orleans Druckenmiller threw a 54-yard touchdown to Bryan Still that helped the Hokies win 28–10 over Texas in what is still considered the greatest postseason victory in school history. Druckenmiller was a first-round selection by the San Francisco 49ers in the 1997 NFL Draft and played in six games in four seasons before retiring in 2003.

Hokies in Their Own Words

KEION CARPENTER

SAFETY, 1995–1998

Growing up in Baltimore, there were only a few guys in my high school who had a chance to go to a Division I college. But with my situation, going through the problems I had with the SAT, Virginia Tech was the only school that stuck with me. They were loyal, and that meant everything to me. A lot of schools, when I didn't improve my score, just went on to the next guy.

Brian Scriven, my coach at Woodlawn High School, didn't want me to get recruited as an "athlete," because, a lot of times, those guys got lost in the shuffle once practice started. That's why Coach Scriven wanted me to become as good at safety as I was at quarterback. We thought safety was going to be the best option.

The first time I met Coach Frank Beamer was during my senior year at Woodlawn. I took an official campus visit, and I was really impressed with the family atmosphere. With Coach Beamer, I got the feeling that he was like a father figure to those of us who grew up in homes with just one parent. He gave me a foundation I didn't have, and my mom felt like she could call him any time and find out how I was doing in the classroom and on the football field.

During my visit, I hung out with Antonio Freeman and spent time with Maurice DeShazo. Antonio was from Baltimore, so I already knew about him. Because I played quarterback, Maurice took interest in me, which was something he didn't have to do because there was no doubt I was going to play safety.

The guy from Baltimore whom I associated with Virginia Tech the most was Vaughn Hebron. I knew he had made it in the NFL, and that impressed me a lot. Because I had such a great experience academically, athletically, and socially at Virginia Tech, I think it helped Vincent Fuller, who went to Woodlawn, and Richard Johnson, who went to Milford Mill, in their decisions to go to Tech.

At first, I thought I would go to Boston College because I had enjoyed the football camp I attended there as a junior. It was the first long trip I took away from home, riding on a train, when I was kind of on my own. You could say I took an unofficial visit while I was on campus, but I liked it enough that I verbally committed to BC. That all changed, though, when my SAT scores didn't improve. Going to Blacksburg was definitely a better move for me and my family. People from home could make the four-hour drive and come watch me play. That was important to me, having my family in the stands if they could make it to a game.

No question that I went through some culture shock as a freshman. You're accustomed to being the best athlete, not just in your school, but in the area, too, but that wasn't the case anymore. I soon realized that I'd never really been challenged. Football and other sports had always come to me really easily, but that's what happens when you're a big fish in a small pond. Looking back on it, there's no doubt that I went through some changes that helped me grow as a person.

Some of the guys who didn't make it just couldn't get over those homesick feelings, but I always kind of thought that they were realizing for the first time that they really would have to work really, really hard to be successful. I guess they couldn't handle the challenges.

We had to stay on campus for a year, which, for me, started in the summer before my freshman season. I had a head start, though, because I had enrolled early, and they paid for summer school. That gave me kind of a head start. You look back to living on campus, and it's a really important time in your career. That's a time that you really get to know other guys, you grow close to people, form cliques, that sort of thing.

Once I moved into an apartment off campus, I felt like I was finally on my own. You had to feed yourself, buy your groceries, eat right, take care of things you'd always taken for granted.

Practice was really, really hard, but the most difficult thing was learning how to pace yourself in those strength sessions. Mike Gentry, man, he pushed you harder than you ever thought possible. I mean, we had to push trucks up a hill, flip tractor tires, things that really took you to another level. I can look back on it now and realize that I was a lot tougher than other guys when I

Keion Carpenter returns an interception 100 yards for a Hokies touchdown in a 21–7 victory over Miami in 1996.

first got into the NFL. I think one of the reasons I made the Buffalo Bills as an unrestricted free agent was because Gentry pushed us so hard, and I was used to working, training, practicing—whatever you want to call it—at a high level.

Another thing that brought my game to a higher level was understanding the schemes. In high school, schemes were vanilla, very easy. It was mostly about just reacting to what you saw in front of you. Once I learned what was expected of me in the secondary at Virginia Tech, I immediately played at a higher level.

A lot of that success I had early in the NFL I have to credit to Bud Foster. He had already taught me so much about making checks and adjustments on the go. I was ready to play free safety in the league, as far as realizing there was so much information that you had to digest and understand before you get out there on the field to play in a game.

Nothing stood out more to me as a freshman than our third game. We were 0–2, and both losses were at home to Boston College and Cincinnati. Now we had to play Miami (which was ranked No. 17), and there was no way we could drop to 0–3. No way. Sure enough, we beat them 13–7, and it turned our season around. But the thing that I'll always remember was watching Ray Lewis taking down Ken Oxendine. We ran an "iso" up the middle, and he hit the fullback and fell to the ground. Oxendine broke to the outside, but that only seemed to make Ray mad. He just jumped up and tackled him something like 30 yards down the field.

We beat the 'Canes that year, and I left my career with a 4–0 record against them. When we knocked them off in my freshman season, that was sweet because we didn't lose again. To be a part of a Hokies team that won 10 straight games and beat Texas in the Sugar Bowl—man, there's nothing in the world, as far as an athletic experience is concerned, you would trade that experience for.

During my freshman year, I didn't play anything but special teams, which I credit completely with helping me block six punts during my last three years. I learned so much from the older players. Just watching how they practiced, how they prepared, how they played—all that really helped when I became a starter in the secondary in my second year. I was splitting time with Torrian Gray, who was a senior. Once I had some guys calling me "Hammer," I knew I had to be doing something right.

If there's one play that probably most people remember me for, it would have to be that 100-yard interception return I had in Miami as a sophomore. It set an Orange Bowl record, which was nice, but the greatest thing was scoring the touchdown and helping us beat the 'Canes.

We beat Virginia in each of my first two years, but they won the last two. That 36–32 game, which was my last game at home, still makes me sick. We came back and put a pretty good whipping on Alabama in the bowl game, but I couldn't stand losing that game against Virginia. They're our in-state rival. It was a like a backyard dogfight. I mean, you took it personally. That's what I consider the true meaning of rivalry.

Still, for all the achievements that made me proud and the setbacks that made me stronger, the greatest single thing was earning my degree. It still hangs on my mom's wall in her house. Sometimes it was hard to stay focused, particularly when I was just one student in an auditorium of 400. I wasn't going to get that one-on-one attention I grew accustomed to in high school. I watched a lot of people get caught up in the shuffle, and I had to remind myself constantly not to slip.

My degree was in residential property management, which benefits me to this day. I have a company with three other Falcons—Allen Rossum, Kevin Mathis, and DeAngelo Hall—and we do all kinds of things in regards to real estate acquisition, management, and sales. Getting that degree, though, was a real grind. I mean, it was the first time in my life that I really felt like I accomplished something truly meaningful, not just to me but to those who worked so hard to give me a chance to become a responsible young man.

In our family, I was the oldest grandchild. My mother, Teresa Harris, still tells me that my diploma was the proudest moment in her lifetime. I had an uncle who had gone to Morgan State, but to take it to the level that I did was pretty special.

Keion Carpenter was a starting safety for the Hokies in 1997 and 1998. He was named All–Big East Conference as a senior in 1998 after he finished second in the league with five interceptions. During his college career, the Baltimore native blocked more punts (five) than any other Virginia Tech player and held the school record with a 100-yard interception return for a touchdown against Miami as a sophomore. Carpenter played in the NFL for Buffalo and Atlanta before retiring in 2006.

1996

After winning the Sugar Bowl in 1995, the Hokies were picked to finish no better than third in the Big East in preseason polls in 1996.

A rash of injuries and suspensions made matters worse throughout the 1996 season, but the Hokies somehow managed to finish 10–2 and play in a Bowl Alliance bowl game for the second season in a row.

After losing to Syracuse 52–21 in their fourth game, the Hokies won their next seven games to earn a share of a Big East championship for the second season in a row. Virginia Tech was absolutely dominant in its last four games, blasting East Carolina 35–14, Miami (Florida) 21–7, West Virginia 31–14, and Virginia 26–9.

Led by defensive ends Cornell Brown and John Engelberger and safety Torrian Gray, Virginia Tech's defense didn't allow more than two touchdowns in any of its 10 victories.

Quarterback Jim Druckenmiller was named Big East Co–Offensive Player of the Year after throwing for nearly 2,300 yards with 20 touchdowns and only five interceptions. Tailback

Ken Oxendine ran for 1,040 yards despite missing two and a half games with a separated shoulder.

The Hokies were overmatched by two-time defending national champion Nebraska in a 41–21 loss in the Orange Bowl. But the 1996 Hokies proved Virginia Tech was finally capable of producing a national contender every season.

1999

Before the 1999 season, a sign was taped to the door of Virginia Tech's coaching offices. It read: "Preparing to Win a National Championship."

Outside of Blacksburg, few people actually believed the Hokies were a national championship contender. But with a menacing defense and electrifying freshman quarterback, Virginia Tech nearly accomplished its impossible dream. The Hokies finished the regular season with an 11–0 record and lost to Florida State 46–29 in the Sugar Bowl.

For four months, much of the nation was captivated by Virginia Tech's football team, and especially quarterback Michael Vick. The Hokies won each of their first seven games by lopsided scores, including a 62–0 rout of Syracuse at home. After beating Pittsburgh 20–17 on the road, Virginia Tech faced its stiffest challenge against rival West Virginia.

On the same day No. 2 Penn State was upset by Minnesota, which opened the Hokies' door to play for the BCS national championship, Virginia Tech nearly squandered a 19–7 lead in the fourth quarter against the Mountaineers. Backup quarterback Brad Lewis threw two touchdowns in the final three minutes to give West Virginia a 20–19 lead.

The Hokies got the ball back at their 16-yard line, and Vick marched his team down the field. The biggest play was Vick's memorable 26-yard run to the West Virginia 36, which put the Hokies in field-goal position. Shayne Graham kicked a 44-yard field goal as time expired to give the Hokies a 22–20 victory.

Virginia Tech walloped Miami (Florida) by a 43–10 score the next week; blasted Temple 62–7; and routed Boston College 38–14 to finish the season with an 11–0 record.

Playing for a national championship for the first time in school history, Vick nearly led the Hokies to an improbable come-from-behind victory. But the Seminoles, who became the first team in NCAA history to go wire-to-wire as the No. 1 team in the country, were simply too much to overcome.

Hokies in Their Own Words

SHAYNE GRAHAM

KICKER, 1996–1999

When I talk to kickers in the NFL about college and how special teams was handled at their programs, they would tell me things like, "The coaches told us we were kicking field goals in period eight of practice, be ready." That was it.

Coach Beamer, our head coach, didn't operate like that when it came to special teams. He would come over to where we were on the practice field and would put us through drills and competitions. He put us through exercises. He may not have had the know-how of pure technique of coaching a kicker, but he would give us the structure so we would train and be disciplined.

Now, he knew how to draw up the blocks and the formations and set returns and create big plays.

The punt block schemes, all that, he drew that stuff up by himself. I saw that during a campus visit the spring of my senior season in high school. He was the person who had the team meetings with special teams and handled the scouting reports of players on the other team. We knew the strengths of guys we were kicking to because he got that information.

It wasn't something that was handed off to somebody else. Special teams was his thing, and he took pride in it, which is why his punt team was called "Pride" and punt block team was called "Pride and Joy." We took so much pride and joy in special teams.

When we were kicking off, we had some of the fastest guys on the team running down the field. He put first-team guys out there: there was no, *This guy doesn't play much, let's get him in there.* This was serious business, and the best of the best were put out there. We didn't put guys out there just to get them on the field. We put guys in there to knock people's heads off. We had guys with the right attitude. Jimmy [Kibble] got the kickoff job the first year, and he did a good job for us; I did extra points and field goals.

I had one extra point blocked my senior year, I had just set the Big East record for consecutive extra points when Ike Charlton had scored on an interception return for a touchdown and we celebrated too much and got a penalty. They moved us back 15 yards for the extra point, and the extra-point attempt got tipped. It fell short in the end zone. That was the first one I missed in a couple of years.

I missed another one against Arkansas State when we scored something like nine touchdowns. The ninth one I missed.

Frank Beamer was pretty good at knowing no one's perfect. He wasn't one who would come yell at me for missing. He knew I was mature enough to handle it and I wasn't going to lose all my confidence.

The people who recruited me included North Carolina, Georgia, Boston College, Virginia, Virginia Tech. Penn State was interested, but they were one of the schools that had a senior kicker coming back, and I knew I didn't want to go there. I wanted to play my freshman year, so I didn't let the recruiting process go very far at schools with a veteran kicker coming back.

Virginia Tech offered me my junior year, and that was a weird situation because at the time they already had Jimmy Kibble, who was from the Manassas area. A lot of people were wondering what they were doing. They offered him first, and he accepted because I think that was his only offer. They offered me, I think, because they would have been given a hard time for not offering a kid from Pulaski.

I didn't expect to want to stay there and play locally. They might have wanted to say that at least they tried. I was down on staying local and thought I wanted to go away. Then, the more I thought about it, Virginia Tech looked like a good choice. I would have a chance to win the job as a freshman and football was the main sport. Tech was also a Top 10 program.

The other thing that made a big difference was the head coach was the special teams coach. You knew you were going to get some attention from the coaching staff because they placed an importance on special teams.

Jimmy had redshirted there my senior year in high school so Tech was going to have two scholarship kickers, which was very rare. I felt confident I could win the job and I devoted my whole life to it. I didn't take any senior beach trips, any vacations. I trained nonstop, kicking and kicking.

That's all I did. When I got in there as a true freshman, I felt like I had really made the transition kicking off the little one-inch block in high school to kicking off the ground. I won the job and the rest fell in place.

Jimmy became the starting punter and was All-ACC. He did a great job.

For years there were no walk-ons at Virginia Tech trying to kick. Now, when you go out there, there are guys out there kicking, trying to get the job as walk-ons. Our first three years at Tech there were no walk-ons because everyone knew we had the place-kicking and punting jobs for three years.

Our senior year we finally had Carter Worley, a recruited, invited walk-on to come out and work and get ready for when there was an open job. Jimmy and I were adequate backups for each other. If I got hurt, Jimmy could kick. If he got hurt, I think I could have punted, but probably not as good as he could have filled in for me as a kicker.

My last year I was there, some of my best friends were guys who walked on and tried to win a spot at kicker.

I think 1995 was the first year Beamer Ball started to get some national attention. We went to the huge bowl system. We had a 10-game winning streak, and Virginia Tech started to make a name for itself. Then we had a blocked punt for a touchdown against Syracuse in 1996 and another one or two against Rutgers.

That was my freshman year. We seemed to have a blocked kick every other game, and people started hearing about our special teams.

Beamer Ball became something of an identity for Virginia Tech because our program was never built around superstars until Michael Vick came along. Even at that, Michael Vick, as much of a superstar as he was, never took that attitude that he was the face of the program and the reason we were so good.

Shayne Graham (left) and teammate Jimmy Kibble hoist coach Frank Beamer onto their shoulders after winning 38–14 over Boston College at Lane Stadium, November 26, 1999, to finish the regular season undefeated. *Photo courtesy of AP Images*

That 1999 team was the best team that ever played at Tech as far as talent and team chemistry. That was the year Michael Vick became a superstar, but we had guys like Corey Moore on defense, Anthony Midget, Ike Charlton, and great linebackers. We had good offensive linemen and very good running backs.

Starters played on special teams. Everybody put their claim on the team, everybody contributed.

Coach Beamer's attitude about special teams and the fact we didn't have five first-round draft picks every year like Miami or Florida State kept away the attention from the stars we had. We had players, but when your special teams is scoring a lot of points, whether it's touchdowns on kick returns or blocks and getting field position, it took away from some good individual players.

There were games where we were ending up with 100 yards of hidden yardage. That's almost two scores in a game, depending on where you start drives.

Shane Beamer was the long snapper and with us all the time in practice. His dad would come over and coach us, but it was funny because we all felt it was our dad coaching us. It felt like there was a family figure out there. You were comfortable and felt you could share with him. There was a trust there, especially when we would be on the sideline and he would ask me, "Can we make this kick?"

I remember that if I told him we should kick a field goal instead of punting and I missed I felt so bad because I let him down. It's the feeling you get when you don't want to see your dad after you let him down. It happened only a couple of time.

I was very realistic and didn't let my pride get a hold of me. He trusted me even more because I would not tell him I could make it when I knew it was risky because of the wind or some other condition out there. Most of the time, I made those kicks.

We had a chance to win the national championship when we played Florida State because our offensive line for three quarters was pounding their defense. Michael Vick was running all over there. I think one of their guys buckled his knee chasing Michael.

But there were just some things that happened that kept us from winning the game. We got a bad spot on a ball that cost us a first down. There was a bad play on the goal line. We were good enough to win the game, but Florida State had a lot of depth.

They were the ones who blocked a punt for a touchdown and returned a punt for a touchdown, and that 14-point swing beat us [46–29]. We were winning in the fourth quarter; it wasn't a rout.

I remember most every kick in my career. You could point out any kick, and I could tell you where it was from and what happened with it.

My most memorable game was my senior year playing at West Virginia just because that one had the most implications. Halfway through that game we realized Penn State had lost. They were No. 2, we were No. 3, and now we had to win to get a chance to play for the championship.

They lost to Minnesota, and we were winning and then we fumbled, and West Virginia scored and went ahead. We were down one with about 1:30 to go. That's when Michael Vick drove the ball down and we kicked a 44-yarder off the right hash in the game's final seconds.

One of the things about me as a kicker is I enjoy the crowd, but when you are going on the field for a kick at the end of the game, it goes to just a buzz, not a loud, screaming mob that you pay attention to. It's just a humming in your ears, a vibration.

I was aiming down the middle with that kick. When you kick off the right hash, guys with a hook might have a more difficult time, but my ball typically doesn't do that. It looks like you are crooked from the right hash, but it's just like lining up down the middle.

I remember there was smoke coming up from that end of the stadium and I could smell barbecue. I saw smoke in the air. I remember that smell and I remember they called a timeout after we just spiked the ball to stop the clock.

I joked around with Caleb Heard, the holder. We had a saying, "Piece of cake," like we had this, were going to make it. He said, "What do you think about this?" and I said, "Cake."

We always spotted the ball on the outside edge of the hash because of the offset of the rush kicking the ball from the right hash. That gap between the center and the guard is opened up so we always spotted on the outside edge of the hash. I remember how comfortable I felt.

Who isn't nervous in a moment like that? But it's all how you control the oxygen through your body and being light on your feet so you can feel the nerves in your body. You don't want to have such a serious heart palpitation that your anxiety is high and you're numb. I looked at it as trying to enjoy every step I took out there.

To me, it is such a strong family. Even today, I stay in touch with a lot of the guys I played with. Sadly enough, those bonds were made stronger by the massacre a couple of years ago. A lot of people who had lost contact reached out for each other.

When you come from a program where people outside the program don't expect a lot from you, it was great to raise everyone's expectations of the program. Not many people gave Virginia Tech much credit back in the early '90s, and we started building that credit and reputation.

Now, every year, we start out in the top 10. That empty spot in the trophy room for a national championship is not some pipe dream anymore. It is an expectation now.

Shayne Graham was named first-team All–Big East Conference in the four seasons he was at Tech. As a senior in 1999, Graham earned Big East Special Teams Player of the Year honors after leading the conference and breaking the school's single-season scoring record with 107 points on 56-of-57 extra points and 17-of-22 field goals. He was

68-of-93 (73.1 percent) kicking field goals in his career. Graham set a Virginia Tech career and Big East record with 97 consecutive extra points. He is the all-time scoring leader in school history and Big East history with 371 points.

2004

When the 2004 season opened, ACC newcomer Virginia Tech was picked to finish sixth in its first season in the conference.

When the Hokies' regular season ended in Miami on December 4, 2004, they were crowned ACC champions after finishing with a 10–2 record. Along the way, the Hokies were on both ends of some of the most dramatic finishes in school history.

Virginia Tech opened the 2004 season against defending national champion USC at FedEx Field in Landover, Maryland. The Hokies took a lead into the third quarter, but USC tailback Reggie Bush and quarterback Matt Leinart rallied the Trojans to a 24–13 victory.

After winning its first-ever ACC game 41–17 at Duke, the Hokies trailed N.C. State 17–16 in the final seconds in their fourth game. Brandon Pace lined up for a winning field goal, but he left his 43-yard attempt outside the right upright, and the Hokies had a 2–2 record heading into October.

Behind senior quarterback Bryan Randall, the Hokies rallied to win their final eight regular season games. Virginia Tech trailed Georgia Tech 20–12 with 5:30 to go, but Randall threw an 80-yard touchdown to Eddie Royal and a 51-yard touchdown to Josh Morgan. Defensive back Roland Minor intercepted two passes in the final 2:31, returning the second one for a touchdown with 56 seconds to play in the Hokies' improbable 34–20 victory at Bobby Dodd Stadium in Atlanta.

After a 27–24 victory over North Carolina and 55–6 rout of Maryland, the Hokies beat rival Virginia 24–10 and Miami 16–10 to win an ACC championship.

Virginia Tech played SEC champion Auburn in the Sugar Bowl on January 3, 2005, losing 16–10 to the undefeated Tigers.

Hokies in Their Own Words

BRYAN RANDALL

QUARTERBACK, 2001–2004

Actually, I received my first scholarship offer after my 10th-grade year from the University of Virginia. That's when things started going uphill for me. I had a really good season in 10th grade, which was my first year playing quarterback. They had me at wide receiver as a freshman.

My 11th grade year I ended up rushing for 1,000 yards and passing for 1,000 yards, the first time that had been done in Virginia high school history. After my junior year I started receiving scholarships from nearly every school in the country. By my senior year, I had my pick of the litter.

Coach Jim Cavanaugh recruited me to Virginia Tech, and I narrowed it down to the East Coast. I didn't really want to go too far from home.

It came down to Virginia Tech, Virginia, North Carolina, and Tennessee. The final two ended up being Tennessee and Virginia Tech, and the thing was, I knew in my heart they wanted me to play safety at Tennessee. They told me they'd give me the opportunity at quarterback, but really the decision was, "What did I want to play?" It was a tough decision. I wasn't really sure for a while what I wanted to do because I really was thinking about the next level, the NFL. What it came down to was that I wanted to play quarterback. I loved the fact of being the leader of the team.

The Virginia Tech coaches told me they were recruiting me as a quarterback and they wanted me to be a quarterback. There really wasn't even a thought of me being a safety.

North Carolina was my first official visit. I was almost sold on UNC when I took the visit there. I was really leaning toward UNC, but when they switched coaches, that just turned me away. Coming out of high school, I was a big basketball guy and I wanted to do the two-sport thing. When I was looking at UNC, I was like, *It would be great to play Tar Heels basketball also.*

I can't really remember what Tennessee told me they would do, but I think they were going to give me the opportunity. Virginia Tech said they would let me do it.

My official visit to Tennessee was incredible because, with the crowd and the stadium, I'd never seen that many people in one place. The stadium was humongous. Knoxville is a football town. I knew it was going to be a great experience wherever I went, so it was a tough decision.

Virginia Tech was the last visit I made officially, and that actually was the first time I saw Mike Vick play in person. He was a redshirt sophomore. The visit wasn't necessarily spectacular because I went when there weren't many students there, during Thanksgiving. I wasn't really going to be sold by the campus that much, but I loved the atmosphere. I liked the coaches, and you could feel it was like family.

It was small town, and I wasn't a big-city guy. That attracted me to it also. When I came close to the end, I actually made my decision before signing day. Everybody wanted to know if my mind had changed. The whole recruiting process, with people calling your house all the time, was kind of fun when it started, but after a while it got kind of annoying. They'll worry you to death, but it was a blessing also to have that many choices.

My coach at Bruton High School in Williamsburg, Kyle Neve, was a punter [who lettered in 1982] at Virginia Tech. I knew he would've loved for me to go there, but he wasn't really pushing me in that direction. To be honest, I really didn't pay attention to Virginia Tech actually until Mike was there.

When they played for the national championship, they were kind of selling me as the next great program.

The guys I kind of bonded with in that first summer session were DeAngelo Hall, Chris Clifton, and Justin Hamilton. Cedric Humes was supposed to be there, too, but he didn't make it. We spent a lot of time together, going to summer school and working out for that whole first month.

As far as conditioning went, you knew the "iron-man" competition was coming, but they didn't have us pushing trucks up a hill or anything like that during our first month in summer school.

What I'll never forget about the actual first conditioning we did was something called the "phase." It was on the track, and I didn't really know what was going on, but some guys were kind of like, "This is the track enema."

Were excited to get out on that track and get started, but they had us run, I want to say, three 400s, two 300s, four 200s, and then five 100s. It wasn't just the freshman. It was the whole team, because everybody comes back to train in the summer session. We were just like, "Woooo! That was a wake-up call." That was the most serious conditioning experience of my life, and I knew if all of them were going to be like that, then I would be in big trouble.

Coach Mike Gentry—he ran it all—and I remember that first day, guys were just laid out, and he was just screaming at us. You know, guys were leaning over, laying down, just worn out. I guess he wanted us to suck it up because he didn't want to hear guys whining. He gave us a piece of his mind.

I believe it's a way bigger jump going from high school to college than it is going from college to pro, level-wise. In college, if you go to a big-time Division I school, you're going to play against big-time teams. Now the majority of them, week in and week out, may drop off, but you're going up against premier, top 10 teams, you're facing some good players.

It steps up again in the pros, but from high school to college is a much more difficult adjustment.

To begin my freshman year, I played behind Grant Noel, who had backed up Mike. I didn't play much at all. I got in a couple of games for mop-up duty, but that was about all I got.

I had a great spring going into my sophomore year, but I didn't win the job. It was weird because there were a lot of questions about whether I would stay at quarterback or not. A lot of people said I didn't have the arm strength and that I was more of a runner. Some fans thought I should be playing defense. The coaches never said it, but I had a feeling that I was kind of on the bubble. I didn't feel like I had won the coaches over.

I don't think I was at the level they wanted me to be. As I look back at it, I believe being put in the position I was in, there's no doubt I was kind of raw coming out of high school. Now I look at guys coming of high school and the schemes that they're in—I mean guys are throwing the ball, they're running four-wides the whole game and using audibles—but we were an option team in high school.

So I never had a chance to really develop as a passer in high school, and in college, you've got to be able to throw the ball. I was still making the transition but I knew I could do it. I knew eventually I'd be able to develop that. After that first year, it was a little rough. I felt like I had the tools and they just needed to be polished.

Because I wasn't really playing in the games, it was hard to tell where my skills were, and then sometimes in practice I wouldn't really have the best day. The thing was, our practices were open to some people, and that's how it would leak out a lot of times. You know, it would go up on message boards—"I've seen him throw the ball, and his lack of arm strength is keeping him from playing"—and from all that, those kinds of rumors would take on a life of their own, just like town gossip.

Going into my sophomore year, I didn't feel like I had won the coaches over because I knew my performance had been less than spectacular, but I felt like, given a spring and another summer in the weight room, I'd be fine. I had a great spring and ended up putting on about 10 pounds to get up to 215. My arm got stronger. I learned the offense better, and people were kind of like amazed and wondering, *Is this the same guy?*

I pushed for that starting job hard that spring and actually, one practice before our Maroon-White game, Grant Noel tore his ACL. He did a great job of rehabilitating his knee and he came back and started the first two games. Grant and I both got significant playing time in the first two games. He played the first two series against LSU, and they put me in for the third series, and I never looked back. That was it. We won the game. I didn't end up throwing a lot of passes, but I was efficient.

Playing after Mike had been there, I felt his presence even though he wasn't there. The standard was set so high. Beginning with the national championship game, we knew we had to win conference titles and play in BCS bowls for it to be considered a successful season. We had the talent to go every year to a BCS, but there would always come a point where we'd have a lot of success early in the season and then lose one, two, or three games at the end, and that became the type of reputation that we had.

Following in the footsteps of Mike, it was kind of hard because of the expectations people had. He set the bar, and we knew that anything less than a top 10 finish was basically unacceptable.

When you're running the team and you're not producing, it can get rough. They'll be calling for your head.

My first start on the road was at Texas A&M, and we ended up beating them. That kind of set me up to look good in the eyes of the fans and the coaches. I think the score was tied, and it was third-and-8. They brought a free safety down in the box and tried to blitz him and six or seven other guys. I wasn't expecting it because I was just a sophomore and I'd never started a game away from home. But it didn't work. I hit Ernest Wilford on an adjusted route, a slant hitch to my right, and he went for 52 yards to set up Lee Suggs' one-yard touchdown run.

I was poised. I felt comfortable, and it was good because I completed my last 10 passes.

After losing at home to Pittsburgh, the Syracuse game up there the next week was really tough. We lost 50–42 in triple overtime. I threw for 504 yards to set a Big East Conference single-game record, but we were sick after missing two field goals [one at the end of regulation and another at the end of the first overtime period]. I was mad at myself for throwing three interceptions. The last one killed us.

A game like that is draining. What a big difference if you win, but to go through all that and lose, it's crushing. You can deal with the physical part of it, but the mental side is tough to handle, particularly after we came home and lost 21–18 to West Virginia the next week.

That was our third-straight loss, making us 8–3. For me, that game was a lot like our season. I remember throwing for [168 yards] and rushing for [125], but we drove all the way down to their 11-yard line and with 12 seconds remaining, I threw an interception in our own end zone. If I had made a better throw, we would've won the game.

I still believe to this day that Lee Suggs got in the end zone on that previous drive when they made a goal-line stand against us.

No doubt, it's tough at the time, but you learn from those kinds of experiences. You have to because you can't afford to feel sorry for yourself and doubt yourself or anybody on your team. I knew I was going to take criticism for that, getting picked at the end of the game, in a loss, two weeks in a row.

You hear it, but that's part of the whole deal. The next thing was, "Well, he can't come through in a big game with everything on the line," or, "He can't produce in the clutch or lead the last drive."

When all that kind of talk is going on, I believe you can take it one of two ways. As a person, I've always felt like we change whether we like it or not, so you can take that and let it bring you down or you can bounce back from it.

I was a sophomore at the time, and it was tough, but I thought, *Man, I've got to learn and grow.* There are going to be ups and downs. I took some hard losses, but at the same time, I believe by the end of my career it made me a tougher person and a better leader.

For us, it felt so good the next game when we beat Virginia 21–9. Talk about needing a win, but then we went down to Miami to play the No. 1 team in the country. I was upset with myself for fumbling twice. One was just a good play by Sean Taylor. He came up and hit me. The other was a poor effort on my part. I just lost the ball. Even worse, we fell short again. We put up some points

[45], but we couldn't stop them [Miami had 56 points and six touchdowns from running back Willis McGahee].

Entering my junior year, I was up to 225. I felt bigger and stronger, but I didn't want to get any bigger than that. It was an important step up because my arm never felt sore the day after practice. I was in better shape and able to handle the workload.

Marcus Vick had redshirted when I was a sophomore and now he was ready to challenge me for the starting job. The big talk at that point was still, "Well, Randall lacks the arm strength to throw the deep ball, and that's what we're missing in our offense. Marcus is going to take us to the next level." Marcus was still learning. He was still young. I knew he was going to have some growing pains.

He and I always had a good relationship through it all. Some people are going to try and make a controversy out of a situation like that. He had a good spring and he was coming along, but I had a year under my belt and I knew the offense better.

I was so hot through the first four games, and I was being mentioned as a Heisman Trophy candidate. When we went to West Virginia, we were ranked third in the country [with a 6–0 record], but we got murdered. It wasn't even a game. They just hammered us. It was bad. It was embarrassing, actually.

That's a rough place to play. No doubt, the fans there are harder on opposing teams than anywhere else. They're just flat-out mean. Our fans are most hospitable. Not that we don't want to win every time we go out there, but there's a line between being competitive and hateful. Our place is loud and rowdy, but we don't have a lot of bad stuff going on.

After losing 28–7 in the West Virginia game, that's when Marcus and I started rotating. I would start the first quarter, and he would play the second. I would play the third, and he would take

Bryan Randall led Virginia Tech to the 2004 ACC championship during his senior season and was named the ACC's Player of the Year.

the fourth, but eventually we got to a situation where, if he was playing well in the second, he would stay in.

I was happy for our team and our fans that we came back after that nightmare at West Virginia and beat No. 2 Miami [31–7]. For me, though, it was a difficult day. I threw a pick on the third series and didn't get back in. Marcus played well in that game. He managed the game well, and our defense was just killing them.

After that, though, it was just trouble for me. I knew Marcus was coming on. We lost to Pittsburgh and Boston College, and everyone was down on us. People wanted to know what was going on because we definitely should've beaten BC, and we'd gone from being unbeaten and ranked third in the country to playing our way totally out of the picture.

Our team was better than that. Expectations were so high going into that season. Everyone was saying, "This team is going to win a national championship," and there's no doubt we had the talent. We had DeAngelo and Kevin Jones. They were absolutely dominating other teams, so it was definitely unacceptable to fizzle out.

When we lost at Pittsburgh and Larry Fitzgerald just went wild on us, that's when it really started getting frustrating for me. I played the first quarter of that game, and we were doing fine, but after I came out to start the second quarter, they came over and said, "We're going to leave Marcus in."

I didn't slam my helmet down or anything, but I was definitely disappointed. I'm a competitor, and I felt like that was my team. I felt I should've been out there and I deserved the opportunity. I felt like I should be leading the team and that it was being taken away from me unfairly. That was hard for me.

I was really steaming after the Pittsburgh game. Even though we had lost at West Virginia, we came back to beat Miami, so we still had a great shot at a conference championship. Losing to

Pittsburgh ruined everything. I would've felt better about it if I had gotten a chance to be out there and do something about the outcome.

But it was really out of my hands, and it hurt me to have no control over the situation. The thing was, everybody was kind of torn. We were losing, the quarterback shuffle thing, the media was coming down on us, our fans were unhappy—there were a lot of things going on, but nobody could blame one reason for our problems. It was a combination of a lot of things. For me, and I'm sure for Marcus, too, the quarterback situation just made it nine times worse.

He and I would talk. During the whole situation, we were friends. We were fine with each other. I didn't have anything against Marcus, because if I were him, I would want to be out there. As competitors, we had respect for each other. People were always saying, "Well, I'm sure they don't get along," or, "They must hate each other," but it wasn't like that at all. I'd say, "I want to win," and he'd say the same thing. We felt like we had to tell the coaches that if you want to play one of us, then play one of us, but we wonder if it's hurting the team to do the shuffle. Anybody could see that it wasn't working.

I had a talk with the coaches after the Pitt game. I told them I was disappointed. Going into the game, I didn't know it was going to happen like that. I was kind of in the dark. As far as I knew, I'd go out there and start the third quarter.

When they pulled me like that, nobody really had allowed me to know what was going on. It was quarterbacks coach Kevin Rogers who came over to tell me Marcus was staying in. The coaches knew I was frustrated. I mean, it was kind of obvious, even though I wasn't going to go out in the public and complain to the media. But to the coaches, I wanted to say, "Y'all know y'all got more respect for me than to leave me in the dark like this. Why not come to me and talk about it? Now, to make everything much, much worse, we're losing."

We talked about the whole situation. I had individual meetings with Coach Rogers, offensive coordinator Coach Bryan Stinespring, and Coach Beamer. It was interesting.

After my junior year, we had a new basketball coach, Seth Greenberg, and I decided that I wanted to play basketball after the bowl game. He gave me the opportunity. I hadn't talked to any of the football coaches, and we had only been back from the bowl game a couple of days when he called and said, "I need you down here tomorrow."

I never told the football coaches, but the way I looked at it was, "That's just the way it goes."

Man, I had the greatest time playing basketball. It was one of the most enjoyable experiences of my life. I was a guard, and it was so relaxing to get away from football and the past season. It was like an outlet, and I actually played in the first game I dressed out against West Virginia.

I hit a free throw and had a putback after I missed a free throw to beat St. John's. It was a home game. We had some success [finishing 15–14 and going 11–4 at home], and a lot of people wanted to give me the credit. But it wasn't about me at all. I was just going out there and playing hard and trying to lead by example.

I didn't have a great spring at all as far as football was concerned. The coaches said I was tired from basketball and that I had been going on for too long without giving my body a rest. I knew there probably was something to that. By the end of spring, Marcus had played better than me, so I knew I was going to have a tough time when summer came around.

At least we knew that the coaches weren't going to try that shuffle thing again. They were going to decide on a starter, and that was going to be the final decision. I was good with that.

[Vick's problems off the field began in February 2004, but Randall still expected none of the first legal issues to affect his status.] When the trouble came, we found out he wasn't going to be with us for that season. When it happened, at least I knew there wouldn't be any controversy to deal with if something does go wrong and I don't perform like I'm capable of performing.

It gave me kind of a path to just relax a little bit and take the pressure off. Entering the season, I wanted to win a conference championship, first of all, and I wanted to be first-team All-ACC in our first year in the league.

We lost to USC at the Washington Redskins' home field in our opener. Then we won a couple of games before N.C. State beat us on a late field goal. But we had started the year with people saying it would be a good season if we went .500. The *Sporting News* picked us to finish eighth—eighth!—in the ACC.

They thought because we lost DeAngelo and K.J. that we'd be rebuilding. It was like 7–4 was going to be a really big achievement.

When we started off 2–2, everybody was saying, "Well, hear we go," but we surprised everybody by winning eight straight. At Georgia Tech, we were down in the fourth quarter and we ran off 22 points in the final six minutes to wipe out a 14–0 deficit and win. People who said we couldn't come from behind had to eat their words. Coming back to win that game was huge.

That gave us a lot of momentum and confidence, because they had us beat, but we found a way to overcome it.

After that, we were in a lot of close games, but we kept finding a way to win. We clinched a tie for the ACC championship with a win over UVA at home. It was senior day. You couldn't ask for anything more.

In my mind, looking at the rivals, UVA and Miami and West Virginia were always the teams we circled on our calendars, but going down to Miami, we were tied with them for the conference lead. Our defense came up huge, and we won 16–10 to take the ACC title. That was so amazing.

It hurt to lose the Sugar Bowl to Auburn, but we really were able to look back at that season and say that we played about as well as we could. To earn ACC Player of the Year honors was more than I could've asked for. It was a great, great way to end my career, a storybook finish.

Bryan Randall was Virginia Tech's starting quarterback during three seasons, from 2002 to 2004. He led the Hokies to the 2004 ACC championship and a Bowl Championship Series game and was named the ACC Player of the Year as a senior. He is Virginia Tech's all-time leading passer, with 6,508 yards, and his 48 touchdowns are the most in school history. Randall is currently with the Richmond Raiders of the Southern Indoor Football League.

Hokies in Their Own Words

JEFF KING

TIGHT END, 2002–2005

I grew up close to Virginia Tech in Pulaski, but I was not a Virginia Tech fan growing up. You wouldn't know it now, but it's true. Tech was still in the Metro [Conference] when I was a kid, and Notre Dame was on TV. Notre Dame was on TV every Saturday.

ACC basketball was on TV a lot, too, and so was the NBA. Sundays was a big NBA day for me because I liked basketball, too.

The first time I went to a Virginia Tech game, I was a sophomore or a junior in high school. I don't think I realized how close I was to a major university. By the time I finished my junior year, I was being recruited by schools up and down the East Coast. Michigan State also came to offer me a scholarship. UNC was high on my list.

As I got around the Tech campus more and the coaches and the environment, I really began to like the place and the people. I committed to Tech the summer before my senior season in high school. I was a Hokie then.

I took two classes in the summer before the official start of my freshman year just to get acclimated to the big change. That's when you transition into the program and become a part of something much bigger than you.

I had about 20 or 30 guys in the program I loved to hang out with. That's a lot of guys on one team to feel close to, and that says a lot about the program.

What you were a part of was a program and school that had high expectations. Virginia Tech had risen to be a national power in football, and we had big-time recruits coming, not saying I was one, but the guys who came at that time.

We had Kevin Jones, who was the No. 1 prospect in the country. We had DeAngelo Hall. Everybody wanted him.

We weren't the sleeper like we were in the '90s. We were a team that people expected to win games. You got a feeling around the program that everyone expected you to be prepared and be on your game and get yourself together as a player.

We won a lot of games when I was there, and it was a collection of talent that Coach Beamer brought in and how we were coached

Tight end Jeff King (90) celebrates his touchdown against Miami, December 4, 2004. The Hokies finished the regular season 10–2 and ACC champions. *Photo courtesy of AP Images*

and the togetherness. Miami was still a national power then, and we were staying on the same field as them.

People forget that we beat Miami 12 out of the last 15 years, or something like that.

Beamer Ball was going full steam then. He was one of those few college coaches who put a number of starters on special teams. He equates special teams to the starting defense and offense and puts a lot of trust in guys. You learn early on at Virginia Tech that special teams has meaning and purpose.

You would always see Coach Beamer scribbling down different things, different schemes to try and get an edge with special teams. He was always working on a way to return the ball differently or block a punt. Special teams did not get stale there. It was because he would be going on the board or a piece of paper scheming.

The punt team, of course, was Pride, and the punt block was Pride and Joy. I was the protector on the punt team.

Here is the thing about Coach Beamer: you always felt like he cared whenever you went up to him. He wanted to win as badly as the next coach, but this guy also cared about his players and that's why he's still at Virginia Tech. That trust gets passed on to players who pass it on to their communities, and people hear about it and say, "I want to play for a guy like that."

Coach Beamer and his coaches wanted to develop players as men. I always looked at him like a father-figure, not just a coach. I know a lot of guys were like that, too. He is not a yeller or a screamer, but he demands things to be right. He leaves his mark on you.

He had his moments, though. He was all about being disciplined, even in the locker room after the game. You better not leave tape on the floor after practice or you would run extra. We did that, and he didn't put up with it. He wanted us taking care of little things.

He is a classy guy, and I feel honored to have played for him. It was a great experience.

The assistant coach I felt close to was Danny Pearman, who is now the assistant head coach at Clemson. I became extremely close to him. You know in college you are with your position coach for hours on end and you see them every day for five years, either watching film or during practice. That's who you got to be close with, your position coach, and that's how the program gets built.

He demanded a lot mentally and physically. His mind-set was game day was supposed to be the easiest day of the week. Tuesday, Wednesday, Thursday were the hard work days, and Saturday was second nature. I really liked that, and I try and prepare the same way now.

My freshman year we beat LSU at home, so that was a big game during my freshman season. Then we went down to Texas A&M and beat Texas A&M. We were the first nonconference team to beat them in 25 years at home.

We kind of fizzled down the stretch and finished 8–4. We had gotten to 6–0 and ranked No. 3 in the country. We were young, and that played a part in how we finished. Bryan Randall was playing for the first time, and we had so many young guys. We played so many big games it caught up to us.

The most memorable game was in the 2004 season when we beat Miami in the Orange Bowl and got to go to the ACC that first year. I caught a big third-down catch to take a knee to run out the clock. That was my fondest memory, and it was our first year in the ACC, so it was big for the program, too.

I caught the third-down pass, but I also caught a touchdown pass early in the game from Bryan. It was a goal line route, a seven-yard route call Z Cadillac. Duane Brown was the tight end, and I was the wing, and he went vertical and cleared it out, and

I trailed right behind him for the touchdown. He cleared it out pretty good.

The third-down catch was a third-and-12. I caught a big corner route to take a knee and win it. That was my most memorable catch. We were on our own 45-yard line and either had to run it and then punt or pass it. Bryan put it where only I could catch it. We didn't want to punt it to Roscoe Parrish. I didn't think they wanted to do that.

So we won the conference by beating Miami and went to the Sugar Bowl to play Auburn, which was unbeaten. To win a game like that at Miami was huge.

We played them every year I was at Tech, and it was always for some sort of positioning conference-wise. We were always near the top with them in whichever conference we were in [the Big East or ACC]. It meant a lot to beat them.

The previous year, 2004, they came into Blacksburg No. 1, and we beat them pretty good. They dropped a sure-fire, wide-open touchdown in the end zone, and we got them. It's always a rivalry between the schools, and we have gained some respect from them over the years. They have their own swagger and confidence.

We have a lot of pride, too, and we both have earned respect from one another. We don't have West Virginia on the schedule anymore, which was a big rivalry, and UVA has been down the last couple of years and has not been the game it should be. Miami has become that big game on the schedule.

UVA beat us one year I was there with Matt Schaub as quarterback. It was at UVA. We beat them the last three years I was there. Early on in my career at Tech they had a lot of good players and really good teams, then the last couple of years we got the best of them.

When I think back on it, that program is built on a lot of people, a lot of guys who worked their tails off. The lunch pail is the signature of the program. That signifies what it means to be a Hokie. You work for everything you get. That's what the program signifies. You ask the NFL guys and they will tell you if you are from Virginia Tech, you are pretty smart and pretty tough because that's what Coach Beamer said all the time. He wanted smart and tough.

> *Jeff King played tight end and special teams for the Hokies from 2002 to 2005 (he was a redshirt in 2001). He had a career-high 26 catches for 292 yards and six touchdowns in 2005, a school record for tight ends. He became the first player in school history to catch a touchdown pass in four straight games. He was named second-team All-ACC. King was selected in the 5th round of the 2006 NFL Draft by the Carolina Panthers.*

Hokies in Their Own Words

AARON ROUSE

ROVER, 2003–2006

The one thing that I will always remember are the Thursday night games where we were running out of the tunnel and people were jumping in Lane Stadium and "Enter Sandman" was playing. The bells and horns were going off. There was something about those night games.

You'd try and sit in class with a game Thursday night and it was hard to separate the two. Class was tough with that Thursday night game coming. Your mind was 80 percent football. You hate to say that; you need to be concentrating on class, but the campus was already buzzing. You were all about what you needed to accomplish.

We played North Carolina, Georgia Tech, and Maryland in some Thursday night games. ESPN liked to cover the Thursday night games at Lane Stadium because there was so much emotion. There was nothing like being there.

When we played Maryland at Maryland on a Thursday night, that sticks out, too. I saw Ray Lewis [with the Baltimore Ravens] on the sideline at the game, and his stepbrother played running back for them. I remember hitting him and saw Ray nod his head like, *Okay, nice job.* It was little things like that made that game special. We put a hurtin' on them.

Of course, the UVA game was special for me, too, because I was from Virginia [First Colonial], and everybody was going to be there. Guys you played with in high school, friends, everybody shows up at the UVA game because everyone knows each other. There are going to be coaches there, government officials, local police, everybody. It's a rivalry game, and everyone who follows high school football in the state is going to show up.

My junior year [2005] I had two interceptions against them and a bunch of tackles [eight] and a tackle behind the line. We won big [52–14], and the game was at UVA. We lost to them once when I was there, and that was tough. Don't ask me about that; I block things like that out of my mind. I get amnesia.

Ask me about the game we played against them my junior year. That I remember. They couldn't do anything against us. They had a tight end who is in the league [NFL] and they had D'Brickashaw Ferguson, who was an All-American. We beat them bad.

That win over UVA was part of a good junior year for me, but I didn't come out of school after three years because my mom wanted me to finish up and get a degree before I made that leap.

Another thing I remember that still sticks out four years later was playing at Georgia Tech at a night game when it was really cold. We were in the visitor's locker room, which is one of the worst in the nation, and everybody was putting on Under Armour stuff, the insulated gear, and I just saw Coach Beamer come around the corner in a full long-johns suit.

It was all white. He looked like this, I don't know, something out of *Andy Griffith*. He had the sleeves and the pants. I used to do a good impersonation of Coach Beamer and have some fun. He was a good guy, a remarkable man who is a lot of fun. All that brainpower that man has is incredible.

I was recruited by UVA and a lot of other schools on the East Coast. Virginia Tech offered me my junior year, and that's when I committed. I played a lot of offense in high school when Tech was recruiting me; that was my bread-and-butter.

I went to defense at Tech because I wanted to play right away and also Virginia Tech was known for defense. I had some size to play defense, and when they gave me an opportunity on that side of the ball, I took it. They had a bunch of receivers there when I got to Tech, so I moved.

I was tall [6'4"] and could run, so I matched up with some of the tall receivers who were coming along. I was athletic and could match up. We had another 6'3" guy, Jimmy Williams. We had Justin Fuller in the secondary, too. We were really good back there.

I learned a lot on the field from Coach Beamer and Bud Foster, but I also learned from Coach Stinespring how to conduct myself as a professional those first couple of years I was at Tech. He was the man who recruited me to Tech and got me going there.

Virginia Tech's Aaron Rouse sacks Auburn quarterback Jason Campbell in the 2005 Sugar Bowl in New Orleans. *Photo courtesy of AP Images*

When you come into college, you have been the star player in high school and you need somebody to tell you how it is in big-time college football. You have to learn your place. I won the President's Award there.

They stuck me at linebacker early and I redshirted. They put some bulk on me, and I went from 190 to 215 pounds, but I could still run. I went to Coach Beamer and, because we had a lot of outside linebackers, asked him if I could play rover. I knew I could still run. He let me move to rover, and it worked out well.

You could approach Coach Beamer and make requests like that. You could go up to him and talk to him, which we all appreciated. I took advantage of that open-door policy. He went to Coach Foster, and they let me play rover to see how I could do.

My junior year I was All-ACC. I remember my first game at rover, the season opener, we went out there and played North Carolina State, and I had a game-saving interception. I had 10 or 12 tackles and two interceptions and some pass break-ups. We won that game [20–16] to start a good season [11–2].

There is a state pride that goes with being a Hokie. And then when you travel the country people know of Virginia Tech football. We have a national identity, and that's something to be proud of. The program has gotten itself on a high level, and you are a part of it for the rest of your life. It means a lot to me to say I played football at Virginia Tech. There is a certain level of respect you get from being a Hokie.

There is some hard work you have to put into it. Those first couple of years I was at Tech, I put a lot of work into going from an offensive player in high school to a defensive player and then making the switch from linebacker to rover.

It's like no other place in the world. It was an experience you couldn't put into words. It is nothing to be seen; it is something to be felt. You could feel the atmosphere all over, as well as see it. Being a Hokie is something to appreciate for years.

When they offered me my junior year in high school, I accepted and never looked back on it. It was a no-brainer then and still is; I'm glad I went. Miami wanted me and so did Maryland. North Carolina was recruiting me hard, along with Georgia Tech.

Tennessee and Navy came around, too. I was a good student and could have picked any school. Georgia was recruiting me, too. You name it, they came around.

In my junior season in high school, everybody was recruiting me, but it was Tech, a school in my home state, that just stepped forward and gave me a full-ride scholarship. While everyone else was recruiting me, they never said the words, "Here, we're paying for your education. It's a full ride."

Tech did that early. Coach Beamer knew what they wanted. I talked to my mom, and she and I knew what we wanted, and we went on and accepted their invitation. We were very grateful and happy with that decision.

It never came down to any other schools. I knew where I was going. I was getting school paid for and I was close enough that my mom could come see me play. I got my degree in sociology.

We knew the NFL was going to be there eventually, so it was important to get the degree. Guys need to understand that you can do both. That was one of the things with Coach Stinespring when he was recruiting me. He said Virginia Tech was going to put me on a path to get a degree, and that made my mom and I comfortable about going to Virginia Tech.

Aaron Rouse was rated among the top strong safeties in the nation going into the 2006 season with uncommon size (6'4", 227 pounds) and speed for a defensive back. In 2005 he won Virginia Tech's President's Award, which is given to the defensive player who showed the most outstanding leadership during the off-season conditioning program and spring practice. Rouse was drafted in the third round of the 2007 NFL Draft by the Green Bay Packers and has played for the Packers, New York Giants, and Arizona Cardinals.

2007

Following the April 16, 2007, shooting on the Virginia Tech campus, the Hokies opened the 2007 football season with heavy hearts. A national TV audience watched Virginia Tech defeat East Carolina 17–7 in its opener, the first game at Lane Stadium after a lone gunman killed 32 people and wounded many others in one of the worst shooting sprees in U.S. history. More than anything else, Virginia Tech's players, students, coaches, and fans showed they were united and would overcome the unforgettable event.

On the field, the Hokies had to regroup after a 48–8 loss at LSU in their second game, the worst defeat in coach Frank Beamer's 21 seasons at his alma mater. Freshman quarterback Tyrod Taylor made his debut against the Tigers and became the team's starting quarterback for the next five games. Taylor led the Hokies to victories over Ohio, FCS foe William & Mary, North Carolina, and Clemson. He started for Tech in a road game at Duke, but injured his ankle during the Hokies' 43–14 victory.

Senior quarterback Sean Glennon was back under center after Taylor's injury. After a heartbreaking 14–10 loss to Boston College, in which Eagles quarterback Matt Ryan threw two touchdowns in the final 2 minutes, 11 seconds, Glennon led Tech to a convincing 27–3 victory over Georgia Tech.

Taylor returned for the Hokies' home game against Florida State, and he and Glennon guided Tech to a 40–21 win. Tech employed a two-quarterback system for the rest of the season. The Hokies routed Miami by a 44–4 score and then beat rival Virginia

33–16. The victory over the Wahoos clinched the ACC's Coastal Division title.

Virginia Tech avenged its loss to Boston College by defeating the Eagles 30–16 in the ACC championship game in Jacksonville, Florida. Glennon and Taylor rotated at quarterback, with Glennon throwing two fourth-quarter touchdowns. The Hokies were invited to a BCS bowl game for the second time in four seasons, losing to Kansas 24–21 in the Orange Bowl.

Hokies in Their Own Words

JOSH MORGAN

WIDE RECEIVER, 2004–2007

I grew up in Washington D.C., so I know what gun shots sound like. I knew those were gun shots that day of the massacre, and it was surreal. I was thinking, *It can't be happening, not here.*

We were in a building near the shootings, the massacre of our people. We ran to D.J. Parker's house and turned on the TV. It was bad. There were people running around the campus and then on the TV they started showing the number of people who died.

It was a countdown, like on New Year's. But this was a count up, it was in reverse, and it was sickening. They kept the body count going up, and we were all devastated. It was four, then seven, then 16, and then more.

They canceled spring practice and gave students the option of going home. If you were passing your class, they said you could take that grade and go home. People left.

That whole next season was like our Hurricane Katrina moment in New Orleans. Everything we did as a football team, we kept the people who died in our minds. It fueled us. We didn't want to forget it. We ended up winning an ACC championship.

East Carolina came to Blacksburg in the first game back, and it was great to see our community come together. Some of the people who survived it came in wheelchairs and were still messed up. Coach Beamer invited them to practice all the time, and it humbled us and made us grateful for everything we had.

It was 32. It was 32 angels in the sky. There was no way we would lose that East Carolina game. It was a close game, they were really good, but we couldn't lose. We felt bad when we lost those couple of games that season. We wanted to win as part of the healing process. We wanted to go undefeated.

One of the things you learn playing at Virginia Tech for Frank Beamer, at least I learned it, is that there are other good players in the program and you better think about other guys on the team and not being selfish.

I was one of the most athletic guys there. I was flexible. I was big, I could run. I was just as fast as guys like Eddie Royal. They used to always tell me I was rare because I was strong and could jump. You think at first they are just being nice to you and making you feel good, but it built my confidence and I finally thought maybe I can take this to the next level, the NFL.

What helped me was I was a basketball player in high school. I was also a quarterback. I didn't have all the wear and tear on my body that all my teammates had from playing pee wee football because I played mostly basketball growing up. My body was still fresh. I didn't start playing football until my high school years.

I was not All-ACC, but you have to look at how many great receivers we had at Virginia Tech when I was there. You are not going to catch 70 passes with guys like Eddie Royal, David Clowney, Josh Hyman. They are going to get their chances, too,

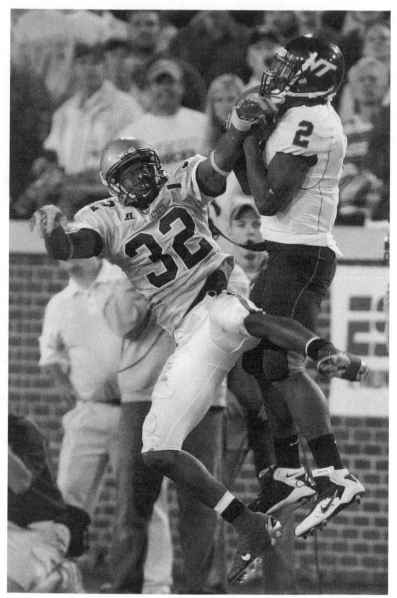

Josh Morgan (2) catches a touchdown pass over Georgia Tech's Jahi Word-Daniels, November 1, 2007, in Atlanta. *Photo courtesy of AP Images*

which was the way it needed to be. You are talking NFL receivers on the field with you.

In every system you are not going to be the main guy, but you always want the ball. You have got to balance out your competitive spirit with fitting in with the team and doing what the team wants you to do. So, at Virginia Tech, with so many good receivers while I was there—guys who are in the NFL now—you had to fit in and not demand to the quarterback, "Hey, throw me the ball." That got me ready for the pros because I didn't think too highly of myself, and that made me work hard.

We had a group of guys all come in as freshmen, and these were really good receivers, and they made me better. They pushed and they wanted to play.

I had the talent to take over the game and do anything I wanted to out on the field, but we had four or five good receivers and had to take care of our chances when they came and know that there were other playmakers out there.

Virginia Tech was the first time I played special teams. I blocked a couple of kicks, I returned a couple of kicks, returned a couple of punts, too. That's what you did at Virginia Tech. You played special teams and, let me tell you, the pros, the people in the NFL, they know that, if you went to Virginia Tech, you learned how to play special teams and you were ready for the next level. That's an advantage of going to Tech.

When I got to the NFL, they put in some things for me to try and block some kicks, but I did well enough at wide receiver that I played more offense than special teams. I went down on the kickoffs a few times and tackled a guy inside the 10-yard line. The first thing they said to me when I got there was, "We know Beamer taught you how to play special teams."

My most memorable game was the Sugar Bowl against Auburn, which was undefeated and fighting for the national championship all season. It was my freshman year, and I probably didn't realize how big that game was for us or how many good players were in that game.

I was watching a DVD of it recently and I paused it here and there and started counting all the guys from that game on Auburn and Virginia Tech who made it to the NFL. I think it was 30 guys.

They beat us 16–14, and I scored two touchdowns. Bryan Randall threw me two bombs to bring us back, one was, like, 80 and another was 35 yards, or something like that. The long pass we used a route with some double moves, and with my speed I got by people. Bryan Randall had a great pump fake on the 80-yarder.

It was after that Auburn game that I thought, *Hey, I can do this, I can play in the NFL.* I was on the same field with a lot of guys who were drafted in the first round, like Carlos Rogers, the defensive back at Auburn.

One of my most fulfilling games was beating Boston College in 2007 in the ACC championship game, because we had lost to them in the regular season. They had Matt Ryan and beat us in Blacksburg in the regular season, and then we beat them. I think I had six or seven catches and a touchdown in that game in Jacksonville.

That was my senior season, and I think, at the time, they told us that our senior class was the class with the most wins ever at Virginia Tech. That was a nice way to go out.

There was a Florida State game, too, that was a good game. We played them in the ACC championship game when we had Marcus Vick. That was in 2005 when we were 11–2.

It's sad to see what happened to Marcus at Virginia Tech. He was a great player. When I see him now, it's like he never left. That was one of the few disappointing things at Virginia Tech.

You get everything you have ever dreamed of at Virginia Tech. Michael Vick was the only reason I knew Virginia Tech existed, seeing him run around on the field, and then I found out how much it had to offer. You get good coaching, you get to play on TV. There are great facilities and great teammates.

What you get at Virginia Tech is a chance for greatness. It's up to you what you do with it because they have everything there that gives you the opportunity to be something great and take off in the world.

Josh Morgan ranks highly in Virginia Tech history, ranking second in receptions (122), fourth in receiving yards (1,817, a 14.9 avg.), and fourth in touchdowns (16). He finished his career with 2,435 all-purpose yards. Morgan led Tech with 46 receptions in his senior season in 2007. He averaged 12 yards a catch for one of the most talented receiving corps in Tech history, which included Eddie Royal, David Clowney, Justin Harper, and Josh Hyman. Morgan's 126 yards receiving against Auburn in the 2005 Sugar Bowl set a school bowl game record. Morgan was selected in the sixth round of the 2008 draft by the San Francisco 49ers. He already has 116 receptions in three seasons for the 49ers. Morgan has two semesters left to get his degree in business management.

2008

The 2008 Hokies probably weren't as talented, experienced, or deep as previous Virginia Tech teams that won conference championships. But through perseverance, hard work, and some luck, they somehow managed to win a second consecutive ACC championship, along with a BCS bowl game.

After losing their season opener to East Carolina in a surprising 27–22 upset in Charlotte, North Carolina, the Hokies rallied to win their next five games. They defeated Georgia Tech at home and North Carolina and Nebraska on the road, winning each contest by five points or fewer.

But with the Hokies struggling to produce much offense, there were still obvious flaws. Virginia Tech lost consecutive games at Boston College and Florida State. After beating Maryland by a 23–13 score, the Hokies lost at Miami 16–14 in a game dominated by the Hurricanes' defense. Left with a 6–4 record and two games to play, the Hokies needed some help in reaching the ACC championship game for the second season in a row.

Somehow, they got it. Virginia Tech defeated Duke 14–13 and then Virginia 17–14 in the Hokies' regular season finale. After other ACC contenders dropped games down the stretch, the Hokies claimed a second-straight ACC Coastal Division title. They met Boston College in the ACC championship game again and prevailed with a 30–12 victory, avenging their earlier loss to the Eagles.

The Hokies played Cincinnati in the Orange Bowl in Miami, beating the Bearcats 20–7. It was Virginia Tech's first victory in a BCS bowl game since a 28–10 win over Texas in the 1995 Sugar Bowl.

Hokies in Their Own Words

CODY GRIMM

LINEBACKER, 2006–2009

William & Mary offered me a football scholarship. That was it. I had some lacrosse scholarships, but I wanted to play football so I walked on at Tech.

My expectations were to try and play. I was not worried about earning a scholarship, it was just to play. I just wanted to take it one step at a time. Dress and play special teams was the first goal. After that came, the next step was to get some snaps with the defense. That came, and I started playing well when I was getting in the game.

It was always one step at a time. I kept working as hard as I could, and it paid off.

I was recruited by Tech, but they never offered me. I guess I was a little short and a little light. I came in my freshman year and weighed 183. I put on 29 pounds, and my sophomore year I weighed in at 212 pounds.

Coach Beamer called me into his office and told me they were going to give me a scholarship that winter before my junior year. They weren't just going to put me on scholarship to keep me from transferring. They wanted me there. That's how they have always been with their walk-ons.

When I came in there the first week, they didn't treat me any differently than they did Macho Harris, who was a huge recruit. They gave me reps. I wasn't getting money, but they coached me hard.

That day I went in to see Coach Beamer, I thought maybe I had done something in school, or somehow had done something wrong. Usually they don't call you and tell you to come to his office unless you did something wrong, or maybe you got a scholarship. I thought I might get a scholarship, or he could be bringing me in to tell me to get a tutor for some class.

I gave my mom a call, and she was excited and so was my dad. One of the reasons I chose Virginia Tech was my parents told me they already had school money saved up and I could go down there. I didn't feel forced to save money by taking the scholarship to William & Mary. I felt good I was able to get a scholarship when I did so they didn't have to worry about spending money on me.

I think a game that showed them I could play was my freshman year when we got pounded by LSU. They threw me in for the whole second half. That was the first time I was actually in on defense and playing against a pretty good team. I played a pretty good half and had some tackles.

It was that game where I felt like those guys were not that much better than me. I felt like in a year or two I could play at that level. LSU won the title that season.

So I came out my junior year and was rotating with Cam Martin every two series. His knee was bothering him, so I started getting the majority of plays toward the end of the season.

They named me a starter in camp before my senior season.

The Miami game my senior season was a memorable game. It was raining hard throughout the game, and they came in highly ranked, and we won. We had this one zero cover blitz where we brought the house, and we ran that a couple of times. We had a lot of different blitz packages for that game, and everything Coach Foster drew up worked.

On the first series of the game Dorian Porch hit Jacory Harris [the Miami quarterback] from behind, and he fumbled. That set the tone.

Coach Foster is so passionate about the game. You can see in the meeting room that he only had a couple of hours of sleep. There was a passion in his eyes. When you see how hard a coach works, you want to work that hard, too. As a player you don't want to let him down.

He was a pretty intense coach. He wasn't afraid to scream at you if you messed up, and he wasn't afraid to pat you on the ass if you did well. I loved playing for him. He took the blame for games we lost, but we knew it was on us.

I loved my time there. The atmosphere around the campus drew me there coming out of high school. Everyone was so nice. You hear about players at other schools going out and getting in fights. At Virginia Tech, we didn't have those issues. I've heard of players at other schools showing up in bars and fighting, and that didn't happen in Blacksburg.

Luckily, I didn't know anyone who was killed in the shootings. I did know people who knew some of those who were killed. I was driving back to my apartment from spring football film study when it started.

On the way home to my apartment police cars were whizzing by me, and I said to my roommate, Matt Reedy, "Something bad must have happened."

I got some texts from a friend who worked in the on-campus clinic about what was happening. They had a police radio there. I turned on the TV, and it was horrible.

I called my dad and my mom. There were so many calls going out to parents from students the cell phone service stopped around campus because the lines were jammed.

It felt good coming back in the fall and getting the team together and trying to get our lives back to normal together. People coming to a football game to cheer, I think, helped put the school back

Cody Grimm (26) carries the Virginia state flag as the team takes the field before the Orange Bowl against Cincinnati in Miami, January 1, 2009. The Hokies won 20–7. *Photo courtesy of AP Images*

together. We took it upon ourselves to have the best season we could have.

My favorite game was probably the Orange Bowl win over Cincinnati. I had an interception to seal the win and I had a sack, as well. Any time you can win a BCS game, it's a big deal.

We had a pretty good defense with a lot of good players all around. We had Brandon Flowers, we had Macho, it was just a good defense on every level. More than that, the one thing I noticed about Tech was that everyone got along, we were all good friends, especially my last two years.

We were hanging around with each other off the practice field, and that is part of the reason we had success. It was a little bit of the coaches and the type of guys they recruited to Virginia Tech. We just wanted to win; the guys were not concerned with individual stats.

I think in the couple of years before my junior and senior years, we might have had better athletes, but this was a better team overall as far as chemistry. A bunch of other coaches will just go get the big-name guys who might not fit together. The boosters want those big-name guys, even though they could create some issues.

Coach Beamer takes a lot into account what their character is off the field. If guys come to Tech and mess around and don't take it seriously, Coach Beamer is not afraid to sit them. He feels pretty comfortable with his position at Tech as far as stability, so he will get after guys if they act out.

We didn't want to let each other down out there. No one wanted to be that person who had to miss a quarter or two for discipline issues. I think Tech had a couple get in trouble at their bowl game this past season and were sent home. We didn't worry about that with the team we had. I counted on guys. Everyone wanted to do the right thing. That's what it meant to be a Hokie.

Cody Grimm was one of the most successful walk-ons in the history of Virginia Tech football. He was not on scholarship for two years, but his junior and senior seasons he became a starter and in 2009 was named an All-ACC linebacker. Grimm was a third-team All-American for the Hokies in 2009. He played in 54 games and had 214 tackles, including 26 tackles for loss and 11.5 sacks. Grimm forced nine fumbles and had two fumble recoveries and two interceptions. He tied a Division I record with three forced fumbles in a game against North Carolina State. Grimm was the Defensive MVP in the 2009 Chick-fil-A Bowl win over Tennessee.

2010

Few Virginia Tech football seasons have started as poorly as 2010. In the span of five days, the Hokies dropped a 33–30 loss to No. 3 Boise State in a highly anticipated Labor Day night showdown and then inexplicably lost to FCS foe James Madison 21–16 at Lane Stadium.

But instead of collapsing, Virginia Tech bounced back like few other teams could.

After starting the season with an 0–2 record, the Hokies won their next 11 games to win an ACC championship for the third time in four years. Behind senior quarterback Tyrod Taylor and running backs Darren Evans and Ryan Williams, the Hokies upset nationally ranked North Carolina State and Miami (Florida) to put themselves in position to play for another BCS bowl game.

After ending the regular season with a 37–7 victory over Virginia, the Hokies walloped Atlantic Division champion Florida State 44–33 in the ACC championship game in Charlotte, North Carolina. Taylor threw for three touchdowns and ran for another one in the victory over the Seminoles. Virginia Tech's 44 points were the most scored in an ACC championship game.

"Those two losses we had at the beginning of the year makes these 11 wins and an ACC championship seem even greater," Virginia Tech coach Frank Beamer said.

The Hokies played in the Orange Bowl for the third time in four years, losing to Pac-10 champion Stanford 40–12.

Hokies in Their Own Words

KAM CHANCELLOR

DEFENSIVE BACK, 2006–2009

The students were like players for us because of all the energy they brought to the stadium. We were just playing as one. We fed off all their noise and support. There was some unity out there.

The Thursday night games were particularly loud. There was a Thursday night game against Clemson at home my freshman year when the stadium was so loud. The fans gave the Tigers a hard time and we won the game. I didn't even play that game because it was my freshman year and I was behind Brandon Flowers at corner, but I felt it.

I was a corner my freshman year, then strong safety sophomore year, then free safety my junior and senior years. Now, in the NFL, I'm a strong safety. Tech got me ready.

Virginia Tech went after the hybrid safeties, tall, strong, fast guys who could play Bud Foster's system. Virginia Tech found those guys and invested in them. What he wanted were safeties who could get into that run defense. He wanted people to make tackles out of the safety spot.

If you are a guy who likes to make hits and make plays, that's the spot for you. It's not too much man-to-man for us big defensive backs. If it is man-to-man, we're on the tight end. You just have to have great technique. They'll teach you that.

I was 6′4″, 230 pounds, and they called me "Big Kid" over there in the secondary.

When we played Tennessee in the Chick-fil-A Bowl, that was a lot of in-the-box for me. They had Montario Hardesty at running back, and he was a good runner, so they had me in there for run support.

I was a productive player at Virginia Tech because I listened to the coaches and I listened to my teammates. That's the one thing about me: I'm a good listener. I will soak up the football, and it shows in my performance and my character. I piece things together, and that helped make me a good player.

The one thing you have to have is a good work ethic. Don't complain, do it. A lot of guys would follow my lead. I wasn't very vocal, but I would lead by example.

Davon Morgan and Eddie Whitley listened a lot. Whitley really paid attention and would ask questions.

When I was coming through I listened to Aaron Rouse, who was another 757 [area code] Hokie. He and I lived near each other. Aaron was a big guy in the secondary, and I looked up to him. I liked how Aaron Rouse was a big hitter, and I wanted to be a big hitter, too.

That's one thing Bud Foster demanded: that you hit people. He was scary sometimes, preaching that stuff to us.

When you mess up, you'd just look over to that sideline and he'd be chewing you out. It'd be too loud to hear what he was saying, but I could read his lips and see how mad he was at me. Bud Foster had the evil eye. You could see the headphones dangling from his side because he had thrown them off.

So when I went back to see a game last year, I saw a player make a mistake, and I went, "What are you doing? You can't do that." That was like me out there when I was a young player at

Tech. I was yelling at the guys and how they had to watch film and know the defense.

I always wanted to be known as the guy who did things right. I was coachable at Tech. Whatever they told me to do, I did it.

Frank Beamer was a players' coach. The players responded to him. He leads and keeps us positive. Here's one thing he did well: if we were ever playing a team that we were supposed to blow out, he took it seriously.

Besides being a leader, the other thing he did was special teams. You look at the special teams and how much we worked on special teams at Virginia Tech. When I got to this level, to the NFL, I understood what was demanded to play special teams. The Seahawks saw that I could be a valuable contributor. They even said anybody who came from Virginia Tech was going to be on their special teams.

Seattle just threw me into special teams, and I dominated special teams up there. I ended up getting double-teamed all season. I was the wedge breaker on kickoffs. I was getting busy. I used to get down there so fast that they had players on the other team going, "Where did you come from, you're not supposed to do that."

I had it down, man. I knew the steps; I knew the yardage. I knew how to get there. I was knocking people out of the way and disrupting their blocking.

In college, I was more of a contain guy, a 3, on special teams. My senior year, somebody got hurt, and I slid inside more at R-4, R-5 against Tennessee. That's when I was playing kickoffs again.

Frank Beamer was all special teams. He would have us for 30 minutes and make sure we got it down pat. We never slacked off on special teams at Virginia Tech because that was the head coach out there running the unit. There was no slacking off.

My two most memorable moments at Virginia Tech? The first was my sophomore season when we played Boston College in the

ACC championship game and it came down to the wire. They were trying to get back in the game and their receiver, [Kevin] Challenger, caught a pass and was running for the end zone, and I dove and made a game-saving tackle. That next play we got an interception and then won the game.

The other game I remember was the Orange Bowl against Cincinnati when I had one of the best games of my career. I had a pick and another pick that they over-ruled, though everybody knew I was in bounds when I intercepted it. That was the game where I got turf toe, but I just shot it up with cortisone and played the second half. It was swollen and like a big cyst. Cincinnati had Tony Pike as the quarterback, and I thought he was a very good quarterback. I liked him a lot, but we won the game.

I went to Maury High School in Tidewater and was kind of leaning toward UVA because my coach went there. I took a visit to UVA and I liked what they were serving, and I was buying it.

It was near signing day when I went to Tech on a visit. I went to a conditioning workout, and there were a bunch of guys from my area there, guys who I recognized who came out of my area, so I felt welcome there. That's when I changed from UVA to Tech.

All the guys were, like, "Come aboard." The coaches were cool, and since I have left Tech, they haven't forgot about me. I know they haven't.

I was being recruited by James Madison, East Carolina, and Richmond. I had a visit to North Carolina, but they didn't offer me.

So every time we played North Carolina, I tried to put on a show for them. I punished whoever had that ball and then looked to their sideline. I didn't give them a chance.

My 40 time was slow, 4.8, so that could have been an issue why they backed off. But a guy like me who is dedicated to hard work is going to get himself in the right position and make things happen. I was willing to work.

Coach Newsome came to one of my games and saw me turn it up out there. It was the Great Bridge game, and I was a quarterback and threw for almost 200 yards and a couple of touchdowns. I also had some big hits in that game; knocked a dude out.

There was another play where I hit the dude, flipped him up in the air, and took the ball from him while he was in the air. That probably helped me get a scholarship. I might have gotten the last scholarship in my class.

We have built a reputation for defense the last 10 years. The motto around there was the defense wins game. We have an offense, but the way Bud Foster looked at it was, we got an offense, but it will have nothing to do with us winning this game. It's on the defense.

That's how we carried ourselves. We carried the team before, and we carried it when I was there.

Being a Hokie means leaving a legacy behind that you were part of a great college football program. There was a sense of accomplishment. You feel honored.

Kam Chancellor was a cornerback, then strong safety, then free safety for the Hokies. He came to Tech as a quarterback before he was moved to defense. He was a backup his freshman season in 2006, but then became the starting rover back as a sophomore. His junior season he made another position change to free safety for the 2008 season and started all 14 games. He had 52 tackles (27 solo), two interceptions, five passes broken-up, seven pass deflections, one forced fumble, and two fumble recoveries. Chancellor played free safety again his senior season and then was picked in the fifth round of the 2010 draft by the Seattle Seahawks.

chapter 3

NATIONAL AWARD
WINNERS

JAKE GROVE

Grove, a native of Forest, Virginia, was one of the best rags-to-riches stories in Virginia Tech football history. A lightly recruited guard at Jefferson Forest High School, Grove left Virginia Tech as a unanimous All-American, winner of the Rimington Trophy as college football's best center, and a second-round choice of the Oakland Raiders in the NFL Draft.

Grove switched from guard to center before his junior season at Virginia Tech and quickly became one of the best players at his position. He helped lead the Hokies to a 10–4 record during his junior season in 2002, which culminated with a 20–13 victory over Air Force in the San Francisco Bowl. The Hokies went 8–5 during Grove's senior season in 2003, which ended with a 52–49 loss to California in the Insight Bowl in Phoenix. Grove was always known as one of Tech's toughest players, playing the last eight games of the 2001 season with a broken hand.

Grove played seven seasons in the NFL, including five with the Oakland Raiders and two with the Miami Dolphins.

Hokies in Their Own Words

JAKE GROVE

CENTER, 1999–2003

I really didn't have the most options coming out of high school. My only full scholarship offer was from Tech. VMI offered me a partial scholarship. I went to VMI to look around and, I don't know, I just couldn't see going there. So I went to Tech, and it felt right. Of course, once I got there, I wanted to make sure I proved to Coach Frank Beamer and all the coaches that it was worth their while to come and recruit me. It took a little while, but I think I got to that point.

I think probably when things kind of clicked for me and I thought I could be a pretty good college football player was about midway through my sophomore year. They had me playing guard, and Steve DeMasi was playing center. They had moved me over to guard, and I was real uneasy at first, but about midway through the season it started to click. Then they moved me back to center the next year, and everything really took off from there. I think playing guard my sophomore year helped me play better center my junior and senior years. I think it really helped me when I got drafted, too. In my first two years in the NFL, I played a lot more games at guard then I did at center.

When it comes down to it, I think Coach Bryan Stinespring had the biggest impact on me when I was at Tech because I worked with him every day. When you work with somebody everyday for five years, you're going to develop a bond. That's a relationship that I hope will keep going. One of the funniest things he ever said to me was, I think, during my freshman year. I wasn't too good back then.

Jake Grove was consensus All-America for the Hokies during his senior season (2003). He was named All–Big East and won the Rimington Trophy as college football's best center as a senior.

I remember I made a pretty good block during practice. It was around Halloween, and he looked at me and said, "You know, Grove, you can tell it's getting close to Halloween because you're masquerading as an offensive lineman." I don't know if you count that as an insult or a compliment. Another time I was running toward the sideline during practice, and I was running kind of fast. He caught it on film and asked me if there was a hot dog vendor over there.

I guess, as the years went by at Tech, I started to get a reputation as a little bit of a dirty player. I think the thing that started that was just in practice, just going hard and guys calling me "Dirty Grove" there for a little while. I think Chad Beasley started that. We used to go at each other in practice every now and then, and I'd grab his face mask, which would make him a little mad.

But it *really* started in that game we had against Miami in 2003. The Miami coach, Larry Coker, made a big deal about it because he said I cut [blocked] one of his players, but the only guy who got a penalty out of the whole thing was Sean Taylor for kicking me in the head. I never got penalized for it. I think I owe Larry Coker a big thank you because he got my name in *USA Today* that week, and I don't think any of our other players had their names in the paper that week. So, hey, I guess it all paid off.

That's definitely one of the games I have memories from. Of course, I'll always remember my first game. When we played Georgia Tech in the first game of my career in 2000, I was about to have a stroke before the game because I was so nervous. I was praying that the game would be canceled somehow. I just wanted anything to happen to make sure the game wouldn't start.

Sure enough, a bolt of lightning came down just before we kicked off and the game got canceled. I don't know if I'd still be here if that didn't happen because I was freaking out. The other games that really stand out for me are the UVA games. I grew up right in between UVA and Virginia Tech—in Forest, Virginia, near Lynchburg—and heard my whole life about that rivalry.

The fact that we won four out of five against UVA when I was there was good. Of course, the Miami games were memorable because you always grew up hearing about those guys, too. My freshman year Miami had Dan Morgan and Damione Lewis. They both wound up being first-round draft picks that year. They were seniors, and I was just starting out, trying to figure out my game. I think I figured out what it takes to be a great player playing against those guys.

But I don't really think about my Tech career in terms of being a great player or whatever. I guess it still really hasn't hit me, even now, all the awards that I was given while I was at Virginia Tech. I've got a lot of those awards and things sitting at my parents' house. I think the thing that means the most to me was when I was named a permanent captain by my teammates in my senior year. It wasn't voted on by sports writers or selected by anybody. It was something that was selected by the people I cared about the most and played against everyday. It meant a lot to me that they would designate me for something like that. I think I got kind of lucky, but I was lucky for a lot of reasons.

Jake Grove was a starting center and consensus All-American for the Hokies during his senior season in 2003. He was named All–Big East and won the Rimington Trophy as college football's best center. He was drafted in the second round by the Oakland Raiders in the 2004 NFL Draft and played five years for the Raiders and one for the Miami Dolphins before retiring after the 2009 season. He lives in Forest, Virginia.

COREY MOORE

If Michael Vick is Virginia Tech's most famous player, then defensive end Corey Moore is a close second.

In three years at Virginia Tech, Moore had 35 sacks before leaving school as the most decorated player in history. He won the 1999 Lombardi Award as college football's best lineman and the Bronko Nagurski Award as the sport's best defensive player. Moore also became Tech's second unanimous All-American and won the Dudley Award as the top college football player in Virginia. He was named Big East Defensive Player of the Year in 1998 and 1999 and the *Football News* Defensive Player of the Year in 1999.

Moore almost didn't end up at Virginia Tech—or even playing college football, for that matter. A native of Brownsville, Tennessee, Moore originally accepted a scholarship to play football at the University of Mississippi. But before his freshman season in 1995, the Rebels were hit with severe NCAA penalties, including a reduction in scholarships. Moore, an undersized defensive end, was among the casualties.

Moore nearly gave up football to enroll at Morehouse College in Atlanta, but instead enrolled at Holmes Junior College in Mississippi. After playing the 1995 season there, Moore signed with Virginia Tech and arrived in Blacksburg as an unheralded junior-college transfer.

During Moore's senior season in 1999, the Hokies finished the regular season with an undefeated 11–0 record. After losing to Florida State 46–29 in the Sugar Bowl, Virginia Tech finished No. 2 in the final polls. With Moore punishing opposing quarterbacks, Tech finished the season ranked first nationally in scoring defense, third in total defense, third in rushing defense, and seventh in passing defense.

"Corey Moore was the freak of college football at the time," Virginia Tech defensive coordinator Bud Foster told the *Hampton Roads* (Virginia) *Daily Press* in 2009. "He was undersized, but nobody could block him. He could out-physical you at the point of attack, and he could run by you at the point of attack.... He's arguably the best player in college football in my time. It would be hard to name another player who had more impact on the game than what Corey Moore had that season."

Bruce Smith returns to his alma mater and looks at the scoreboard as quarterback Tyrod Taylor watches the action during Virginia Tech's 28–21 win over Georgia Tech, November 4, 2010. *Photo courtesy of AP Images*

BRUCE SMITH

Frank Beamer might have put Virginia Tech football on the map, but defensive end Bruce Smith was its first truly great player.

Known as the "Sack Man" during his college career, Smith became one of the NFL's most feared pass rushers during his Pro

Football Hall of Fame career. Smith capped his remarkable Virginia Tech career by winning the 1984 Outland Trophy as college football's best lineman.

A native of Norfolk, Virginia, Smith was one of the country's most recruited players during his senior season at Booker T. Washington High School. But Smith chose to play for Virginia Tech, which was still a fledgling football program at the time.

During Smith's Pro Football Hall of Fame enshrinement speech in 2010, Smith said former Hokies coach Bill Dooley helped persuade him to stay close to home.

"At the time the Hokies were not known as the football powerhouse that they are today," Smith said. "But Coach Bill left a lasting impression on me when he said, 'If you come to Tech, you will receive an excellent education. And if you can play, they will find you.' Coach, you were right."

Smith is still the most beloved player in Virginia Tech history and is often serenaded by cheers of "Bruuuuce!" during games at Lane Stadium.

Smith had 71 career tackles for loss during his four-year college career, totaling more than five times the length of a football field. He had 46 career sacks, including 22 during his junior season in 1983, when he was named All-America by the American Football Coaches Association. He was named a consensus All-American during his senior season in 1984.

Smith was the No. 1 pick of the Buffalo Bills in the 1985 NFL Draft. He played 15 seasons for the Bills, helping them reach the Super Bowl four times. After four seasons with the Washington Redskins, Smith retired as the NFL's all-time sack leader with 200 during his 19-year career. Smith made 11 Pro Bowls and was a first-team All-Pro nine times. He was named Associated Press

Defensive Player of the Year two times and was named to the NFL's All-Decade Team for both the 1980s and 1990s.

MICHAEL VICK

One of the most electrifying players in college football history, Vick helped lead the Hokies to the 1999 national championship game and won an ESPY as the national player of the year.

As a redshirt freshman in 1999, Vick finished third in Heisman Trophy voting after throwing for 1,840 yards with 12 touchdowns and rushing for 580 yards with eight scores. He appeared on the cover of *ESPN The Magazine* in 1999 and nearly led the Hokies to an improbable comeback from a 21-point deficit against Florida State in a 46–29 loss in the Sugar Bowl. Tech finished No. 2 in the final polls with an 11–1 record.

Vick, a native of Newport News, Virginia, led the NCAA in pass efficiency in his first season at Virginia Tech, setting an NCAA record for freshmen with a 180.4 rating. It also was the third-highest rating in NCAA history. Vick was invited to New York for the Heisman Trophy ceremony after finishing behind Wisconsin running back Ron Dayne and Georgia Tech quarterback Joe Hamilton in voting.

Vick's second season at Virginia Tech was derailed by injuries, but he managed to lead the Hokies to an 11–1 record. He didn't play in Virginia Tech's 21–14 loss to Miami, which was the team's only defeat of the season. He played his final college game against Clemson in the Gator Bowl in Jacksonville, Florida, and was named the game's MVP after throwing for 205 yards with one touchdown and running nine times for 19 yards.

After only two seasons at Virginia Tech, Vick was the first pick by the Atlanta Falcons in the 2001 NFL Draft. He played six seasons for the Falcons, but pleaded guilty to federal felony charges surrounding his involvement in a dog-fighting ring, for which he served 21 months in prison. He signed with the Philadelphia Eagles in 2009 and was named the NFL's Comeback Player of the Year in 2010.

Hokies in Their Own Words

MICHAEL VICK
QUARTERBACK, 1998–2000

Jim Cavanaugh first started recruiting me when I was a junior at Warwick High in Newport News, Virginia. The first time I saw Virginia Tech play in person was in Charlottesville in 1997. After that game, I met the coaches and all, but I didn't take my official visit until January of '98.

It was just a regular weekend where I went down and hung out with Corey Moore, André Kendrick, a guy named Cory Bird, Al Clark, who was the starting quarterback—I got to know him really well—and Shyrone Stith. We were all really tight.

Virginia Tech and Syracuse were the two schools I narrowed my final decision down to. I was on my way to Georgia Tech, but after I went to Virginia Tech, I knew it would come down to the Hokies or the Orangemen. The thing with Syracuse, though, was I didn't want everyone comparing me, a black quarterback, to Donovan McNabb, so with all things being equal, there was no doubt that Virginia Tech was the best choice for me.

My high school coach, Tommy Reamon, told me any school I committed to had to keep their word that they would redshirt me as a freshman. I didn't want to play early. I needed the time to kind of figure out what I had to accomplish academically. That was the right thing to do.

I didn't go down there early, like in June or anything, so my first exposure to practice was the day freshmen had to report. Coach Mike Gentry used the off-season to make us push trucks in that parking lot right next to Lane Stadium. We'd be pushing a pickup truck that's in neutral and we had to move it 50 yards. We had to push it down a little hill and then push it up a small hill that wasn't big but was sloped enough to make a big difference.

That was tough, but it made us strong as hell, I'll tell you that.

My year in the freshman dorm I roomed with Ronyell Whitaker. I didn't meet him until we got there, but we had a ball together. When I moved off campus, I roomed with Emmett Johnson and Reggie Harris [Johnson].

I knew I wasn't going to play as a true freshman, but I still dressed for every game. It was great for me because I got to experience the whole travel thing, to understand what it took to be a college quarterback as far as responsibility and preparation are concerned. Just to understand the whole deal was big—from coming out of the tunnel to watching the game from the sideline, and from talking to my teammates to having discussions with my offensive coordinator.

Looking back on it, I can see I didn't really understand at the time what was going on, but it allowed me to soak it all in and enjoy the trip, so to speak. It wasn't until that December that everything clicked for me and I started really understanding the offense and learning how to read coverages. Once I did that, the next spring was a wrap.

Heading into my first season on the field, you can say that I knew what was about to happen, but I didn't really. I was nervous. I was a little scared. I was a little excited. A lot of different emotions were going through me, but at the same time, I didn't want to disappoint all those people who thought I was going to be this great quarterback.

The whole time leading up to that season, I kept hearing things like, "We've got Michael Vick at quarterback, and he's going to step into the lineup and carry this team. He's going to put everybody on his shoulders and fulfill the expectations of being, like, another Jim Druckenmiller and take us back to the level where we need to be."

I was thinking, *Man, that's a lot of pressure.* That was a lot on me, particularly for a guy who had never played a college snap.

So, yeah, I was excited and a little scared, but once I got out there, I just realized it was maybe even a little easier than high school.

During those first few games, we were blowing them out, but I was shocked. After we opened with James Madison and won 47–0, I thought, *Man, this is going to be easy.* But I couldn't believe it. At the same time, I was thinking, *It's not supposed to be like this. This can't be college football.*

So I thought, *Well, okay, this was James Madison. Maybe it'll be different later on.* I got hurt against them and didn't start the next week against UAB, but I came back against Clemson and threw three interceptions. The thing was, I made the biggest play of my life— and I think the biggest play of my college career—on third-and-11 to seal the deal.

They were coming back, and then suddenly we had the momentum. From that point on, things really slowed down and started to come easily for me.

Against Clemson, even though we won 31–11, I had those three picks, and it was just 14–11 when I converted that third-and-11 by hitting my tight end, Derek Carter, who's still a very good friend of mine to this day, for 15 yards.

When I was coming to the sideline, my position coach and offensive coordinator, Rickey Bustle, pulled me aside and told me, "A young, inexperienced quarterback who was rattled after throwing three picks couldn't have made that throw if he wasn't focused." Once he told me that, man, I had the confidence I needed to raise my game to another level.

The very next week, at Virginia, I knew it was our rival and I had to bring my A game, and I just built off what happened the week before. I had a great game, even though I only threw nine passes. I had seven completions for 222 yards. [The Hokies won 31–7.]

When we went to Rutgers the next week, I put a move on a guy that was so crucial, and I guess that was the first time I looked over to the sideline and it was like, "Oh, my God, did you just see that?"

So we kept winning, and I'll be the first to tell you, it wasn't just me out there making plays. No, we had André Davis, Shyrone Stith, Ricky Hall, Jarrett Ferguson, Cory Bird, Nick Sorenson, Corey Moore, Anthony Midget, and great players on special teams—man, I could go on forever because that team was loaded with great players.

We got to West Virginia, and I'd never seen anything like it. The place was packed, and they were trying to rattle us from the minute our bus left the airport. It was just nasty, man, with some of the people hacked off and yelling things at you about your momma and saying degrading things that you had to just tune out. It was bad.

For us to escape that place with a win was so huge—easily the biggest game of the year for our team. What it showed me was that our team wasn't going to quit, no matter what. We got the ball back with 1:50 left and needing a field goal to get out of there with a victory. I remember we had no timeouts, and the ball was on our 15. Because we were in the two-minute offense, I was calling my own plays.

There was a play near the sideline where this DB for West Virginia had me at the sideline. All he had to do was push me out of bounds, but instead he looked over at one of our guys who was ready to put a block on him.

I'll never forget looking into his eyes and watching him turn toward my teammate and then letting me right past him. We already had the first down, but that move cost them another 14 or 15 yards. It was enough for us to get in position [for Shayne Graham's 44-yard game-winner].

The last three games of our regular season weren't all that close. We beat Miami after they took a 10–0 lead and we scored 43 straight points. I had that big run [75 yards] against Temple, and then I was 11-for-13 against Boston College, but it should have been 13-for-13 because two of the balls were dropped. That's okay because I had my share of mistakes, too.

About halfway through that year, things started to really change for me off the field, too. It got to where I couldn't go anywhere without getting recognized and being asked to sign. Some of it was fun, but really, all I ever wanted was to just go out and play football.

I'm still like that now, even though I've gone to three Pro Bowls with the Falcons. Everybody wants to talk about the commercials or the highlights or things like that, but it would suit me perfectly if all I had to do was just be a quarterback. I'm not complaining about it, you know, because it's helped put some extra coins in my pocket and made my life completely different—you know, in a good way. It's nice not to have to worry about scraping up money to pay bills or buy clothes and food and stuff like that. That's the way it was for us growing up. My mom always had to be tight with money, just to make sure we had enough to eat.

It was also kind of weird for me on campus because that was the first time people started passing stuff they wanted me to sign during class. Some of it was pretty funny, but not being used to all that attention was just crazy for somebody who doesn't seek out attention. Being a leader of our football team is one thing, but being outspoken just doesn't come naturally to me.

Having said that, it still was pretty cool going to New York for the Heisman Trophy presentation. Everybody knows I came in third [behind Wisconsin's Ron Dayne and Joe Hamilton of Georgia Tech], but they wanted me to go first with the cameras and interviews and all that. I was cool with it.

My mother, Brenda Boddie, went with me, and we had a great time. She was just blown away by the whole thing, though. It was crazy enough for me to meet guys like Marcus Allen or just to be around all these famous football players, but for my mom, she didn't know what to say.

Everybody talked about how great I played in the national championship game, and while you can say we laid everything on the line and played as hard as we could, it was still disappointing because we couldn't get anything going, offensively or defensively, in the fourth quarter.

I had another really good spring before my sophomore season in 2000, both on the field and in the weight room, but I made a mistake by not staying in Blacksburg during the summer. Instead, I just wanted to hang out with my homeboys in Newport News, which was cool because I could be myself and not worry about other people looking at me like I was something special.

Looking back on that situation now, though, I probably would've had a better season if I had stayed at Virginia Tech during the off-season. I did that the year before and had the season of my life.

You look at the scores of my sophomore year, especially early on, and the games weren't all that close, but I never felt like I played as good as I should have. The season was more of a grind. That game at Boston College [a 48–34 win for the Hokies] is a perfect example of what I'm talking about. Everybody was caught up in how many yards [210, including an 82-yard score] I ran for, but I had a terrible game, completing five of 17 passes for 61 yards and one interception. I can't take satisfaction from having such a bad day as a passer. I don't care if I run for 1,000 yards in a game. It would be better if I completed, like, 12-of-12 passes for 300 yards, a couple touchdowns, and no picks.

That's the same way I look at things in the NFL, and I'm preparing for my sixth season as a professional. I can run, but as a quarterback, my job is to move the ball downfield and involve as many people as possible.

I always felt like that pass I connected with André Davis on against West Virginia was the best I ever threw in college. It was 64 yards, right on the money and led him just right. Of course, he did a great job on his end. That game was pretty satisfying after we put up a bunch of points [48] on the Mountaineers, but that day belonged to André, man, with those three straight touchdowns he had in the third quarter to help us pull away.

That trip we had to Syracuse was one hell of a battle. They sacked me [eight times, including six in the first half], and Dwight Freeney was unstoppable coming off the edge. We couldn't do anything to neutralize him. I'm not surprised he's as good as he is now with the Indianapolis Colts because he was in my face all day.

I'd never heard that kind of noise like they had that day in the Carrier Dome. I mean, you couldn't hear yourself think. We never

Michael Vick is considered perhaps Virginia Tech's greatest player ever after he led the Hokies to the 1999 national championship game against Florida State as a freshman quarterback.

did settle down, but at least we got out of there with a 22–14 win [the first Virginia Tech victory at Syracuse since 1986].

We needed a field goal to beat Pittsburgh the next week, but I knew I was in trouble after getting sacked and having my ankle twisted so badly. With Miami coming up, I knew it was the biggest showdown we could've hoped for, with us ranked No. 2 and the 'Canes No. 3.

I did all the rehab that was possible to get out there, and they definitely made the right call in having Dave Meyer start for me. It didn't take long for me to realize that I had no chance of helping my teammates that day. We had a sweep called to the left side, and all I could see was daylight in front of me, but I tried to push off and get that burst I need to turn on the jets. I had no juice, just nothing at all.

There comes a time in a situation like that where you have to realize that you're not helping your team if you're out there and you can't perform like you should. What was worse for me was knowing that it wasn't just that I wasn't helping but that I was hurting my team. That's a pretty helpless feeling.

We beat Central Florida and ended the regular season with an easy win over Virginia, but nobody felt like we had accomplished anything special because we had no chance to play for the national championship. We could've beaten Miami, I know, if my ankle had healed up. And we would've had a chance to win the whole thing that year, but it just wasn't meant to be.

Another distraction was all the Heisman talk, and I can't lie about getting too caught up in it. I did think about it too much. Maybe because I'd gone up there the year before and it was such a surprise and all, I started thinking too much about stats. You can't do that as a football player, particularly as a quarterback and as the leader of your team. That's not my job, to put up numbers, as much as it is to make plays and get as many of my teammates involved as I possibly can.

Going to the Gator Bowl was a huge letdown. We didn't even want to be there, but I know that I used that game to take out all my frustration on Clemson. I didn't just want us to beat them. I wanted us to play a dominant game from start to finish. We did that, but finishing 11–1 that year wasn't even close to being as satisfying as 1999 was when we had the same record.

Once we got into December of that year, I was thinking really hard about applying for early entry to the NFL Draft, but honestly I didn't consider myself a first-rounder. I thought third or fourth round was more realistic. But once we got into the new year, it was pretty clear from everything I heard and all the stuff people were telling me that I had a chance to go No. 1 overall.

The next three to four months were kind of a blur. I had my pro day and burned it up, so I had a good idea that there was a good chance I'd be the first guy drafted. For the longest time, what seemed like forever in April, I thought I was going to San Diego. I was cool with it. After meeting with their people and spending time talking about the offense with Chargers quarterbacks coach Mike Johnson, I was ready, but then everything shook up with the Falcons getting involved and making the trade a few days before the draft.

Once they talked to my agent and it was obvious they'd do what was necessary to sign me, then I knew I'd be [going] to Atlanta.

Michael Vick is considered by many as Virginia Tech's greatest player. The electrifying quarterback led the Hokies to a 22–2 record in his two seasons as the starter. As a freshman in 1999, Vick led Tech to an 11–0 record during the regular season. The Hokies lost to Florida State 46–29 in the Sugar Bowl. Vick finished third in Heisman Trophy voting in 1999. He was the No. 1 pick by the Atlanta Falcons in the 2001 NFL Draft and was voted to the Pro Bowl three times in his first five seasons. After serving 21 months in prison for his involvement in a dog-fighting ring, Vick signed with the Philadelphia Eagles in 2009. He was named the NFL's Comeback Player of the Year in 2010, the season in which he led his team to an NFC East title.

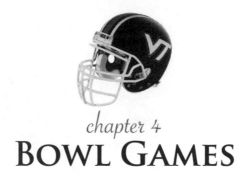

chapter 4
BOWL GAMES

1947 SUN BOWL
Cincinnati 18, Virginia Tech 6

Virginia Tech had to use snow plows and construction equipment to clear its practice field after snow covered Blacksburg before the Sun Bowl. The weather wasn't much better when the Hokies played Cincinnati at Kidd Field in El Paso, Texas, on New Year's Day 1947. The Hokies finished 3–3–3 under coach James Kitts during the 1946 season, but were still invited to play in their first bowl game.

Three inches of snow fell on the ice-covered field on New Year's Eve, and both defenses dominated action the next day as a result. The Hokies reached Cincinnati's 2-yard line late in the first quarter, but were turned away from the end zone on four straight running plays. After Cincinnati took a 12–0 lead with two touchdowns in the third quarter, another Virginia Tech scoring threat was thwarted by an interception.

The Hokies made it 12–6 in the fourth quarter and were driving for a potential tying touchdown late in the game. But Cincinnati halfback Harold Johnson intercepted a pass and returned it all the way to Tech's 25-yard line. The Bearcats added a third touchdown and won the game by an 18–6 score.

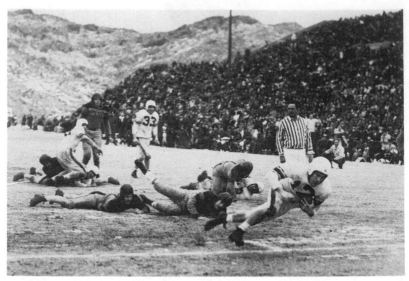

Cincinnati's Harold Johnson scores in the third quarter as the Bearcats defeat Virginia Tech 18–6 in the Sun Bowl before a shivering crowd of 10,000 on January 2, 1947. *Photo courtesy of AP Images*

1966 LIBERTY BOWL
Miami (Florida) 14, Virginia Tech 7

The Hokies waited nearly two decades to play in their second bowl game and were again greeted by frigid temperatures when they faced Miami in the 1966 Liberty Bowl on December 10, 1966, in Memphis, Tennessee.

The Hokies went 8–1–1 under coach Jerry Claiborne in 1966. Virginia Tech's defense was led by All-America safety Frank Loria and defensive end George Foussekis. The Hokies also had a reserve defensive back named Frank Beamer.

The Hokies defense made its mark early in the game, blocking Miami's first punt. Virginia Tech took over at the Hurricanes'

12-yard line and needed only five plays to score a touchdown on Tommy Francisco's two-yard run for a 7–0 lead. Tech's defense held Miami to only 16 yards of offense in the first half, and the Hokies had a 7–0 lead at the half.

But Miami's fortunes changed after halftime. The Hokies appeared to block another Miami punt in the third quarter, but were penalized for roughing the kicker. The miscue helped the Hurricanes tie the score at 7–7. In the fourth quarter, Miami used a 10-play, 70-yard scoring drive to pull away for a 14–7 victory. Virginia Tech's offense gained only one first down in the final three quarters.

Hokies in Their Own Words

TOM STAFFORD

QUARTERBACK, 1963–1966

I came out of Jones Valley High School in Birmingham, Alabama, and Coach Jerry Claiborne had some ties to the high school coaches in that area because he had coached with Bear Bryant, who was the coach at Alabama at the time. I was a big Alabama fan growing up because I had been born and raised around Birmingham.

I ended up with three scholarship offers coming out of high school—from Auburn, Georgia Tech, and Mississippi State. One of the high school coaches knew Coach Claiborne and recommended me to him, and I ended up visiting Virginia Tech. When I came to Virginia Tech, it was kind of like it was home as soon as I got there. I don't know why I knew that, but I just knew it.

I graduated from high school in 1963 and enrolled at Virginia Tech that fall. I really didn't know anything about Virginia Tech and had never even heard of it before I went up there. In 1963 I played on the freshman team, and we played about five or six games. We played West Virginia and Tennessee, and they spanked us about 55–0. It was a different place at that point in time. Freshman teams were a pretty big deal back then.

Bob Schweickert was the quarterback on the varsity team and was a senior in 1964. I played as a sophomore, but at defensive back. I didn't start as a sophomore, of course, but played that season and didn't get redshirted. We played Florida State that season, and they had receiver Fred Biletnikoff and quarterback Steve Tensi. I had to guard Biletnikoff most of the day. Somehow and some way, we kept that game close, made the right plays, and won the ballgame 20–11. It was the biggest victory we'd ever had at Virginia Tech. But it probably would have been better if I had been redshirted. Bobby Owens was the quarterback my junior season in 1965, and I backed him up.

I remember going up to Syracuse late in the season during my sophomore year. We got a bad call on a tackle-eligible play late in the game, and it was the only game in my career when I thought we got a raw deal. I really thought we had won the game, but we lost it after a great effort. Well, that night, I found out how special a place Virginia Tech was. We flew back to Roanoke and took some buses back to Blacksburg about 3:00 or 4:00 in the morning. A couple of miles outside of Blacksburg, probably 1,000 people met the buses, and the team got out of the buses and walked with the fans back into town. I had never heard of that and never seen that. First, we had lost the game, and it wasn't even on TV. I knew it was a special place then.

I moved back to quarterback before my junior season because I guess there was a lag in the process of having quarterbacks come through. Schweickert had been there for four years and Owens was there for three years. The young quarterbacks had not come through yet. I think it was a recruiting thing. They hardly ever played a quarterback until his senior season. I think it was just the nature of the beast. We had a good team coming through and didn't have an experienced quarterback, but I guess I had the game experience and the maturity in the system, so I think it was just a natural move for me. I think it probably just took me that long to mature as a quarterback. I think I showed more promise as a defensive back early.

I was fortunate during the years I played at Virginia Tech. Schweickert's teams were a good group of athletes who had a lot of success. My group, which came out of the 1963 and 1964 recruiting classes, had some really good teams. I was fortunate the whole time I was there and played around some great athletes. Tom Francisco, Terry Smoot, and Tommy Groom were in the backfield. We had some great players in the backfield, particularly during my senior year. Ron Davidson, Frank Beamer, and Frank Loria had come in and made up most of the secondary during my senior season in 1966. It was a good ballclub.

I made my first start at quarterback at Tulane in the first game of my senior season in 1966. I remember it was hot. We had prided ourselves on conditioning, and I think we went down there in pretty good condition, but I don't think we were really prepared for the humidity down there. Plus Tulane had a pretty good ballclub. They had a quarterback named Bobby Duhon who ended up getting drafted. It was a hard-fought game and a low-scoring game, but we lost 13–0. I remember our coming out and blowing them off the ball for the most part, but then it stalled because of a penalty or something. I remember thinking, *Boy, we're really blocking well.* But they got tougher as the night went on, and I don't think we had quite jelled as a ballclub yet.

It was a horrific loss for us. It was a very tough game for us to lose. For some reason, we felt like we had a team that could win all of its ballgames. We really thought we could win all 10 games. Of course, after coming right out of the chute and losing, it was pretty devastating. I remember there being a lot of tears in the hotel room that night. I think that probably made us a better team by not winning that ballgame. It was a good experience.

I had a really good game against Tulane running the ball, but I had a terrible game throwing it. Actually, I couldn't even hold the ball because there was so much sweat. Our centers were sweating all over the ball, and I couldn't even hold it. I think Bill Brill, one of the newspaper columnists, said that "my passing could be best described as miserable," or something like that. I never did like Mr. Brill after that. He was pretty brutal to us a few times.

We came back to Blacksburg, and they worked us hard on Sunday. We kind of fought through the first three games and then hit our stride after that. We crushed George Washington 49–0 the next week, and I probably had the best game I had at quarterback. George Washington had some pretty good athletes back then. We tied West Virginia 13–13 and missed an extra point for the win. So we were 1–1–1, and it was kind of like, "Okay, we thought we were going to be 3–0. What's going on around here?" I think we just kind of kicked it in gear after that, and everything started jelling and we just had a heck of a run after that.

We went to Kentucky the next week, and that game was a lot bigger for other people than some of us because we had a lot of kids on that team from the Louisville area, and Coach Claiborne and a lot of his staff came from Kentucky. We didn't play Kentucky my freshman season, but we played Tennessee and got beat 55–0. That same year, Kentucky beat that Tennessee freshman team by about 30 or 40 points. So here we were playing the team that beat

A native of Birmingham, Alabama, Tom Stafford played defensive back his first two seasons and then moved to quarterback before his junior season in 1965.

the team that killed us during our freshman season. I think we were two evenly matched teams, but our intestinal fortitude just wouldn't let us lose the game. Frank Loria just made one hell of a play at the end of the game. It was your typical Jerry Claiborne–coached game: the offense went out, didn't turn the ball over or make a lot of mistakes, and took advantage of field position and scored when it had the opportunities; and the defense went out there and made some things happen. I think it was your typical Claiborne defensive masterpiece.

We played Vanderbilt in the Tobacco Bowl in Richmond and won the game 21–6, but it was not a good effort on my part. I think I threw two or three interceptions that day. But as a team, we had enough going at that point to overcome a mistake here or there. Vanderbilt had this lineman named Scott Lemay, who was an All-American and just terrific. I remember Bob Griffith and Donnie Bruce were on the right side of the line, and they were supposed to double-team him because we had a dive play or something on the first play of the game. It was supposed to be a safe play. But neither one of them touched him, and he came back into the backfield and about killed our tailback. They came back to the huddle and looked at each other and said, "That son of a bitch is fast, isn't he?" That was one of the things about it, we had a lot of fun during the games.

Against Virginia, we went to Charlottesville and just kind of rolled on them pretty well. There weren't a lot of stars on the 1966 team—I don't know if we had anyone you could classify as a star—but we had a lot of good kids. We were overachievers, and Virginia had a quarterback who was the ACC Player of the Year, Bob Davis, and we went down there and didn't have much trouble with them at all in a 24–7 win.

We had to play Florida State again. The game was on TV, and we were hitting our stride about that time. I had two touchdowns, one to Tommy Francisco and one to Ken Barefoot. We won 23–21, but it didn't feel that close. Florida State was probably the strongest team we played until we faced Miami in the bowl game.

We didn't do much against Wake Forest or William & Mary, but I never felt like we were in danger of losing either one of those games. Winning was the only thing that was important back then. Sometimes you had better performances than at other times, but winning was all that mattered. We didn't critique the past performance all that much back then. We'd critique the game film on Sundays and then move on to the next game.

We closed the 1966 season against Virginia Military Institute, and it was one of those games where it all came together. VMI was always a problem for us back in those days. You never knew if you were going to go in there and they were going to lay one on you. But we got on a roll that day, and it was just like a snowball. I think I probably played about a quarter-and-a-half that day, even though we had some scouts there watching us. The score got out of hand pretty early. I think Francisco scored about six touchdowns that day, and we won 70–12. Of course, our team went out there the year after I left, and I came back to watch the game, and VMI pulled off the upset. So you never really knew what was going to happen in that series.

I remember one of our backup quarterbacks, Freddie Cobb. He was on the scout team for four years, and he could throw the football like crazy. But that wasn't Claiborne's game. Claiborne's game was ball control, don't turn the ball over, make short passes, and be a good running quarterback, too. Well, Freddie was none of the above. He could just drop back and launch it. Finally, after four years on the scout team, he got into the VMI game. Of course, what did Freddie want to do? He wanted to throw the ball, and we were already ahead about 50–0. He launched a couple, and Claiborne pulled him out of the game. Claiborne put him back in the game, and he launched another one. He wanted to show what he could do finally, but Claiborne got a handle on it pretty quickly because the game was getting out of control. But after four years of waiting, Freddie finally got in a game, and that was probably as rewarding to us as winning, as far as I'm concerned.

We played in the Liberty Bowl at the end of the season, and honestly, I think getting the bid was probably the No. 1 thing for us. It was a confirmation of our being a good football team, and that was probably as important as anything. We worked hard before that game; Claiborne wasn't ever going to let that change. But we had some injuries and a car accident before the Liberty Bowl that made us make some changes at some key positions. We had a linebacker playing fullback, and one of our captains was out. I was hurt. I nursed a groin pull for half the season, and I got to the point where I couldn't run, and that was mostly what I did. We had some problems.

I remember the last play of the first half. Ted Hendricks, who they called "Stork," came across the line while we were running some sort of option, and he just about killed me. One of my teammates picked up my broken face mask, and we went into the dressing room. I didn't even know where I was until we came back out for the second half. I was knocked out, but kind of walking-around knocked out. I remember going into the locker room and doing all the halftime scheming and everything, but I just didn't know where I was.

We competed with Miami for about two-thirds of the game, and then I think we were just worn out, and they beat us 14–7. We had some chances, but I think the reward was going to the game and getting the bid. I know that doesn't ring well in today's world, but I think it was true back then. It was a good time and a good ballclub. We were a bunch of overachievers, is what we were.

I'll never forget Coach Claiborne. We were at the Wake Forest game during my senior season. Back then, the way you got plays into the game was to run substitutes into the huddle. Well, it was third down and about two, and he was running a substitute in. Coaches take up a lot of clock and put the pressure on the quarterbacks. Well, he ran the substitute in late and I had to call a timeout to keep from getting a penalty. I kind of just turned and kicked my foot on the ground and walked back to the huddle. I did it and didn't think anything about it. The play he brought in was the exact play that I had called in the huddle.

After every ballgame, the quarterback got on the bus and sat next to Claiborne so you could go over the game. All of the other players would be in the back of the bus enjoying themselves, and the quarterbacks had to sit up there with Coach Claiborne. We went through every play. Every single play. Well, we took a bus back from Wake Forest to Virginia Tech, and Claiborne stopped the bus right in front of the Coliseum. Right in front of the whole team, he looked at me and said, "Get off." He said, "I'm not too pleased with you." I said, "Well, what did I do?" He said, "You kicked the dirt." I looked at him and said, "Gosh, Coach, the play got in late and all I did was kick the dirt. By the way, I had the same play called in the huddle." He said, "I don't care. You don't kick the dirt. Don't let that happen again." Then he told me to get back on the bus.

You can kind of see what kind of person he was. He was very set in his principles and something as minor as that was very important to him. I could never figure out if he felt I was showing him up or he just didn't like that kind of behavior. Coach Claiborne liked his quarterbacks to be a little too clean. Schweickert was the proto-typical Claiborne quarterback. Schweickert was Mr. Everything. I love him. He was very clean, and everybody wanted their daughter to marry Bob Schweickert or their sons to be just like him. He was just a great guy and a great representative of Virginia Tech.

But some of us weren't cut that clean. I'd be out at practice and have something called, and a lineman would come back to the huddle and say, "Boy, I can throw a pass better than that." I'd say something with a little testiness to it, and maybe even put in a little bit of a minor cuss word in there. Next thing I knew, somebody would kick my rear end. It was Coach Claiborne. He'd say, "We don't need that kind of talk in the huddle." I'd say, "Well, Coach, let them get back here and try it." All he would say is, "We don't need that kind of talk in the huddle." So every once in a while, he'd be punting me in the rear end. He was a good man and a very sincere man and probably a great influence on a lot of kids who went to Virginia Tech during that time. He never played favorites and would call anybody out.

Living in Miles Hall was always a good time. We didn't have a lot of money back then, so most of the trouble we got into was pretty innocent stuff. Whether it was water balloons or bottle rockets or Frisbee. But one time there was a terrible snowstorm. I don't know how it happened. For some reason, a football game got scheduled, and Miles was going to play the dorm next to us. There must have been a foot of snow out there. The other dorm was licking their chops. They said, "Here's our chance to really put a hurtin' on some football players." But the rules were that you had to play in your jockstraps. So we were out there in a foot of snow playing football, and every third play or so, we'd have to run inside to get warm.

You can get the impression that we didn't play much football up there and just had a lot of fun. During my junior year, I wasn't playing much because I was behind Bobby Owens. We were sitting around, talking about running long distances and about running to Roanoke. I don't know how it happened, but somebody got a pool together. It was a dollar a man, and we decided to see who could run to Roanoke. Back then, $40 was a lot of money sitting out there, so I decided I was going to run to Roanoke without stopping. I'd never run more than 100 yards in my life.

Back then, they didn't have Interstate 81, so one of my teammates and I started running, and we ran through Dixie Caverns and up and down the hills and everything. The guy who was with me ran for about an hour and then quit. I said, "Well, I might as well just do this thing." A bunch of my friends, including Milt Miller, drove their cars down and escorted me on the highway. They went on down, watched a movie at the theater in Salem, had dinner at some hamburger joint, came back, and found me still on the road. They stretched a long piece of twine across the road near Salem and said, "This will be the end of it. You don't have to run any further." I still have that finish line to this day.

It took me about five hours to run that far, and I came back that night and stayed in the shower for a couple of hours. The next day at practice, I could hardly get loosened up, and Coach Claiborne asked, "What's wrong with you?" I was hobbling around and told him, "Milt Miller stepped on me." They didn't know any different until after my senior season, when I told Coach Claiborne. He got a kick out of it. We had some fun kids.

What does it mean to be a Hokie? I don't know that I've ever thought about it in those terms. I know what it feels like. There's been something about that school since the day I arrived there.

Everybody thinks we just became something when Michael Vick came through there. I think Vick certainly put us in the national spotlight, and we started to get blue-chip players after that. But I've been to other schools, and a lot of fans just go to the games for entertainment. They go to see other people, to be seen, and it's an occasion like going to the movie theater.

But that's not the way it is at Virginia Tech, and it's never been that way. I think people at Virginia Tech believe that when there's a football game, they have a role to play. Their role is not to be a spectator. They believe they have to play their role, whether it's hollering and yelling or playing. They actually believe they're part of the game. The fans feel like they have an impact on the game, and it's always been that way. People feel like they have a vested interest in the success of Virginia Tech.

Tom Stafford was Virginia Tech's starting quarterback in 1966 and led the Hokies to an 8–2–1 record. A native of Birmingham, Alabama, Stafford played defensive back his first two seasons at Tech and then moved to quarterback before his junior season in 1965. He threw for 610 yards and five touchdowns during the 1966 season, leading the Hokies to victories over rivals Virginia, Florida State, William & Mary, and Virginia Military Institute.

1968 LIBERTY BOWL
Ole Miss 34, Virginia Tech 17

Playing in Memphis for the second time in three seasons, the Hokies fell victim to an Ole Miss quarterback named Archie Manning. Virginia Tech took a 17–0 lead in the first quarter at Memphis Memorial Stadium on December 14, 1968.

On the game's second play, Virginia Tech scored a 58-yard touchdown on a trick play, in which Ken Edwards ran from a muddle huddle. The Gobblers huddled at the line of scrimmage, and quarterback Al Kincaid casually flipped the ball to Edwards. After the Rebels fumbled, the Hokies recovered and added another quick touchdown on Terry Smoot's seven-yard run. Tech added a field goal at the end of the quarter for a 17–0 lead.

But from that point, nothing went Virginia Tech's way. Manning threw two touchdowns in the second quarter to cut Virginia Tech's lead to 17–14 at the half. Ole Miss halfback Steve Hindman put the Rebels ahead for good with a 79-yard touchdown run on the opening play from scrimmage in the second half. The Rebels recovered three Virginia Tech fumbles, intercepted two passes, and scored 34 consecutive points in completing their comeback.

Hokies in Their Own Words
AL KINCAID
QUARTERBACK, 1965–1969

I grew up in Tuscaloosa, Alabama, and people have asked me for years how I ended up playing football at Virginia Tech. The short answer is basically because Coach Bear Bryant said I wasn't good enough to play at Alabama. I had played quarterback at the high school in Tuscaloosa and was all-state, and I thought I was a great player. But Coach Bryant came to see me one day. I thought he was coming over to offer me a scholarship.

It was right after Joe Namath and Ken Stabler played quarterback, and Alabama was throwing the football a lot, and I couldn't throw it a lick. So Coach Bryant asked me, "Do you really want to play quarterback?" I said, "Yeah, Coach, I really do." So he looked me straight in the eye and said, "Well, you can't play for us." You want to talk about an 18-year-old kid who was crushed. But Coach Bryant said he knew of a good place for me and he'd help me go there. I remember asking him where, and he said, "V.P.I." [Virginia Polytechnic Institute, or Virginia Tech]. I remember looking at him and saying, "Coach, where is V.P.I.?" I had heard of V.P.I. and VMI, but I really didn't know one from the other.

Coach Bryant told me one of his former coaches, Jerry Claiborne, was coaching at Virginia Tech. Coach Bryant told me, "You can play for Jerry because they won't throw the football but five or six times a game." Basically, that was really the reason I went to Virginia Tech. I had an appointment to West Point, and it really came down to West Point or Virginia Tech. I had a few offers from others schools, such as Vanderbilt and Auburn, but I decided to go to Virginia Tech. I wasn't sure if I was ready for the full military commitment at West Point. Of course, when I went to Virginia Tech, I was in the corps for two years, and then I could make a choice.

I didn't actually visit Virginia Tech until spring practice after I signed. Frank Beamer and I came in at the same time. We were both quarterbacks and became good friends. They were signing about 65 freshmen every season back then, and I think we both thought we were going to be the quarterback when we got there. I think they signed about eight or 10 quarterbacks that season. Bob Schweickert had been *the* quarterback and had graduated, and Tom Stafford was the quarterback on the varsity team during my freshman season.

When I went up there, the first year or two during fall practice, they put me at defensive back. I'd never played defensive back a day in my life. But during my first season in 1965, when I was playing on the freshman team, a couple of quarterbacks got hurt the week before we were supposed to play our first game against the freshman team from the University of Tennessee. So the coaches threw me back over there. I practiced three or four days, went to Knoxville, started at quarterback, and went both ways.

In 1966 Stafford was still the starting quarterback. Then I separated my shoulder during fall practice and was redshirted. We played Miami in the Liberty Bowl that season, and I made all the trips and stood on the sideline. I came back the following season and started the next three years.

I made my first college start at the University of Tampa in 1967. I don't know whether it was the heat, my nerves, or a combination of both of them, but I remember going out and starting the first half, and at halftime they had to give me an I.V. because I was so dehydrated. People have kidded me about that for years. I don't know if it was the heat or nerves or what. We won our first seven games that season but then lost our last three and finished 7–3.

In 1968 we opened the season against Alabama in Birmingham, and of course, the next year we opened up against the Crimson Tide in Blacksburg. Those were two years that Alabama was kind of down. I think they finished 6–5 both of those seasons, and Scott Hunter was the quarterback. He was the guy they signed instead of me. It was a thrill to come down to Birmingham and play because I knew a lot of the Alabama players, having grown up and lived in Tuscaloosa.

We went 7–4 in 1968 and played Ole Miss in the Liberty Bowl in Memphis. It was Archie Manning's sophomore year and my junior year. A lot of Virginia Tech people still remember the first play of the ballgame. They kicked off to us, and I ran a quarterback sweep on our first play on offense and flipped it to Ken Edwards. We ran the swinging gate on the play. Kenny went about 85 yards for a touchdown and scored right off the bat. It was a play we had practiced a lot, and Coach Jerry Claiborne was known for running a trick play in every game. I ran a sweep and kind of bent over like I was tying my shoe, and the rest of the team was lined up in the middle of the field. I flipped it underhanded to Kenny, and he took off down the field. That was the first time we had run that play in a game. We scored another touchdown and went up 17–0 in the first half, but then the floodgates opened. Archie brought his team back, and Ole Miss won the game 34–17.

I don't know that we ever really bounced back from losing to Alabama at the start of my senior season in 1969. We had gone to the Liberty Bowl the season before and had basically everybody coming back. I think it was one of the few times we were ranked in the top 20 before the season started, and everybody was excited about Alabama coming to Blacksburg. We had played a close game against them in Birmingham and thought we had a chance to beat them at home.

So it was really devastating when we lost to Alabama, 17–13, to open the season in 1969. I still remember both of those games, and we had a chance to win both of them. Those two games are what I enjoyed the most and looked forward to more than anything else. I always wish for Coach Claiborne's sake that we could have beaten Coach Bryant.

We went to Wake Forest the next week and played awfully, and then lost to Richmond and Kentucky. Things became unraveled. I hurt my knee in the fourth or fifth game and missed the rest of the season. It was a rather disappointing senior season, to say the least.

We all lived in Miles Hall at the time. There were so many things that happened up in there, and some of them I can't even tell you about to this day. But I'm about to get Frankie Beamer in trouble. It was the week before we played Alabama in Blacksburg at the start of the 1969 season. At that time, there were really only a few girls enrolled at Virginia Tech. We always had to go to Radford College to find dates. We had a scrimmage the Saturday before we were going to play Alabama, and I was dating a girl from Radford and got Frankie a date with a girl from down there. So we drove down to Radford after the scrimmage, and there was maybe a 12:00 curfew that night.

Well, we didn't get back in time for curfew that night. We didn't think there would be any problems. One of the coaches lived in the dorm, and we didn't think he would check curfew on a Saturday night. Frankie was rooming with Mike Widger at the time, and I was rooming with Randy Treadwell. I got back to my room about 2:00 in the morning, and Randy said, "They had a bed check at 12:00." I said, "Oh, my gracious," and then went up to Frankie's room. I told him they had had bed check, and we went down to meet the coaches, but they were in a meeting.

So we went to lunch and class and came back, and there was a note on my door to see Coach Claiborne. I went up to Frankie's room and asked him if he got a note, but he didn't. Widger had told the coaches that Frankie had gone to the bathroom when they came into the room for bed check, and the coaches didn't go down to the bathroom and check. So Frankie didn't get caught; it was only me. Well, tears came to Coach Claiborne's eyes, and tears were coming from my eyes, too. He told me, "Here you are our quarterback, and you've been starting for three years. We're playing Alabama this week, and you're missing curfew. I think I ought to kick you off the team."

When it was all said and done, he didn't kick me off the team, but he took away my laundry money for the entire season and my four tickets for all the home games. So it was a pretty expensive

Al Kincaid was Virginia Tech's starting quarterback for three seasons, from 1967 to 1969, and later became head football coach at Wyoming and Arkansas State.

date. For years, I used to kid Frankie about giving me some money since he didn't get caught.

After graduation in 1970, I went down to Florida and tried to play on one of the golf mini-tours. I thought I wanted to be the next Jack Nicklaus and found out I wasn't as good as I thought I was. I was initially going to be able to play football and baseball at Virginia Tech. After starting on the freshman team in 1965, I went in to see Coach Claiborne and said, "Well, I guess I can start practicing with the baseball team now." Coach Claiborne said, "Yeah. Of course, you've got a chance to maybe start next year. But if you don't go through spring practice, you won't have a chance." So I went through spring practice and redshirted during the 1966 season. The next year in 1967, I started at quarterback and thought, *Boy, I got it made now.* So I went in and asked Coach Claiborne about playing baseball, and he said, "Sure, but we're changing the offense." In the end, I never played baseball at Virginia Tech and kind of turned to golf.

I started helping coach football at a high school in Florida and sent some letters back to Virginia asking for a job. In 1971 the superintendent of schools from Giles County High in Pearisburg, Virginia, called me down in St. Petersburg, Florida, and asked me if I was still interested in coaching. He said they started practice that day and the head coach quit. So I flew up there the next day and took the job on the spot, and that's how I got started in coaching.

I was the head coach in Pearisburg for three years and then went to the University of Alabama as a graduate assistant under Coach Bryant and was there for two years in 1974 and 1975. I went to East Carolina as the offensive coordinator under Pat Dye, and then he took the head coaching job at Wyoming, and I went with him in 1980. He only stayed at Wyoming for one year before getting the Auburn job. Wyoming offered me the job to replace him. I was 33 years old and probably the youngest head coach in the country. I got the job in 1981 and stayed there until 1986.

Having played under Coach Claiborne and coached briefly under Coach Bryant, I would have hoped that some of that would have worn off on me. But I never really tried to emulate Coach Claiborne or Coach Bryant. Everyone has his own style of coaching, but certainly both of them had to be big influences on me.

There were no gray areas with Coach Claiborne; everything was always in black and white. Coach Bryant was always known as being a tough disciplinarian, but Coach Claiborne was every bit of that, if not more. I used to just cringe when I'd have to go into his office and sit down. I probably had as much respect for him as a person and coach as anybody I've ever been around. I remember when I became the head coach at Wyoming in 1981, and he was coaching at Maryland at the time.

I had recruited the Washington, D.C., area and used to get the *Washington Post*. There were a few articles in there kind of getting on Coach Claiborne and saying how he was outdated as a coach and this and that. I remember writing the *Washington Post* a letter as one of his former players and a Division I coach, and I wrote that if there were more coaches like Jerry Claiborne in the coaching profession, then it would be a much better profession.

After I left Wyoming, I moved back to Alabama and got out of coaching. I went back into coaching and was the head coach at Arkansas State, but I was only there for two years and left in 1991. When I took the job, their board of trustees voted to go to Division I-A, but they forgot to tell me about it. I went up to Temple in 1998 as the offensive coordinator for Bobby Wallace, who was a good friend of mine from Alabama.

During my only season at Temple, we went down to Blacksburg and played Virginia Tech. We hadn't won a game, and Virginia Tech was undefeated. We were starting a freshman quarterback for the first time after two of our quarterbacks had been hurt the week before. Somehow, we beat them in their homecoming game, and ESPN called it the biggest upset in the history of college football.

That was the first time I'd been back to Virginia Tech for a football game since I'd played. It was kind of the best of times and the worst of times. Temple was talking about building some new facilities, and Frankie had showed us around the day before. Frankie and I always had been close. My first year at Virginia Tech, it was too far to go back to Tuscaloosa for Thanksgiving, so I had dinner with him and his family. As thrilling as it was to finally win a game at Temple, I felt really bad for Frankie and felt bad for Virginia Tech.

Al Kincaid was the Hokies' starting quarterback for three seasons, from 1967 to 1969. He helped guide Virginia Tech to the 1968 Liberty Bowl and had a 14–7 record in his first two seasons as a starter. Kincaid coached high school and college football for more than two decades. He was the head coach at Wyoming and Arkansas State and retired from coaching for the third and last time in 2000. He currently lives in Birmingham, Alabama, and is a sales representative for a sporting goods manufacturer.

1981 Peach Bowl
Miami (Florida) 20, Virginia Tech 10

The Hokies faced another future Hall of Fame quarterback in the 1981 Peach Bowl, and they left Atlanta still searching for their first bowl victory.

The Hurricanes were led by sophomore quarterback Jim Kelly, who would later lead the Buffalo Bills to four Super Bowl appearances. Miami took the opening kickoff and drove right down the field, with Kelly throwing a 15-yard touchdown to Larry Brodsky for a 7–0 lead at Atlanta's Fulton County Stadium on January 2, 1981. The Hurricanes added another touchdown early in the second quarter on Chris Hobbs' 12-yard run.

Tech's offense had a couple of chances to score in the first half, but tailback Cyrus Lawrence threw an interception at the Miami 1 on a trick play. Quarterback Steve Casey also was intercepted while trying to throw a touchdown on a fourth-down play.

Dennis Laury kicked a 42-yard field goal for Tech in the second quarter to cut Miami's lead to 14–3 at the half.

Virginia Tech scored its only touchdown of the game on its opening possession of the second half. Lawrence dove in from the 1-yard line to make it 14–10 with 8:52 to go in the third quarter. Lawrence ran 27 times for 137 yards with one touchdown, but Virginia Tech was never able to muster enough offense to come back in a 20–10 loss.

1984 INDEPENDENCE BOWL
Air Force 23, Virginia Tech 7

Virginia Tech's vaunted defense was led by All-America defensive end Bruce Smith, who earned the moniker "Sack Man" because of his ability to harass opposing quarterbacks. The NCAA nearly sacked Smith before his final college game, but Smith took the issue to court, and judges in Louisiana and Virginia ruled he was eligible to play.

But even with Smith leading the defense, the Hokies were never able to break Air Force's high-powered wishbone offense in a 23–7 loss at Independence Stadium in Shreveport, Louisiana, on December 15, 1984.

After the Falcons took a 3–0 lead on a 35-yard field goal in the first quarter, Eddie Hunter's 33-yard run moved Virginia Tech inside Air Force's 20-yard line. Maurice Williams scored on a three-yard run to give Tech a 7–3 lead at the end of the first quarter.

The Falcons took a 10–7 lead at the half after the Hokies fumbled the ball away at their 2-yard line. Air Force's Pat Malachowski recovered, and then Jody Simmons scored on a three-yard run.

Air Force broke the game open in the fourth quarter with two touchdowns. The Falcons intercepted Virginia Tech's option pass, and Mike Brown scored on a two-yard run for a 17–7 lead. The Falcons' final touchdown came on quarterback Bart Weiss' 13-yard run.

1986 PEACH BOWL
Virginia Tech 25, North Carolina State 24

The Hokies waited nearly 100 years for their first bowl victory, and it came in dramatic fashion in the 1986 Peach Bowl at Atlanta's Fulton County Stadium on New Year's Eve 1986.

Trailing 24–22 with less than two minutes to play, Virginia Tech's offense took over at its 20-yard line. Quarterback Eric Chapman moved the ball to the Tech 44 with a pair of passes to tight end Steve Johnson. After another pass completion and four straight running plays, the Hokies faced fourth-and-3 at the N.C. State 37 with only 20 seconds to play. Chapman completed a nine-yard pass to Johnson to move to the Wolfpack 28.

With 15 seconds to play, Virginia Tech tried to complete a long pass. But the Hokies were penalized for holding on the play, moving the ball back to N.C. State's 38. Chapman again threw a deep pass on the next play, and the Wolfpack was penalized for pass interference, moving the ball to the 23-yard line.

Coach Bill Dooley sent kicker Chris Kinzer onto the field with only four seconds to play. Kinzer, whose field goals had helped win five games and settle a tie during the regular season, booted a 40-yard field goal as time expired to give the Hokies a dramatic 25–24 victory. The Hokies won their first bowl game and sent Dooley out a winner in his final game as their coach.

"In the huddle before the kick, I just told everybody to get a piece of somebody," Kinzer said afterward. "The whole thing was perfect."

And it was a perfect ending to Virginia Tech's first bowl victory.

Hokies in Their Own Words
CHRIS KINZER
KICKER, 1985–1988

I grew up in Dublin, Virginia, which is about 20 miles from Blacksburg, and went to Pulaski County High School. I was always a Virginia Tech fan, and it was a dream come true that I was able to go down there and play football. I always wanted to play for the Hokies. I can remember many times when my grandmother would call me in to listen to Virginia Tech football. They were called the Gobblers back then, and she would say, "Come in here and listen to these Gobblers whoop up on Bear Bryant and Alabama!" Of course, Tech would always get the hell beat out of them when they played Alabama, but to this day I can still remember listening to Virginia Tech games on the road. I'm just a big Virginia Tech fan.

I had been recruited by not only Virginia Tech, but Wake Forest and a few other schools. My grades were fine, but I was having problems with the SAT, so I went to Fork Union Military Academy for a year and was able to get my score up. After a year at Fork Union, I ended up at Virginia Tech.

I was a freshman in 1985, and there was a senior kicker, Tom Taricani. They gave him a shot kicking the field goals and extra points to start the season, but he didn't do so well. I took over in Game 6 and held on to the job for the remainder of the season.

The first game I kicked at Virginia Tech was against William & Mary. I ended up the season 5-for-7 on field goals and 20-for-21 on extra points.

The 1986 season was really a fun time. We opened the 1986 season against Cincinnati at home, and I missed a couple of field goals in that game that I normally would have made. We ended up losing 24–20. But then I reeled off 17 field goals in a row. After the Clemson game, I didn't miss again until Richmond, which was the next-to-last game during the regular season. I had a nine-game stretch without missing a field goal.

I'll never forget kicking at Death Valley. It's a great place to play football. It's so dad-gum loud and it's a great atmosphere, it really is. When we played against Clemson, their program was still really good, and we won 20–14. I kicked four field goals against Syracuse in the Carrier Dome, which, of course, is a perfect environment for a kicker, and we won 26–17. We beat East Tennessee State pretty good, 37–10, to move to 3–1 going into the West Virginia game.

The West Virginia game in Blacksburg was probably one of the hardest-hitting football games I've ever seen. Of course, the games against West Virginia every year were always physical football games. I kicked two field goals in that game, and we won 13–7. I kicked a 50-yard field goal in that game against about a 20 mph wind, and to this day I still don't know how I made it.

We came back the next week and tied South Carolina 27–27. That was a heck of a football game. They had a quarterback, Todd Ellis, who was really a prolific passer, and they had Sterling Sharpe, who was a great receiver. I think they threw for about 450 yards on us. We played Temple and lost 29–13, but they ended up forfeiting the game because they used an ineligible player. I really thought it was a strange game and a strange place to play

Chris Kinzer is best remembered for making this last-second, game-winning, 40-yard field goal to beat North Carolina State 25–24 in the 1986 Peach Bowl in Atlanta. It was Tech's first victory in a bowl game.

the game. For some reason, the game ended up being played in Norfolk, Virginia, and they were a good football team. They had Paul Palmer, who was a great running back and a finalist for the Heisman Trophy.

We beat Virginia pretty good, 42–10, in a rainstorm down in Blacksburg. I didn't do anything but kick extra points and kick off during that game, but we won, and that was all that mattered. To be honest, we weren't a very good offense in the red zone that season. When you get the ball down inside the 20-yard line, you'd like to put it in. But if you look at the stats, I had just as many field-goal attempts as extra-point attempts. We were just not very effective down there. It's good for a kicker and good for stats, but you'd rather have six points than three.

I had a lot of big kicks during the 1985 season, but my last field goal in the Kentucky game was one of the biggest because we didn't have any timeouts and the clock was running. Kentucky had scored with about two minutes to go and was successful on a two-point conversion to go ahead 15–14. It was pretty muddy, and conditions weren't really too good. We had no timeouts and got the ball, and Erik Chapman, our quarterback, drove us right down the field. He had a couple of really big fourth-down completions, one to Donald Wayne Snell. With about 15 seconds left, we ran a play off the right side to about the 33-yard line. I ran in and lined up for a 50-yard field goal as the clock was winding down. Luckily, it went through, and we won the game 17–15. We beat Richmond and Vanderbilt to finish the season and got a Peach Bowl bid, which was a really big deal back then.

I could have never imagined how that game would turn out. N.C. State was beating us 24–22 late in the fourth quarter. We had a fourth-down play with about 15 seconds to go. We completed a pass to move to State's 28-yard line, which was in my range, but we got called for holding and had to run the fourth-down play again. Erik Chapman dropped back and threw for the end zone. Fortunately, they grabbed David Everett near the goal line and were called for pass interference. We got the ball at the 23-yard line, which set us up for the 40-yard winning field goal try, and then they called timeout. I came back out and lined up and kicked the ball pretty good, and then they drilled me on my follow-through. But the kick went through, and we won the game 25–24.

When I made the game-winning kick at Kentucky, they jumped on me, and it was a helluva pile. So that was one of the reasons I ran toward the N.C. State sideline after I made the field goal in the Peach Bowl. They about killed me in the Kentucky game. I was running down the sideline and was pointing my finger at them. At the last second, there were a couple of their gentlemen who were shooting me the bird. Of course, the camera was on me and, being young and dumb, I returned the favor. It's something I regret. I shouldn't have done that. Somebody should have grabbed me and thrown my butt on the ground.

When I got back to Virginia and watched the game on tape, I couldn't believe how nervous I was. I was a nervous wreck watching the game, even though I already knew the outcome. But when you're out there on the field playing, you're really not nervous because you're so focused on what you're doing.

Having grown up so close to Virginia Tech, I was a Tech football fan my whole life. You'd always see Virginia Tech get to a bowl game and lose. They'd get to another bowl game and lose. The big deal at the time was that was the first bowl win in the history of Virginia Tech. So to help to bring my institution some publicity was very gratifying. There were a lot of individual awards I gained from that, being an Associated Press All-American and a *Playboy* All-American and all of that, but I really felt a lot of pride and still have a lot of pride in helping Tech win its first bowl game.

Coach Beamer took over the program before my junior season in 1987. In all fairness to Coach Beamer, Coach Dooley was someone who really stressed running the football between the tackles, and we didn't throw the football a whole lot. Coach Dooley was just like his brother at Georgia; he was a run 'em out, grind 'em out kind of guy. We were on probation [for NCAA rules violations committed during the Dooley era] and limited in the amount of scholarships we could give. The guys who were already in the program were recruited by Coach Dooley and recruited to play his offense. Coach Beamer came in and was more open-minded and wanted to throw the football a little bit more, and it takes a while to make that change and recruit the type of kids you want to run your offense. So we struggled there for a couple of years. We just didn't have the personnel in place to do what Coach Beamer wanted to do.

Coach Beamer was a great coach. Beamer would talk to you, whereas Coach Dooley's assistants did a lot of the work. He would talk to the team, but he wouldn't have a whole lot to say to you outside of practice. Coach Beamer would talk to you more and ask about how things were off the field. As a fan, I sure am glad they didn't get rid of Coach Beamer. Like any other fan, when things don't go well, everyone is always going to question decisions when mistakes are made. That's just human nature. But the rest is history. They've run off an incredible history of going to consecutive bowl games, and not a lot of schools can say that.

After graduation, I chased that dream of trying to play in the NFL for a couple of years and went through a few tryouts. It never really panned out. After my senior season, I still had to finish my degree at Virginia Tech. To the credit of Coach Beamer and Dave Braine, who was the athletics director at the time, they really stayed on me. When I would run into them somewhere, they would always say, "Hey, you've only got one semester left to get your degree, you need to finish." They would always remind me to come back and get my degree. So after a couple of years of trying to kick in the NFL, I eventually went back and got my degree.

For so long, I thought Virginia Tech didn't get the respect it deserved. It's down in the country and it's a hard place to get to for a lot of people. You always fought people calling it the "Cow College." But I'll never forget sitting there in my dorm room in Blacksburg when Coach Beamer got the job after Dooley resigned. They were interviewing Beamer on TV, and he said, "I hope one day we can compete and win a national championship." I was sitting there thinking, *This guy must be smoking marijuana or something.* But you know? Damned if we didn't almost do it a few years ago. And for the past decade we've been in the national championship picture. I guess I never saw that potential, but it didn't matter what I thought because Beamer saw it and he's seen it through. That's a credit to him.

Chris Kinzer was Virginia Tech's place=kicker from 1985 to 1988. He still holds school records for consecutive field goals made, 17 in a row, and 22 field goals in a season, both set in 1986. During that season, Kinzer made game-winning field goals as time expired against West Virginia and North Carolina State in the Peach Bowl. He was named second-team All-America by the Associated Press and All-America by Playboy. *Kinzer teaches physical education and health at Walker Grant Middle School in Fredericksburg, Virginia, where he lives with his wife, Jennifer, and daughter, Rebecca.*

1993 INDEPENDENCE BOWL
Virginia Tech 45, Indiana 20

Frank Beamer's first bowl victory as his alma mater's coach was nearly as dramatic as the final seconds of Bill Dooley's final victory in 1986.

The Hokies had a 14–13 lead over Indiana with only 35 seconds left in the first half of the 1993 Independence Bowl in Shreveport, Louisiana, on New Year's Eve 1993. With the ball at Virginia Tech's 49-yard line, Hoosiers quarterback John Paci dropped back to pass. He was hit by Hokies defenders George DelRicco and DeWayne Knight. The ball popped into the air and landed in the hands of defensive end Lawrence Lewis, who ran 20 yards for a touchdown to make it 21–13 with 23 seconds to play.

But the Hokies weren't done. Indiana took the ensuing kickoff and moved to the Tech 42. After a nine-yard pass, Virginia Tech thought time expired and started to run to their locker room. But officials ruled Indiana called timeout and put one second back on the clock. The Hoosiers lined up to try a 51-yard field goal, but Tech's Jeff Holland blocked the kick. The ball bounced into the air again, and Tech's Antonio Banks scooped it up and ran 80 yards for a touchdown. Tech scored 14 points in the final 35 seconds to take a 28–13 lead at the half.

"I've never, ever seen a half end that way," Lewis said afterward. "They wanted the extra second, so they got the extra second, and look what happened. They should have just went on and took it as it was."

Virginia Tech quarterback Maurice DeShazo was named the game's most outstanding player after completing 19 of 33 passes for 193 yards with two touchdowns. But Virginia Tech's defense and special teams, which would become the staples of "Beamer Ball," were the real heroes of the 1993 Independence Bowl.

"It sure made for good TV, didn't it?" Hokies coach Frank Beamer said.

1994 GATOR BOWL
Tennessee 45, Virginia Tech 23

Another Manning spoiled Virginia Tech's postseason hopes in the 1994 Gator Bowl, which was played at Ben Hill Griffin Stadium on the University of Florida campus on December 30, 1994. The Gator Bowl's traditional home in Jacksonville, Florida, was undergoing renovations after the city was awarded an NFL franchise.

Virginia Tech's defense had no answer for Volunteers freshman Peyton Manning, who completed 12 of 19 passes for 189 yards with one touchdown in Tennessee's 45–23 victory. Volunteers tail-back James "Little Man" Stewart ran for two touchdowns and passed for another score as Tennessee took a 35–10 lead at the half.

Tennessee had seven plays of 20 yards or more and amassed 495 yards of offense. The Volunteers won six of their final seven games after Manning was named the team's starting quarterback.

"Too many long plays defensively, just too many long plays," coach Frank Beamer said. "And early on we did what we couldn't afford to do—turn the ball over. It's tough to overcome that."

Virginia Tech couldn't overcome a series of self-inflicted wounds. The Hokies fumbled four times, losing one, and quarterback Maurice DeShazo was intercepted twice. DeShazo scored Tech's only touchdown of the third quarter on a seven-yard run.

1995 SUGAR BOWL
Virginia Tech 28, Texas 10

Virginia Tech's 28–10 upset of Texas in the 1995 Sugar Bowl at the Louisiana Superdome in New Orleans on New Year's Eve 1995 still stands as the greatest bowl victory in school history. And the Hokies weren't even supposed to be playing in the game; they were awarded the coveted bowl berth after co–Big East champion Miami was dropped because of NCAA sanctions.

After falling behind the heavily favored Longhorns 10–0 in the first half, Virginia Tech grabbed momentum when Bryan Still returned a punt 60 yards for a touchdown to cut Texas' lead to 10–7 with 2:34 left in the half.

Hokie Marcus Parker (34) carries the ball for a touchdown as Tre Thomas of Texas (17) looks on at the Sugar Bowl, December 31, 1995. Virginia Tech won 28–10. *Photo courtesy of AP Images*

With Virginia Tech leading 14–10 in the second half, quarter-back Jim Druckenmiller threw a 54-yard touchdown to Still to make it 21–10. Still touched the ball only seven times, catching six passes and returning one punt, for a total of 179 yards.

"We want to get the ball in his hands as much as we can," coach Frank Beamer said afterward. "It always pays off."

Tech's defense harassed Longhorns quarterback James Brown throughout the game, sacking him five times and forcing three interceptions. The Hokies defense scored the game's final touchdown after Cornell Brown sacked Brown and caused a fumble. Tackle Jim Baron scooped up the ball and returned it 20 yards for a touchdown.

"We've been working in this program to move up to the top of the college football world," Beamer said. "That's another step for us. Beating a great team like Texas makes it even better. It's a great night for the Hokies."

1996 ORANGE BOWL
Nebraska 41, Virginia Tech 21

In a game that coach Frank Beamer billed as the biggest in school history, Virginia Tech went toe-to-toe with two-time defending national champion Nebraska in the first half of the 1996 Orange Bowl. But the Cornhuskers proved to be too deep and too talented in the second half of a 41–21 victory at Pro Player Stadium in Miami on New Year's Eve 1996.

After Nebraska took a 24–21 lead at the half, it scored on its first four possessions of the second half to blow the game open. The Cornhuskers, who were 17-point favorites, scored 17 points in a 10-minute span in the second quarter, including a defensive touchdown on a botched option play by the Hokies.

Virginia Tech lost despite quarterback Jim Druckenmiller throwing for three touchdowns and tailback Ken Oxendine running for 150 yards and catching three passes for 60 yards. The Hokies had 407 yards of offense.

Nebraska ran for 279 yards and didn't commit a turnover.

"We didn't have an error-free game, the one error really hurt," Oxendine said afterward. "We ran the ball on them. They couldn't stop us until the fourth quarter."

Unfortunately for Virginia Tech, its defense couldn't stop Nebraska, either.

1998 Gator Bowl
North Carolina 42, Virginia Tech 3

Virginia Tech was ambushed by a motivated North Carolina team, which was upset it was snubbed by the Bowl Alliance and because its coach, Mack Brown, had left for the University of Texas.

With Tar Heels defensive coordinator Carl Torbush acting as interim coach, North Carolina scored touchdowns on offense, defense, and special teams in a 42–3 rout in the Gator Bowl in Jacksonville, Florida, on New Year's Day 1998.

"I think we know an Alliance team when we see one, and this is certainly an Alliance team, in my opinion," Hokies coach Frank Beamer said afterward. "Of all the teams we've played in a bowl game, North Carolina wouldn't take a back seat to any of them."

With Torbush coaching from the press box, the Hokies were held to a season-low 185 yards of offense and lost three of six fumbles.

North Carolina quarterback Chris Keldorf completed 17 of 28 passes for 290 yards and three touchdowns, and cornerback Dre' Bly blocked one punt and recovered another one for a touchdown.

UNC defensive end Greg Ellis recovered a fumble in the end zone to give the Tar Heels a 22–0 lead only seven seconds into the second quarter.

"This is a pretty good whupping they gave us," Virginia Tech running back Ken Oxendine said.

1998 MUSIC CITY BOWL
Virginia Tech 38, Alabama 7

On a cold and blustery day in Nashville, Virginia Tech ended its bowl drought and futility against the Southeastern Conference, routing Alabama 38–7 in the inaugural Music City Bowl on December 29, 1998.

The Hokies also set the stage for their breakthrough season in 1999.

A sellout crowd of 41,600 braved freezing rain and a frigid wind chill to watch the Hokies end a 10-game losing streak against the Crimson Tide. It was Virginia Tech's first victory over an SEC team and most lopsided victory in a bowl game.

"It was time for us to get a bowl win," Virginia Tech quarterback Al Clark said. "Like an alumnus told me earlier, it doesn't make sense to go to all these bowls if you can't win them. And to beat a team like Alabama, that's a great stepping-stone for Tech."

Virginia Tech had a 10–7 lead at the half, but pulled away behind All-America defensive end Corey Moore in the second half. The Hokies intercepted three passes, blocked two punts, and recovered a muffed punt return in scoring 28 consecutive points.

"We've talked a lot about trying to get up that ladder," said Virginia Tech coach Frank Beamer, who lost to the Crimson Tide as a Hokies player in 1968. "I think we took some steps. We've got to keep building our program and take nothing for granted."

Beamer couldn't have known how high the Hokies would climb the very next season.

2000 SUGAR BOWL
Florida State 46, Virginia Tech 29

Virginia Tech didn't win a national championship when it played Florida State in the 2000 Sugar Bowl in New Orleans, but the Hokies probably earned the respect of anyone who watched them play on college football's biggest stage.

After falling behind by 21 points in the first half, Virginia Tech rallied behind electrifying quarterback Michael Vick and took the lead going into the fourth quarter. But Virginia Tech's defense had no answer for FSU star Peter Warrick, who had six catches for 163 yards and two touchdowns in the Seminoles' 46–29 victory. The teams combined for more than 900 yards of offense in the highest-scoring Sugar Bowl ever.

"I'm proud of the way we came back," Virginia Tech coach Frank Beamer said. "We were down 28–7, and it could have gotten ugly. I know I'd be miserable if we had gotten beat 55–7. We came back and played hard. We just didn't make enough plays."

The Hokies couldn't contain Warrick, who caught two long touchdown passes and scored again on a punt return. It marked the first time in 11 years that the Hokies surrendered a touchdown on a punt return.

"Peter Warrick kind of made a statement tonight," Beamer said.

So did Vick, the Hokies' sensational freshman quarterback, who ran for 145 yards and passed for 225. Vick scored on a short run in the last minute of the first half, and then the Hokies got two long punt returns from Ike Charlton and scored nine points less than 10 minutes into the third quarter. The Hokies took a 29–28 lead on Andre Kendrick's six-yard run just before the fourth quarter.

Florida State regained the lead on Chris Weinke's 14-yard touchdown pass to Ron Dugans, which came after the Seminoles converted a fourth-and-inches play in their own territory. Warrick put FSU ahead for good with a 43-yard touchdown catch with 7:42 to play.

"I thought we had them on the ropes," Vick said. "But Florida State is Florida State. They're going to make it a slugfest all the way to the end."

The Hokies took most of FSU's punches until the very end.

2001 GATOR BOWL
Virginia Tech 41, Clemson 20

In what would be Virginia Tech quarterback Michael Vick's final college game, the Hokies exorcised their Gator Bowl demons in a 41–20 rout of Clemson on New Year's Day 2001.

After being routed by Tennessee and North Carolina in its previous two trips to the Gator Bowl, the Hokies jumped on Clemson early in the game, taking a 14–0 lead on Vick's 23-yard touchdown pass to Jarrett Ferguson and six-yard scoring run in the first quarter. After taking a 21–10 lead at the half, Virginia Tech scored two more touchdowns in the third quarter to blow the Tigers off the field.

"After the way we played the last two times, if we didn't do better this time, the Gator Bowl people weren't going to have us back," Virginia Tech coach Frank Beamer said. "We weren't as consistent as we'd have liked, but overall our defense played well and came up with big plays, and offensively we got some big plays. It was a great win and a great start to next year."

Vick finished his final college game with 224 yards of total offense and was named Gator Bowl MVP. He completed 10 of 18 passes for 205 yards with one touchdown and ran for 19 yards and one score. Hokies tailback Lee Suggs ran for 73 yards and three touchdowns.

"I wasn't going home feeling the way I felt that night," said Virginia Tech tailback André Kendrick, who played on the 1997 team that lost to North Carolina 42–3 in the 1998 Gator Bowl. "That was embarrassing. I just wanted to win this one. I didn't care how."

2002 GATOR BOWL
Florida State 30, Virginia Tech 17

In a rematch of the 1999 national championship game, Virginia Tech's defense again had no answers for Florida State's high-powered offense in a 30–17 loss in the Gator Bowl on New Year's Day 2002.

Once again, Virginia Tech led the Seminoles going into the fourth quarter, after quarterback Grant Noel fired a 55-yard touchdown to André Davis for a 17–13 lead with 40 seconds left in the third quarter. Davis caught five passes for 158 yards with one touchdown in his final college game.

But FSU scored 17 straight points in the fourth quarter. On the first play of the final quarter, FSU quarterback Chris Rix threw a 77-yard touchdown pass to Javon Walker to give the Seminoles a 20–17 lead. The Seminoles stopped the Hokies on fourth-and-1 on the ensuing possession, and then Rix found Walker for a 50-yard pass on the very next play. Xavier Veitia kicked a 35-yard field goal for a 23–17 lead with 10:13 to play.

The Seminoles put the game away on Rix's 23-yard touchdown pass to Walker with 2:14 remaining. Rix threw for 326 yards with two touchdowns, and Walker set a Gator Bowl record with 195 receiving yards on four catches with two touchdowns.

"I think it's pretty simple," Virginia Tech coach Frank Beamer said. "There were too many long plays for them, and we didn't take advantage of field position. When you put those two things together and you're playing a good football team like Florida State, you won't win it."

Hokies in Their Own Words

ANDRÉ DAVIS

WIDE RECEIVER, 1998–2001

I really only got interested in Tech because my cousin, Richard Bowen, was a walk-on offensive lineman on the team and he encouraged me to come down there and look at Tech. At the time, I was being recruited by lots of I-AA schools like Massachusetts, Maine, and Delaware. So I thought I was going to make my decision out of one of those schools. But Richard told me to send my tape down to Tech and have them take a look at it. I said, "It can't hurt. Why not?"

About two weeks later, Terry Strock, who was the receivers coach at Tech at the time, told me to come down and check it out. It was kind of weird because I was on a recruiting trip at the University of Delaware when I started thinking about Tech. I did the whole recruiting trip at Delaware, and then my parents decided that we were going to go on down to Blacksburg that Sunday and meet up with everybody. Well, I didn't get to meet anybody when I went down there because it was such a quick trip. I was there for maybe four hours at the most. I remember seeing Tech players Nick Sorensen and Dave Meyer walking through the hallways, but that was about it. I had lunch with Coach Strock and visited the campus and made my decision to go to Tech when I came back home.

Coming from my area [Niskayuna, New York, which had a population of 20,295 as of 2000], there weren't a whole lot of people getting I-A offers, so if somebody was going to offer me a full scholarship to get an education and play football, I was going to take it. I remember leaving the campus that night and telling my parents I was going to sign there but I wasn't going to do it right away. I didn't want everybody to think I was just going to make a snap decision like that.

I remember I got to Tech and redshirted the first year. It was probably, like, halfway through my first season when I realized I belonged at a place like Tech. There I was, playing with guys who were considering schools like Florida and Florida State coming out of high school, while I was trying to make a decision between places like Maine and Delaware just a few years earlier. It made me realize I could compete on that level.

But I don't think it really hit me until that national championship year in 1999 when things really started taking form for me. I knew I could play, but I don't think I really knew what my potential could be and how much potential I really had until that year when some things started happening.

It's funny because I really didn't want to be a punt returner when I first got started at Tech. But I remember we were down at the Sugar Bowl and Ricky Hall got hurt. They really didn't want me to do it right then, but Coach Beamer told me he wanted me to start working at punt returner to be ready to do it for the next season. I remember talking to my friends and parents and telling them I would've rather been a kick returner instead of a punt returner because I didn't want that ball hanging up there and have 11 guys breathing down on you all looking to kill you, but the faith that Coach Beamer had in me was really something. I decided it was just another opportunity to play, and I'm glad I wound up making the most out of it.

I was lucky enough to have some big games at Tech. In my junior year, that West Virginia game where I had three touchdowns on three different plays stands out in my memory. I think that let people see my ability and know I could make big plays. You always expect to do those kinds of things, but you don't think about it when you're out there. I just remember watching *Sportscenter* and reading the newspapers the next morning and realizing how big of a game it really was. It really let me know that I could do it and put all the things together that I was able to in that one big game.

Of course, I played with Michael Vick, and there's probably three games that I remember of Mike's. There was one up there against Temple in Philadelphia, and the Boston College game up there in Massachusetts. He had so many sick runs in that Boston College game where it seemed like he was making all 11 guys miss. Then, there was the national championship game, of course. I remember a lot of people talking about how he couldn't do what he did against Florida State in the Sugar Bowl against guys in the NFL—it was just college guys. But there were a lot of guys, like the guys from Miami, who went on to the NFL that he was doing those kinds of things to. In my mind, and I think in a lot of other people's minds, it was confirmation that he could do it against anybody.

André Davis was named an All-America punt returner during his junior season in 2000. He ranked second in the country, averaging 22 yards on 18 punt returns and returned three for touchdowns.

There are a lot of people I'll never forget from my years at Tech. For me personally, I can't thank Wayne Ward enough. That dude had my back. Any time we were out there on special teams, we were always talking about big blocks. I remember the one year we roomed together, every week we were looking to set Wayne Ward up to get that Hammer Award.

The Hammer Award is pretty much the big hit award. It's something the guys on the team really look forward to. It's really about making sure we make the play because you'll see a lot of guys whiff sometimes.

Most of the guys I keep in touch with were guys in my recruiting class. Dan Wilkinson was my roommate in my freshman year. Jarrett Ferguson and Wayne Ward also lived on my hallway and we got close. I still keep in touch with those guys today probably once a month. They were all a big reason why Tech is still such a special place to me.

André Davis was a standout receiver for the Hokies and was named an All-America punt returner during his junior season in 2000. His 87-yard punt return against East Carolina in 2000 was the second longest in school history. Davis is the fourth-leading receiver in Virginia Tech history, with 103 catches for 1,986 yards and 18 touchdowns. Davis was selected in the second round of the 2002 NFL Draft by the Cleveland Browns and played for Cleveland, New England, Buffalo, and Houston through 2009.

2002 SAN FRANCISCO BOWL
Virginia Tech 20, Air Force 13

After being victimized by Florida State's Peter Warrick and Javon Walker in previous bowl games, Virginia Tech cornerback Ronyell Whitaker found some sense of redemption in Virginia Tech's 20–13 victory over Air Force in the San Francisco Bowl on New Year's Eve 2002.

With the Hokies leading 20–13 in the final seconds, Air Force quarterback Chance Harridge completed a fourth-and-10 pass to the Virginia Tech 10 with 17 seconds left. After two incomplete passes, Harridge scrambled for the end zone after dropping back to pass and finding no receivers open. He was met at the 4-yard line by Whitaker, who forced a game-ending fumble.

"If you've got Air Force where they've got to throw, you feel like you've got them," Virginia Tech coach Frank Beamer said. "But we didn't have them. They're an upset special waiting to happen. They were down near the end zone, and everybody was holding their breath."

Virginia Tech trailed 10–0 in the first quarter, but rallied to take a 17–10 lead on Lee Suggs' one-yard touchdown run with 4:55 left in the first quarter. The teams traded field goals, setting up the final frantic seconds at the end.

Virginia Tech finished the 2002 season with a 10–4 record, its sixth 10-win season in school history. More importantly, Virginia Tech's senior class won its 40th game, making it the most successful class in school history.

"For these seniors to go out as the all-time winningest class is pretty significant," Beamer said.

2003 INSIGHT BOWL
California 52, Virginia Tech 49

Virginia Tech got a glimpse of another Super Bowl–winning quarterback when it suffered a thrilling 52–49 defeat against California in the Insight Bowl in Phoenix on December 26, 2003.

The Hokies and Bears combined for more than 1,000 yards of offense in a shootout in the desert, as Virginia Tech quarterback Bryan Randall dueled with California's Aaron Rodgers on nearly every possession.

California won the game on Tyler Fredrickson's 35-yard field goal as time expired.

"You could say that if we scored every time we got the ball, we would have won, but we didn't," Virginia Tech tailback Kevin Jones said. "So we can't pin it on the defense or offense. The team lost."

Virginia Tech's offense certainly did its part. Randall completed 24 of 34 passes for 398 yards and tied an Insight Bowl record with four touchdown passes. Hokies receiver Ernest Wilford caught eight passes for 110 yards, and Jones ran 16 times for 154 yards and one touchdown.

Virginia Tech's defense surrendered 530 yards of offense, and Rodgers, who would later lead the Green Bay Packers to victory in Super Bowl XLV, completed 27 of 35 passes for 394 yards and two touchdowns.

"We knew their quarterback was good," Beamer said. "He was as accurate a guy as any I've seen and he's a heckuva player. You've got to make plays. That's the bottom line and we didn't do that tonight."

2005 Sugar Bowl
Auburn 16, Virginia Tech 13

After winning an ACC championship in its first season in the league, Virginia Tech took undefeated Auburn to the wire in a 16–13 loss in the Sugar Bowl in New Orleans on January 3, 2005.

Trailing 16–7 late in the fourth quarter, Hokies quarterback Bryan Randall threw an 80-yard touchdown to Josh Morgan to cut the Tigers' lead to 16–13 with 2:01 to play. Randall broke the school's career touchdown pass record with 48.

But Auburn recovered an onside kick and ran out the clock to finish the season with a perfect 13–0 record.

"We didn't do some things that we've really been doing well," Beamer said. "We dropped a few balls, we had some mental errors in the kicking game, we weren't sharp in the passing game at times, and the tackling wasn't consistent at times."

It wasn't a good formula against Auburn, which narrowly missed out on playing for a BCS national championship after winning an SEC title. Trailing 6–0 in the second quarter, the Hokies drove to Auburn's 2-yard line. On third down, Randall ran a quarterback draw and seemed to have a clear lane into the end zone. But safety Will Herring stuffed Randall inside the 1-yard line. Beamer elected to go for a touchdown on fourth down, but fullback Jesse Allen dropped Randall's pass.

"We made them throw from the 1," Auburn coach Tommy Tuberville said. "We convinced them they couldn't run, and that was the key."

Auburn took over at its 1-yard line and drove down the field. John Vaughn kicked a 24-yard field goal for a 9–0 lead. The Tigers added a touchdown on the opening drive of the second half, and Virginia Tech couldn't climb out of a 16–0 hole.

"We had a chance to go up 7–6, and I felt we were lucky to be down 6–0 at the time," Beamer said. "I felt even if we don't make it, we'd have them backed up. They did a nice job of moving the ball."

2006 GATOR BOWL
Virginia Tech 35, Louisville 24

After nearly imploding with a series of mistakes and egregious penalties in the first half, Virginia Tech rallied from an 11-point deficit with 22 fourth-quarter points in a 35–24 victory over Louisville in the Gator Bowl on January 2, 2006.

After committing five 15-yard penalties in the first quarter, the Hokies were lectured by coach Frank Beamer before regaining their composure to break a two-game losing streak in bowl games.

Louisville went ahead 24–13 early in the fourth quarter, but then Virginia Tech quarterback Marcus Vick threw a 54-yard pass to David Clowney and tailback Cedric Humes scored on a 24-yard run on the next play. Vick threw a pass to Josh Morgan for a two-point conversion, making it 24–21 with 13:04 to play. After Hokies defensive end Chris Ellis sacked Hunter Cantwell and forced him to fumble, Vick threw a 48-yard pass to Clowney on the ensuing play.

On second-and-goal, Vick threw a five-yard touchdown to tight end Jeff King for a 28–24 lead with 6:09 to play. On Louisville's next play, linebacker James Anderson intercepted Cantwell's pass and returned it 39 yards down the right sideline to seal the 35–24 victory.

"I want to remember the second half," Beamer said. "I don't want to remember the first half."

Vick finished 11-of-21 for 203 yards and two touchdowns, and Humes ran 22 times for 113 yards with one touchdown.

"We were lucky to win this one," Beamer said. "At the same time, I'm proud of our football team. We got back to Virginia Tech football in the second half. We knocked off the penalties and played good, tough football. I was proud of that. I was proud that we ended up the day playing the way Virginia Tech is supposed to play. I thought our kids gave great effort and kept battling."

Hokies in Their Own Words

DAVID CLOWNEY

WIDE RECEIVER, 2003–2006

Virginia Tech found me because I found them. My senior year in high school, we had a big playoff game at Delray Beach Atlantic against Pompano Ely, which is a powerhouse school down here. I had a 99-yard touchdown catch and sent Tech the tape of that play.

They saw the tape in Blacksburg and asked me to come up and take a visit. It was just a go route on first down. I caught it and outran everybody to the end zone. They liked the speed.

North Carolina, Minnesota, and Toledo were recruiting me for football, and all the Florida schools were recruiting me for track, but Tech came late. I sent the tape, and, out of nowhere, Tech came, maybe 10 or 11 days before the signing date.

I canceled a visit to one school and went up to Virginia Tech. I had a great time. The facilities were incredible. The whole presentation was nice. I had to make a decision between Toledo and

Virginia Tech. That's what I had left because other schools said I was waiting too long; they started taking back offers.

I was a high 4.3, something like 4.38 or 4.39 in the 40-yard dash. I was fast and could have run track in college, but I wanted to play football.

We had some great receivers at Virginia Tech when I was there, but that is the type of team you want to be on. I played as a true freshman and was one of the only ones, if not the only one, who played as a true freshman.

The receivers, we called ourselves the Fab 5 of college football, that's how good we were. It was myself, Josh Morgan, Eddie Royal, Justin Harper, and Josh Hyman. You're talking some NFL guys in that group, and we all took care of business on the field. We had a poster done and were on the game program.

My junior year, Marcus Vick was the starting quarterback, and that was my best year. My senior year, Marcus was supposed to be there again, but he ended up getting dismissed from the team, and we had Sean Glennon as the starting quarterback.

I actually had a first-round and second-round grade for the NFL Draft coming out of my junior year. My intentions were to leave and come out early, but a lot of family members wanted me to stay in school and get my degree [in residential property management and real estate].

My coaches wanted to use my speed to stretch the field and open up things underneath. The defense would have to watch me going deep, but that just cleaned things out for people coming underneath or a run play. A had a high yards-per-catch average [18 yards] because of deep balls.

I loved playing football. I loved the go route. We ran the ball a lot because we had good backs, but I would only get two or three catches a game. They had to be loud when I made them.

David Clowney (87) reaches for a pass in front of Miami defender Marcus Maxey (24) during a game at Lane Stadium, November 5, 2005. *Photo courtesy of AP Images*

Even if I didn't get a catch, I went out there blocking my butt off every game. I had a great game against Miami my junior year. My catches weren't there, but you can measure your game by getting open, blocking, and things like that.

Duke was always a good game, but that was Duke. There was the Gator Bowl game against Louisville that we won. There was a 60-yard bomb from Marcus they called back, but I had another long catch from Marcus in that game.

Marcus was a very good quarterback, a natural. He was a real quarterback. Everybody thought because his last name was Vick he wanted to run. He hated running. He was a dropback passer.

I enjoyed my time at Tech, even if I didn't get seven or eight catches a game. It would have been nice to get a lot of balls thrown my way; any receiver would like that. But we won at Tech, and that was the important thing. It was a great time for me.

The coach who had the most influence on me was Coach Tony Ball, who is the receivers coach at the University of Georgia right now. He had the most impact on me. He recruited me out of high school, and when I talked with him while I was still in high school, he told me exactly what he expected out of me. He taught me how to run precise routes and how to get open.

He had me read this one book, *The Art of War*, which explains how to be a leader and become a better man. That helped me be a leader for our team. If I did go out there and drop a pass, I had no doubt in my mind I was going to come back and catch a 60-yarder. Tony Ball had a lot of trust in me as a player.

We had a lot of wins, and you want to be part of a team that is doing well. We had running backs who carried us and that's how we played, but when we had to throw it, we could throw it. If I had to do it all over again, I think I would still go to Tech.

Being a Hokie means having heart and never giving up and staying strong. Even at your worst moments, those games when you are down 10 or 15 points, you come back and fight and make things happen and don't quit.

Being a Hokie is determination.

I have my own foundation, the David Clowney Foundation, which helps inner-city youth, giving scholarships to kids who can't afford it. Like myself, if I had not gotten a full scholarship to Virginia Tech, my parents would not have been able to send me to college.

We were not slum poor, but we weren't wealthy either. Brandon Flowers and I are from the same place in Florida, and we have the leading murder rate in the state of Florida because of gang activity. I try and stress to kids that gang life is not the way to go and you don't have to sell drugs to make money. You don't have to be in a gang to have friends.

When the earthquake happened in Haiti [in January 2010], we used my foundation to go down there and try and help people, especially the kids. We were able to build tents for people because they were living under sheets. We took food, diapers, water just to get them going again.

I was at New York [with the Jets] at the time, and they gave us some clothes that were donated. The whole trip was a big success.

After that I ended up going to Ghana, which is one of the poorest countries in Africa. We showed the kids how to play American football. Yes, there was some civil war there. It's not always a safe place for those kids, but we ran a camp for them.

I told guys back at Virginia Tech what I was involved in. Different guys have different reasons for why they do things, but I don't try and tell people to do this or do that. Just because I have a certain mind-set about children doesn't let me tell people what to do. I do things my own way.

If they do make it to the NFL, I do pray and hope they give back to the kids. I really hope they can do something.

I have a David Clowney celebrity weekend for my foundation for kids in south Florida, and a bunch of different guys show up. I have a celebrity basketball game, but we also show kids how to play football. We go over technique, things like that. It is a benefit to kids. That's why we do this. It's for the kids.

David Clowney is ninth all-time at Virginia Tech in receiving yards and averaged 14.7 yards per catch in his career. He led the Hokies in receiving in 2005 and 2006 and was drafted in the fifth round of the 2007 draft by the Green Bay Packers. Clowney has also played for the New York Jets and is currently under contract with the Carolina Panthers.

2006 CHICK-FIL-A BOWL
Georgia 31, Virginia Tech 24

After jumping out to a 21–3 lead over Georgia in the first half, the Hokies imploded in the second half of a 31–24 loss in the Chick-fil-A Bowl in Atlanta's Georgia Dome on December 30, 2006.

The Hokies took a commanding lead with three touchdowns in the second quarter. Tailback Brandon Ore ran for a pair of one-yard touchdowns, and receiver Eddie Royal threw a 53-yard touchdown to tight end Sam Wheeler on a trick play.

But Virginia Tech turned the ball over on four straight possessions in the second half—three by quarterback Sean Glennon—and Georgia turned three of those miscues into 18 points. The Bulldogs cut Tech's lead to 21–6 on Brandon Coutu's 52-yard field goal early in the third quarter. Bulldogs coach Mark Richt then gambled with an onside kick, and his team recovered. Georgia quarterback Matthew Stafford threw a six-yard touchdown to Martez Milner to make the score 21–13.

Glennon was intercepted on Virginia Tech's ensuing possession, and then Georgia's Kregg Lumpkin scored on a three-yard run. Stafford threw a pass to Milner for a two-point conversion to tie the score at 21–21 with 12:39 left. Glennon fumbled on the next possession, setting up Coutu's 28-yard field goal to give the Bull-dogs a 24–21 lead. Then Glennon's interception set up another Georgia touchdown, making it 31–21.

"When you turn the ball over, you're going to lose against a good football team, and Georgia is a good football team," Beamer said. "They played better than we did in the second half, and we helped them. Tonight, we lost because we turned the ball over."

Virginia Tech's senior class finished with a four-year record of 39–13, narrowly missing a chance to become only the second class in school history to win 40 games.

Hokies in Their Own Words

SEAN GLENNON

QUARTERBACK, 2004–2008

Coming out of high school in northern Virginia, I wanted to go to college relatively close to home. Now, when I say relatively close, I wasn't really looking to leave the ACC region.

I narrowed it down to about four or five ACC schools, and I don't know exactly what it was about Tech. Just the coaches, the players, the atmosphere at Tech—without being able to completely describe it, I just felt more at home there and more at ease at Virginia Tech than I did anywhere else.

To be honest with you, the only things that were holding me back from Tech were, one, the offense wasn't tailor-made for a drop-back quarterback, and two, they weren't in the ACC. They were in the Big East.

Then, I woke up one morning in July [2003], and suddenly Tech was going to the ACC. That kind of shot Tech to the top of the list because one of my two concerns was erased. Now, my only concern was the offense, and I'd been talking with Kevin Rogers, who was the quarterbacks coach. He said, "You know, Sean, the ACC move could work out not just because you want to play in the ACC, but it's more of a passing conference than the Big East was. We're going to have to adapt a little bit. You can be the beginning of that."

He said we were getting some great receivers in, and we did. I also had an inkling Eddie [Royal, who played with Glennon at Westfield High in Chantilly, Virginia] was going to come with me. So those factors pushed me over the edge.

To this day, I am so thankful for the time I was able to spend with Coach Rogers at Tech. I'm not going to lie. I hated Coach Rogers in the beginning. He freaking rode me into the ground. It was to the point I would come off the practice field, and Cory Holt, who was in my class and whom I became very close with over our careers, would be there. I'd tell him, "Man, I just can't do this anymore. Coach doesn't let me breathe. Every mistake I make, he's screaming."

As much as I hated the instruction at first, Coach Rogers actually sat me down at the end of that first year and told me he was nervous. You know, Marcus [Vick] was suspended. Bryan [Randall] was the kind of quarterback who took a lot of hits and, at any moment, could get injured because he was always running and didn't throw the ball away much.

[Rogers] said he was just doing everything in his power to get me ready in case I had to go in. I love the guy to death off the field. I learned more in a month with him than I did in my whole high school career. He was a huge reason I came to Virginia Tech.

After I played a little bit in my freshman season, I did ask to be redshirted in my second year. I said, "It's not that I don't want to

Sean Glennon (7) looks to pass under pressure from Georgia defensive back
Quentin Moses (94) during the 2006 Chick-fil-A Bowl. *Photo courtesy of AP Images*

do what's best for the team or anything, but I think what's best for me is to sit out. Yeah, it's fun going in for the fourth quarter when we're up 40 points, I don't want to sit here and say I don't want to play. It's just not worth me losing another year of eligibility doing mop-up work."

Marcus was back and was a junior. I knew he had two years of eligibility left, and I didn't want to have only one year of eligibility left by the time Marcus left. Of course, it turned out Marcus made an early exit, so I had the opportunity to play the next season instead of having to wait two years.

When I played in '06, more than half of my interceptions came in two games, and the Thursday night game against Boston College [a 22–3 Tech loss] and the Chick-fil-A Bowl [a 31–24 Tech loss] are really the only two games I wish had never happened. I know people look at it as I played on a roller coaster that season, but I threw five or six interceptions in just those two games.

The rest of the season I actually played pretty well for the most part, I thought. There were games that were definitely better than others, but those two games I mentioned are the only ones where I thought, *Wow, I really hurt our team today.*

We lost to Georgia Tech that season, but it was the first game where I went in to it feeling like not all of my teammates were in my corner. I know I wasn't the mold of Virginia Tech quarterback that had come before me in recent years. I know there were some guys in the locker room who were in other quarterbacks' corners because Virginia Tech was known for having mobile guys at quarterback and things like that.

So after that game was the first time a few guys you might not expect came up to me—and I'd gotten beat up in that game; just took a beating and kept getting back up—to say, "Hey, we really respect you. We're behind you."

I really didn't care about what the fans thought about me when it came to criticism, but it always helped to have the locker room behind me. I'm not sure why none of that translated the game after the Georgia Tech loss into the Boston College game, but it did give me confidence moving forward.

After the disaster in the Chick-fil-A Bowl, I was getting a lot of heat from the media and stuff like that. I just really dedicated myself to getting better and getting stronger in the off-season. It wound up being the best off-season of my career.

I knew coming into my junior year Tyrod [Taylor] was a big recruit, and eventually, there was going to be some controversy at our position. Honestly, I did not anticipate it in the first year at all, let alone the second game [at Louisiana State].

I guess the thing that upset me the most about that situation, and I loved all the coaches at Tech and all my teammates and I appreciate all they'd done for me, but I thought the LSU game was handled poorly. We could've had Peyton Manning at quarterback that day. It just wasn't in the cards for us. We couldn't stop them.

When [quarterbacks] Coach [Mike] O'Cain came to me the week after the game and told me, "We're putting Tyrod in," I was like, "What?" I didn't even know that was an option. Now I realized I had to have a really good season because I knew the next season Tyrod was going to be nipping at my heels, but I didn't believe he was going to really play that first year up until that moment.

I actually went on and had a really good season. I was so low after watching Tyrod play for the next three games, but then I got back in against Duke after he got hurt, and I think every pass I threw in that game was perfect. From that point on, I just decided I was going to have fun. For the next six- or seven-game stretch, I played the best football I'd ever played in my life. At one point,

I think I had the longest streak in the nation without throwing an interception.

It dawned on me after the season that with Tyrod getting a whole year under his belt, and once he actually understands this offense, the whole off-season was going to be filled with controversy. I know fans tried to make it out as me versus Tyrod and there was a real schism on campus dividing us, but the truth is, Tyrod and I never said one bad thing about each other, we never shot a dirty look at each other.

He's never verbalized it to me, but I know he felt uncomfortable by it all. It wasn't his fault. He was kind of thrust into it, and to be honest, I don't know if he even wanted it. Athletically, he was ready from the time he was 10 years old, but he didn't know half our offense as a freshman. I was never bitter toward Tyrod, and he never once acted arrogant or rubbed my nose in it. We actually maintained a decent relationship. We weren't best friends, but we talked a lot. We helped each other. It was a working business relationship.

I actually sat down with the coaches after the Orange Bowl and said, "Look, just be honest with me. I'm not going to get mad or anything, but just tell me if the writing is on the wall and Tyrod is going to take over this team next year, because it's really important for me to continue my football career. If this is where my stock is going to be at its highest for the next level, then I'm going to go take my chances [in the NFL]."

I put in my papers with the NFL draft advisory board and was projected to be a sixth-round pick. So there was a good chance I could maybe get drafted late. The coaches said, "No, we have every intention of playing both of you like we have been." So I stayed there, but in the back of my mind I was nervous that things weren't going to go my way. It ended up that my instincts proved to be correct the next year.

After the ECU game at the start of my senior year, when we lost, I went home and was talking to my now ex-girlfriend and told her, "I know it's going to happen again." I just knew it. Sure enough, I came in on Monday and Coach O'Cain told me to stay after our meeting. That's when he told me they were going with Tyrod. I still got to get in and play in a few games and rotated in and out with Tyrod like I did the year before.

I remember the Maryland game especially because it was my last Thursday night game in Blacksburg. I don't care what any-body says—Thursday night in Blacksburg is awesome. I really have to take my hat off to the fans because they make Thursday night games really special. There's nothing like coming out of that tunnel for a Thursday night game. We won that game, and it was big, and I played well, so I felt good about that one.

For a while, I was kind of a pissed-off, bitter guy about things, but the brain has a funny way of working. Now, I can't even remember some of the games I didn't play in. It's almost like it didn't happen.

You know, I probably had a lot of the really tough moments where some people might have broken, but 80 percent of my career at Tech was awesome. I made a lot of friends. I had a lot of fun. I got to play on a team that was on national TV every week and played in big bowl games. I was a big part of that for a few years. Those are things I'll never forget.

Sean Glennon was the 2007 ACC championship game MVP and ended that season with a 12–3 record, with 12 touchdowns and five interceptions. In his Hokies career, he threw for 4,867 yards and 28 touchdowns. In 2008 he won the Paul Torgersen Award. He signed with the Minnesota Vikings as an undrafted free agent in 2009, but was released when quarterback Brett Favre was signed to the team.

2008 Orange Bowl
Kansas 24, Virginia Tech 21

After winning the ACC championship for a second time, Virginia Tech ran into a Cinderella team in the Orange Bowl in Miami on January 3, 2008.

Kansas, which was playing in a BCS bowl game for the first time in school history, intercepted three Virginia Tech passes and used its stifling defense to defeat the Hokies 24–21 at Sun Life Stadium. It was Virginia Tech's fourth consecutive defeat in a BCS bowl game.

"It's disappointing, that's for sure," Beamer said. "It's a game we had control of, and if we play normal Virginia Tech football, we're going to win."

The Hokies did not play like themselves, however, with their three turnovers leading to 17 points for the Jayhawks. Kansas cornerback Aquib Talib returned an interception 60 yards for the game's first score. Kansas took a 17–0 lead in the game's first 23 minutes, thanks in most part to Virginia Tech's miscues. In addition to the turnovers, the Hokies dropped a touchdown and missed a field goal.

After the Hokies cut Kansas' lead to 17–7 on Branden Ore's one-yard touchdown run late in the first half, "Beamer Ball" put them back into the game in the second half. Justin Harper scored on an 84-yard punt return after taking a lateral on a reverse from Eddie Royal, making the score 17–14 with 11:35 to go in the third quarter.

But the Jayhawks went back ahead by a 24–14 score on quarterback Todd Reesing's two-yard scoring run with 10:57 to play. Virginia Tech did not quit, however, and quarterback Sean Glennon fired a 20-yard touchdown to Harper to make it 24–21 with three minutes to go. The Jayhawks recovered the ensuing onside kick, ending the Hokies' comeback hopes.

"Give Kansas credit," Beamer said. "They made the plays, and we did not make enough. Usually when you turn the ball over three times against a good team, you are going to have a hard time winning."

2009 ORANGE BOWL
Virginia Tech 20, Cincinnati 7

After defeating Boston College in the ACC championship game for the second season in a row, Virginia Tech found itself in all-too-familiar territory on New Year's Day 2009. The Hokies were back in the Orange Bowl, playing another upstart opponent at Sun Life Stadium.

This time, however, Virginia Tech didn't hand Cinderella a glass slipper.

With tailback Darren Evans running for 153 yards and one touchdown, and Virginia Tech's stingy defense intercepting four passes, the Hokies routed Big East champion Cincinnati 20–7 to become the first ACC team to win a BCS bowl game since 1999.

"All year, all year, all year we've been the underdogs," Virginia Tech cornerback Victor "Macho" Harris said. "We had to scratch and claw our way to a victory. It says a lot about the character on our team."

The game started poorly for Virginia Tech again, just like against Kansas in the Orange Bowl the previous season. Cincinnati

Tyrod Taylor (5) runs past Cincinnati's Brandon Underwood (8) for a touchdown during the 2009 Orange Bowl. *Photo courtesy of AP Images*

took the opening kickoff and drove the length of the field before Tony Pike threw a 15-yard touchdown to Marshawn Gilyard for a 7–0 lead with 13:08 to play in the first quarter.

But Virginia Tech's defense stiffened, and quarterback Tyrod Taylor got its offense going in the second quarter. Taylor scrambled

17 yards for a touchdown to tie the score at 7–7 with 13 minutes to go in the first half. Dustin Keys added a 43-yard field goal to make the score 10–7 on the final play of the half. Keys kicked a 35-yard field goal to give the Hokies a 13–7 lead with 8:32 left in the third quarter.

Virginia Tech's defense helped put the Bearcats away from there. Cincinnati was backed up deep in its own territory, and Pike rolled to his right and tried to throw back to his left. But Tech defensive end Orion Martin never bought Pike's fake and made a diving interception at the Bearcats' 10-yard line. Evans scored on a six-yard touchdown run to make the score 20–7 with 11:29 to play.

On Cincinnati's next drive, it faced fourth-and-goal from Virginia Tech's 1-yard line. Pike tried to run for the end zone, but he was stuffed by Barquell Rivers with 7:25 to play. Pike's fourth interception of the game came five minutes later, ending Cincinnati's chances of coming back.

"We don't always play well, but we always play hard," Beamer said. "That's what we did tonight."

The Hokies ended their four-game losing streak in BCS bowl games and ended the ACC's 0-for-8 drought in BCS play.

Hokies in Their Own Words

Tyrod Taylor

Quarterback, 2007–2010

I don't think I ever told anybody before, other than Coach Beamer, my mom, and my dad , but I actually gave Coach Beamer a verbal commitment way before I told everybody else. I knew for a long time I was going to Virginia Tech.

I remember coming to watch [Michael] Vick play [in 2000] against Virginia, and [Lane Stadium] seemed a lot smaller then. I remember he got hurt, but he came back and [Tech] ended up beating them. It was just a great feeling in that stadium. I told myself right then I'd love to play in that stadium.

I guess the best way to describe how Tech made me feel on my early recruiting visits was that it was like a family. I went to other schools, but nobody had the family atmosphere and showed me that they cared more than Tech.

That was important to me. Also, I felt like I had the best opportunity to play at Tech. It worked out for me.

Every time I came up for a visit to Blacksburg, they'd put me with a player whom I knew or played against in high school. Nobody else could do that for me. There was so much connection with my area—the 757 area [code]—I guess it was impossible for it not to feel like a family.

When I got to Tech, playing in my freshman year on the road against LSU in my first game [a 48–7 Tech loss] actually helped me. I'll never turn down playing experience over just learning from the chalkboard because I feel like the best way to experience it and learn from something is actually being out there. It's one thing to be watching it and learning from film, and another thing to be out there in the fire. That helped me more than anything else in my career— getting to play early and learning from my mistakes after that.

Sean [Glennon] and I started rotating a lot [at quarterback], so we tried to make each other better throughout the whole process. I learned from him and he learned from me.

It was a tough situation to be in, being in a two-quarterback system and not even knowing when you're going to get your next play. It was kind of a situation where we would stand beside the coach and wait for when he felt like putting us in. That's how it was. We made the best out of it and just tried to go out there and make every play work.

While it was tough, I knew how it was going to be when I came to Tech. Sean only had a couple more years when I got there, so I knew it was only going to be a matter of time before I had the chance to go out there and have the team to myself.

Even though I didn't know if I was going to play or redshirt when I first got to Tech, I wanted to prepare myself like I was going to be the starter from day one. I think that helped me in my preparation, so when it was time for me to take over, I went in there and did it.

I think during my sophomore year things started slowing down for me. During my freshman year, I was just out there playing off talent. I knew all the things they asked me to know, but when it was time for me to actually play, it was just me going out there and making a play just like it was in high school.

Even though it started slowing down for me in my sophomore year, it slowed down even more in my junior year because it was finally my team. I was starting my third year in the offense and my third year with the guys around me. You could tell the difference.

One of the biggest changes for me was going from my freshman to my sophomore year and going from an experienced group of receivers to an all new group of receivers. After my sophomore and junior years, I spent a lot of time with those guys trying to get better. You could see the confidence I had in those guys and the confidence they had in me during my junior and senior years.

All of them grew with me. Danny [Coale] came in to Tech with me and is one of the guys who could've played as a true freshman, but there were so many guys that were experienced at receiver when I was a freshman that there was no need for him to play. He really made great strides, and so did Jarrett [Boykin] and Dyrell [Roberts], especially Jarrett because Dyrell got hurt [in 2010].

Jarrett played the X receiver in our offense, and because of that, I'd say he had to grow a little quicker than all the other guys. The X receiver in our offense gets the ball a lot.

I know there were people criticizing the way I played sometimes, but I just avoided it. If anything, I used it as motivation. That's what I did throughout my career. Even when it came down to winning ACC Player of the Year [as a senior], well, I felt I was the best player in the ACC every time I stepped on the field. That's just me, but everybody isn't going to feel that way. I used that as motivation to go out and prove to the people who didn't think I was the best wrong.

As far as anything that happened in terms of criticism while I was at Tech, I wasn't frustrated by any of it. With my throwing motion, when the stats aren't as good as they should've been at times, people find things to be negative about. That's just the nature of the game, especially for a quarterback.

The quarterback is looked on and scrutinized more than any other position. I knew that when I played quarterback as a five-year-old. The quarterback is going to be the player that everybody depends on, but at the same time, he's going to be the one who gets the most negative things said about him, too.

My career at Tech was just a process of developing over the years. I showed some things my first two years, but my junior year was really my coming-out party.

I would say the Nebraska game in my junior year [Tech's 16–15 victory featuring an 88-yard touchdown drive in final 1:23] is my favorite memory of a game. It just showed I had the poise to make the big play when I needed to. I think that lit our fire as an offense and we continued on for the rest of the season.

It's a great feeling to have a moment like that Nebraska game in my personal book of my career. That's one video I never get tired of watching. You might see some things you get tired of seeing sometimes, but the Nebraska game is something I never get tired of watching. It was a great feeling for me and for the team.

There were a lot of guys who were a part of that moment— Danny making the great catch, Dyrell making the great catch, the line holding up for 11 seconds [on the touchdown pass]—there were a lot of things that contributed to that drive. It was great to be a part of it.

Going into my senior year, people were talking about us as national championship contenders. I don't think we bought in to it all that much, but I also think we deserved to be mentioned as contenders. I think we had the team and the confidence for it. We just didn't go out there and finish the first two games against Boise State and JMU.

If we had gone out there and just lost by 20 in both of those games, then I would've said, *Yeah, the guys weren't ready.* I just think it was a lack of focus and maybe the short turnaround kind of hurt us on the JMU game. I'll never blame it on that, because we knew the setup going into the season. We just had to deal with it.

I remember talking to John Graves right after the JMU game about what we needed to do. We came together and had a team meeting. I think it was more just about everybody being on the same page. I think at some points during those first two games it was like the Tech offense against the Tech defense and we were competing against each other. It shouldn't be like that. We should feed off each other's energy and play off each other.

To run off an 11-game winning streak after that, I mean, it's hard to win 11 straight in any sport. That just shows the talent we had on our team. Losing those first two games was a big learning experience for the guys on our team, especially for the guys who are going to play in years to come.

You never want to finish the season the way we did [with a 40–12 loss to Stanford in the Orange Bowl]. We had a great undefeated run in the ACC, but we didn't finish the bowl game. That's always going to be in the back of my head because I was a senior and it was my last game at Virginia Tech. At the same time, that 11-game run was one of the greatest runs in Virginia Tech history. Still, being a competitor, I'm always going to hate losing—especially the way we lost that Orange Bowl.

Looking back at it, any college football player should be better than he was the year before, especially if he's playing a lot. That was my goal—just keep getting better every year. I didn't take any steps back during my career. I'm proud I was able to leave my mark at Tech in that way.

Tyrod Taylor shared quarterback duties with Sean Glennon as a freshman and took over the job for the following three years. His sophomore year, he was named ACC Championship Game MVP in a decisive 30–12 victory over the Boston College Eagles. He then led the team to a 20–7 win over the Cincinnati Bearcats in the Orange Bowl. His senior year, 2010, the Hokies started 0–2 but then were led by Taylor on an 11-game winning streak, finishing the season with an undefeated ACC record. For his efforts, Taylor was awarded ACC Player of the Year and ACC Championship Game MVP in a 44–33 win over Florida State.

2009 CHICK-FIL-A BOWL
Virginia Tech 37, Tennessee 14

Virginia Tech has produced plenty of great running backs through-out its history, but few of them accomplished what Ryan Williams did during his freshman season in 2009.

Williams capped his brilliant rookie season by running for 117 yards and two touchdowns, leading the Hokies to a 37–14 rout of Tennessee in the Chick-fil-A Bowl in the Georgia Dome on New Year's Eve 2009. Virginia Tech won back-to-back bowl games for the first time in school history.

After Tennessee tied the score at 14–14 late in the second quar-ter, the Hokies scored the game's next 23 points to produce a rout. Williams, who became Virginia Tech's single season rushing leader with 1,655 yards, scored the game's first two touchdowns. He set an ACC record with 21 rushing touchdowns and 22 total touchdowns.

"Ryan was something tonight, particularly at the start of the second half," Beamer said. "We got after them good."

Virginia Tech's offense scored on four of its first five second-half possessions, with quarterback Tyrod Taylor scoring on a one-yard run, Matt Waldron kicking two field goals, and David Wilson adding a late touchdown.

Virginia Tech's defense intercepted a pass by Tennessee's Jona-than Crompton early in the first quarter to set up Williams' first touchdown. Crompton later fumbled when he was sacked by Tech's Nekos Brown, and John Graves recovered at the Volun-teers' 13-yard line. Graves' fumble recovery set up Matt Waldron's 22-yard field goal.

Virginia Tech's defense didn't allow any second-half points, the fifth game in a row the Hokies shut out an opponent after halftime.

2011 ORANGE BOWL
Stanford 40, Virginia Tech 12

A Virginia Tech team that won 11 games in a row after losing its first two of the 2010 season was simply no match for No. 4 Stanford in its finale.

Stanford quarterback Andrew Luck threw four touchdown passes, including three to unheralded tight end Coby Fleener, and the Cardinal routed Virginia Tech 40–12 at Sun Life Stadium in Miami on January 3, 2011.

It was Virginia Tech's most humbling bowl loss under coach Frank Beamer. Stanford finished in the top five of the final rankings for the first time since its 1940 team finished undefeated and ranked No. 2 in the country.

"They're really good, and we helped them be good," Beamer said. "There were a couple of long plays against our defense, and then the game got away from us. The thing kind of snowballed."

Stanford's offense had a lot to do with it. The Cardinal produced six plays of 30 yards or longer, including Luck's touchdown throws of 41, 58, and 38 yards to Fleener.

Virginia Tech quarterback Tyrod Taylor ran for 22 yards and passed for 222 yards with one touchdown and one interception in his last college game.

The Hokies' finale was as disappointing as their first two games of the 2010 season. After losing to Boise State 33–30 on a last-second touchdown pass in the Labor Day opener, Virginia Tech lost to FCS foe James Madison 21–16 at home five days later. But after starting 0–2, Virginia Tech won its next 11 games, including

Running back Ryan Williams leaps over a pile of Tennessee players during the 2009 Chick-fil-A Bowl. Virginia Tech won 37–14. *Photo courtesy of AP Images*

a 44–33 victory over Florida State in the ACC championship game in Charlotte, North Carolina.

"I am still proud of my boys for the whole season," Taylor said. "We had a heck of a season, and it's nothing to hold your head down about right now."

chapter 5

VIRGINIA TECH'S ALL-AMERICANS

XAVIER ADIBI
Linebacker, 2007

Along with Vince Hall, Adibi formed perhaps Virginia Tech's best linebacker tandem during their three seasons together. Though he enjoyed a breakout performance as a junior, Adibi exploded as a senior in 2007, earning first team All-America honors from the American Football Coaches Association. In 2007 Adibi led the Hokies with 115 tackles, including 12 tackles for loss, along with three sacks and two interceptions. He was named All-ACC and was a third-team All-America selection by the Associated Press. Adibi was drafted in the fourth round of the 2008 NFL Draft by the Houston Texans. Adibi's older brother, Nathaniel, was a standout defensive end at Virginia Tech.

Hokies in Their Own Words

XAVIER ADIBI

LINEBACKER, 2004–2007

I never really was a big Virginia Tech fan growing up. I didn't know a lot about the school or the program until my brother went there. I knew nothing about them. I wasn't thinking about going to school there.

I was a big-time Miami fan growing up. I almost went there. When I first started getting recruited, Miami was my favorite, but then I almost went to Tennessee. I took my visit there and would have signed with Tennessee on the spot. But the thing they did wrong was they didn't ask me if I wanted to commit.

Randy Shannon was coaching the defense for Miami. He was a good recruiter for them and he could talk to the kids coming through them. So, those were my best two options at first: Tennessee and Miami.

When I took my visit to Virginia Tech, Marcus Vick was my host, and I played against him in high school. We would talk on the field after games in high school, so I knew him. I was hanging around him on my visit to Tech and was around Aaron Rouse and Jimmy Williams, and it felt like I was home again.

There were a lot of 757 (area code) guys. I decided that I didn't want to play too far from home. It felt right. It was very hard not to go to Miami, but I never regretted not going there.

It was too bad about Marcus. He helped get me to Tech, and I wish things would have worked out for him. The off-the-field troubles got in his way.

He could have been one of the best quarterbacks, if not the best, to go through Virginia Tech. He wasn't as fast as his brother, but he was so much better as a passer. He could just put a touch on the ball and he had a lot more poise in the pocket. He could stay in the pocket and take the hits and deliver a good throw.

My sophomore year was the most talented team I played on. We had him and four wide receivers on that team who are in the NFL playing now. Eddie Royal, Justin Harper, David Clowney, and Josh Morgan. We were stacked with Marcus throwing to them.

Frank Beamer had to do what he had to do with Marcus. Beamer is a very loyal person who cares a lot about his players. He will do anything for his players, and I was blessed to play for him. It was pretty hard for him to do what he had to do with Marcus.

My brother went there right after the Michael Vick era, and everybody was sky high.

The coaches were amped up about everything and they live and breathe football. The program was really moving forward.

I played linebacker at Virginia Tech, but I didn't play linebacker until the last five games of my senior year in high school. I played defensive end and running back at Phoebus.

When you think Virginia Tech, you think defense. Coach Bud Foster loves to get those athletes, so I moved over to defense. They love to get those tall, rangy athletes who can run. If you can run and are athletic enough, you can play for Coach Foster because he will find a scheme for you.

They did an excellent job of recruiting 757 and getting these Tidewater players in there.

Bud Foster loves speed, but you have to be able to hit people, too. He wants you to hit, so after we did all our stretching, then came the pursuit drills. You have to run through the line. They act like they pitch the ball to the running back and then you have to haul ass to the cone at the other side of the field.

The coach has to give a thumbs up for you to pass the drill. The first defense does it, the second defense does it, the third defense does it. If you don't get the thumbs up, you do it again. After the first week and a half you realize the coach is not backing up from this, this is something we better do or we will run all day.

It worked for us because you saw 11 guys getting on the ball. You could see it on the film.

We did not have a strong, run-up-the-score type offense around the time I was there. We had the receivers, but we wanted to run the ball and be physical. Virginia Tech could score when Mike Vick was there, but we got a reputation for stopping people with defense after that. He is so talented, he made the offense look very dynamic. He took the offense to another level, either out-running people or throwing the ball deep to André Davis.

They were stacked on defense, but it looked like a lot of offense with Vick around. It wasn't a complex offense, but he made it look very complex and that's why Tech's defense was overlooked. It was better than people thought.

My most memorable game was probably against Boston College and Matt Ryan in the ACC championship game my senior year. It was the second time we played them that season. He picked us apart the first game [a 14–10 BC win] and it looked like he was going to do it again in the championship game in '07.

They were driving on us and needed to score. Ryan went back to pass, and the ball was tipped, and I grabbed it and ran it in for a touchdown with 11 seconds to play. That was my football [jersey] number, 11, so I thought that was pretty neat. Barry Booker, our defensive tackle, tipped it.

We were playing cover 9, a quarter-half defense. I was responsible for any back leaking out of the backfield coming to the boundary side. If a back leaked out or a receiver from the opposite side came across on a drag, I had him. I kept looking around to see if anyone was going to show in my area.

I saw Matt Ryan starting to throw, the ball was tipped, I grabbed it and took off. That sealed the game for us [30–16].

Linebacker Xavier Adibi returns an interception against North Carolina during a game at Lane Stadium, September 29, 2007. *Photo courtesy of AP Images*

Bud Foster was very aggressive on defense, but I didn't blitz a lot. He liked keeping me in coverage, and I had eight interceptions in my college career. He would bring a lot of blitzes from the strong side, a lot of those usual NCAA blitzes coming off the strong side with the Mike and Sam and had the boundary end backing off.

He liked the boundary corner blitz with Brandon Flowers and this other blitz he had called Rake. The Mike and Will crossed with the strong safety coming right down the middle. The linebackers would cross into the A gap, which would open everything up for the strong safety coming right down the middle.

The Boston College game was big for me and all the UVA games were big for me because of Al Groh, their coach. I refused to lose to UVA. I didn't like them at all.

I can remember Al Groh coming to my high school. I was ranked No. 1 in the state and my teammate Phillip Brown was No. 2. He called Phillip in the room first, and his meeting was real quick. He offered him a scholarship right on the spot.

When I went in there and sat down, he started talking about how UVA had recruited a bunch of older brothers of younger guys who ended up going to Virginia Tech. He talked about the Lewis brothers and Vick brothers. His take on it was because he lost all those brothers to Virginia Tech that, if I wanted to go to UVA, I had to recruit them.

He said I had to come to them, like they were USC or something. I was mad, but I didn't say anything. My dad was pissed and was upset about it. I refused to lose to them.

The best fight they put up against us was my first season at Tech. They were stacked with players. They put up a fight, but we still won.

Of course, before you get on the field for anything on defense they give you a look on special teams. I was the punt protector for the Pride team, the punt team. Beamer was a genius with those special teams. The first thing the Houston Texans coach said to me when I got to the NFL was, "I don't have to worry about you playing special teams, you already know what's going on, you played at Virginia Tech."

It meant the world to me to go to Virginia Tech. There were a lot of guys who paved the way for me. The Bruce Smiths, the Corey Moores, and Michael Vick. I wanted to pave the way for the guys after me, especially linebackers. I think I am one of the only linebackers to be mentioned as All-America, but I want some others to go there and have the benefit of playing in that system and going to school there. Vince Hall was a great there, too, an All-America talent at linebacker.

The Boston College game and the UVA games were the highlights, but the lowlight was the massacre. I was living off campus and I was just waking up that morning. The first call was from my brother, and he asked, "Are you all right?" I said, "Yeah, what are you talking about?"

He told me don't go to class, turn on the news. My phone started to ring off the hook. My parents called three or four times. The death count kept going up, and I couldn't believe something that tragic was happening.

I went to the store the next day, and it was like summer school. There were not a lot of people around. It was a ghost town. Some teammates and I went to a candlelight service, and it was tough to be there. It was bad. I have lost people to tragic accidents before; that hit home.

I didn't want to cancel spring ball because I didn't want that guy to cause any more issues on our campus. He was affecting us all again.

When we got on the field for that first game against East Carolina, it was very emotional. We ran out of the tunnel for that game and there was all kinds of emotion in the stands. There was no way in hell we were going to lose that game.

CORNELL BROWN
Defensive End, 1995

Brown became the first Virginia Tech player to earn consensus All-America honors when he was named to five All-America teams as a junior in 1995. Brown was named first-team All-America by the

Associated Press, United Press International, the Football Writers Association, *Sporting News*, and *Football News*. Of course, Virginia Tech fans knew Brown was going to be great as soon as he stepped on campus. As a true freshman in 1993, Brown started 10 games and logged more snaps than any other defensive lineman on the team. The next season, Brown led the Hokies in sacks and was fourth in tackles. Brown's best year came in 1995, when he led the Big East in sacks and tied for third nationally in sacks and tackles for loss. He helped lead Virginia Tech to a 10–2 mark in 1995, when the Hokies won a Big East title and the Sugar Bowl. For his work, Brown was named National Defensive Player of the Year by *Football News* and Big East Defensive Player of the Year. Brown missed three games because of a knee injury as a senior in 1996, but was still named All-America by the Walter Camp Foundation and was one of four finalists for the Lombardi Award. He posted eight sacks, five other tackles behind the line, 19 quarterback hurries and 58 total tackles during the '96 season. Brown received his degree in consumer studies and a master's in education. His No. 58 jersey was retired in 2002, and he was inducted into the Virginia Tech Sports Hall of Fame in 2007. Today he is the outside linebackers coach at Tech.

Hokies in Their Own Words

CORNELL BROWN

DEFENSIVE END, 1993–1996

When I arrived at Virginia Tech, the culture with the fans was not exciting, not at all. That was the feel I got from them. They knew

Coach Beamer's team would play hard and to the end, but they would say things like, "We knew you were going to lose."

We couldn't find a way to pull games out the year before I got there. I remember going out one time after we started the season 2–0 my freshmen year and hearing the students say, "Don't worry, they'll find a way to make this a bad season."

I was thinking, *How can they be like that?*

In hindsight, you see how we had not won consistently for so long and people were conditioned to believe the Hokies were not going to get it right. People fell in that mode that our team was not going to win.

But we turned a corner in 1993. That was the first fall I was on campus. We were 2–0, lost to Miami, but then finished 9–3. We went to our first bowl game, which was the Poulan Weedeater Bowl in Louisiana. We beat Indiana in that bowl game, and off we went.

That 1993 team was basically the same team that lost seven or eight games the year before in the fourth quarter. They had talent, but just didn't finish. They had the experience when they came back in '93 and finished games and pulled them out.

That was a major turning point for the program, and people got behind the program again. It is strange what winning can do for anybody in any city, at any school. Winning brings happiness and becomes infectious. Everybody started to put in the work.

There were some people who wanted Coach Beamer fired, but they would have had to pay some money to him to make a change. They didn't buy out contracts back then, and that turned out to be a good thing for Virginia Tech. He got some time.

Guys came in and played for themselves, but Coach Beamer also created a family atmosphere where we understood we were in this together. He was not looking for accolades, he just wanted to mold people into solid young men.

He is about being respectful of other players and other teams. That's what he portrayed, and it has showed up in his program year after year. He was the same guy in a winning situation and losing situation. Now, it's 18 years later, and he has Tech as a top 10 program.

When I came to Virginia Tech, there were hedges in the south end zone with 5,000 seats. There were bleachers. Now it is all enclosed. People can't imagine that stadium before the winning started.

Now it is Hokie Nation. Now it's big. They don't say, "You'll find a way to lose." Now, it's Virginia Tech will win.

So here's what happened. You take Tidewater, for instance. There were a lot of players in there, and other schools were coming in there, northern schools, and around the South, and they were grabbing Tidewater guys.

Now, those guys were coming here. There was a lot of talent in there, and, finally, by winning, Tech went in there and sold the same thing Penn State was selling when they were going in there: winning.

My most memorable game was my first game playing in Lane Stadium against Bowling Green. I caused a fumble on the first drive, and we ended up scoring. Another drive, the quarterback had to throw the ball away because I was coming after him.

I was coming off the field, and a buddy of mine, Bruce Garnes, was jumping up and down and saying, "You can play, you might be well worth having around here."

Lester Karlin, the equipment man, came up to me and said, "Man, you're worth all the recruiting we did for you. You need anything, you let me know."

I said to him, "Well, if you mean that, I need you to cut this jersey down because it's too big for me." I wore No. 58.

I played as a true freshman. I was 6'1½"and 215 pounds, which was extremely light for a defensive end. I always played to the open field, what they called the Stud End, which made us feel good back then when they said because they thought you were something special. They put the athletic guy to the field, plus I was a smaller guy, and most teams want to run it into the boundary. We put our bigger guys to boundary side for the pounding.

Playing well in the Bowling Green game gave me some more confidence to play on that level. I took off from there and started a lot of games.

The next game after that we beat Pittsburgh [63–21], and we beat them bad. What was funny was my brother, Reuben, was at Pittsburgh. He was an offensive tackle. We had to go nose-to-nose a few times.

We were talking trash, and I could hear him go back to the huddle, yelling at the other offensive linemen not to let me intimidate them. He kept saying, "Are you kidding me? You letting that kid intimidate you?" That was pretty funny. He kept saying, "He ain't that good."

Athletically, they were talented because they had a lot of guys who went to the pros. The next year we pounded them, too. They came to Blacksburg, and we had to call the dogs off [45–7]. We talked after the game; I gave him a hug. I couldn't rub it in.

The third season I was there, 1995, we played the Sugar Bowl against Texas. That got Tech into the national spotlight and set things up for that Michael Vick team that played for the national championship.

We went down there to the Sugar Bowl, and nobody thought we should be there. We started the season 0–2 and beat Miami and didn't lose another game. We won nine straight and got into the Sugar Bowl.

At the beginning of the week, getting ready for that game with Texas, the media kept asking us questions about being in the big game and how we were going to react being on that big stage with somebody like Texas. They asked if we were just happy to be there. I was upset we were getting treated like that. Texas was never questioned like that. Truthfully, we were there to win the game. We didn't care anything about being around New Orleans and all the hype.

I was talking to Bruce a few days before the game and said, "If they don't score on the first drive, they won't win the game."

They punted on the first drive, but they scored on the next two drives and led 10–0. He looked at me said, "It don't look too good."

The sideline never got down. There might have been a little question in some guys' minds that maybe this was not our time, but we snapped to it and said we're going to pull it out. We did win it. We rolled over them the second half.

I know Texas took us lightly. That was Ricky Williams' freshman year. He had 1,000 yards rushing, and they had a quarterback, James Brown, who was a great runner. They had names all over the place, top draft guys. They had All-Americans.

We played against them the way we always play. We play aggressive and we are going to attack. That's what we do now. We are going to force you to change what you do to play us.

That junior season when we started 0–2, Bruce Smith came and talked to us before that third game of the season against Miami. He was an NFL star, and we listened how he told us to go out there and have fun. He was very encouraging and told us it was great just to have the opportunity to play ball and not to worry about being perfect.

Being a Hokie means there is a lot of pride in helping build something from basically nothing. It is a program that came from nowhere. Frank Beamer came to Virginia Tech, replacing a coach who almost got the school the death penalty from the NCAA. We hadn't won. A lot of people had lost faith, but he brought the team out of the ashes, and look at it now. That is truly a prideful thing.

EUGENE CHUNG
Offensive Tackle, 1991

Chung was the first Virginia Tech offensive lineman to earn All-America honors as a senior in 1991. He proved to be a wall while protecting the quarterback's blind side at left tackle, allowing one sack in 730 plays for the Hokies in 1991. Chung started as a freshman for the Hokies and was voted the team's best lineman in 1990. He was named the National Lineman of the Year by the Washington Gridiron Club in 1991. Chung became the first Korean-American ever taken in the first round of the NFL Draft when the New England Patriots selected him No. 13 overall in 1992. Chung played with the Patriots from 1992 to 1994 and also played with the Jacksonville Jaguars, Indianapolis Colts, Green Bay Packers, San Francisco 49ers, and Kansas City Chiefs before retiring.

BILLY CONATY
Center, 1996

Conaty inherited one of the most unenviable positions in Virginia Tech football history when he was pegged to replace unanimous All-America center Jim Pyne in 1994. By the end of his senior season in 1996, Conaty also was named an All-American by *Sport-ing News* and had become Virginia Tech's most dependable player in history. As a senior, Conaty saw action on 98 percent of Virginia Tech's offensive plays, and graded a winning percentage in 10 of 12 games. He led the Hokies with 65 knockdown blocks that year, as well. He finished his career by setting an all-time school record for starts and consecutive starts with 48. He achieved that iron-man mark despite breaking both of his ankles over the course of the 1995 and '96 seasons. Conaty broke his right ankle in the final game of the regular season as a junior in 1995, underwent sur-gery in November, and returned five weeks later to help the Hok-ies defeat Texas 28–10 in the Sugar Bowl. Conaty broke his left ankle during preseason camp before his senior season in 1996, but returned in time to start against Akron in the season opener. An undrafted rookie free agent, Conaty played seven seasons in the NFL for the Buffalo Bills, Minnesota Vikings, Dallas Cowboys, and Arizona Cardinals. Conaty attended Rutgers Law School after retiring from pro football and currently works as a sports agent.

CARROLL DALE
Wide Receiver/Defensive End, 1959

After earning second-team All-America honors as a junior in 1958, Dale became Virginia Tech's first football player to earn first-team All-America honors during his senior season in 1959. Dale, a native of Wise, Virginia, led the Hokies in receiving in each of his four seasons and finished his career with 67 receptions for 1,195 yards and 15 touchdowns. He entered Virginia Tech as an offensive end and defensive end in 1956. After seeing varsity action as a reserve in the first game of the 1956 season, Dale started the remaining 39 games of his college career. As a junior in 1958, he was named

Southern Conference Player of the Year and won the Jacobs Blocking Trophy. In 1959 he was named Virginia Tech's team captain and was named All-America by the Football Writers of America and Newspaper Enterprise Association. He was named Associated Press second-team All-America in 1958 and '59. Dale spent more than 10 years as a player in the NFL and started for three consecutive championship teams for legendary Green Bay Packers coach Vince Lombardi. Dale was inducted to the Virginia Sports Hall of Fame in 1976 and the College Football Hall of Fame in 1987. Dale's No. 84 jersey was the first to be retired by Virginia Tech.

ANDRÉ DAVIS
Wide Receiver, 2000

There have been few Virginia Tech players who were more explosive big-play weapons than Davis. An acclaimed sprinter on Virginia Tech's track team, Davis also was a three-year starter at wide receiver on the football team. Davis was even more dangerous returning punts, and earned first-team All-America honors from the American Football Coaches Association as a punt returner. During his junior season in 2000, Davis returned 18 punts for 396 yards for a school-record average of 22 yards per return. He tied another school record by returning three punts for touchdowns in a single season, including an 87-yard return against East Carolina, which was the second-longest in Tech history. A three-time Academic All–Big East selection, Davis ranks third on the school's career list with 1,986 yards receiving and 103 catches. His 18 career touchdowns are second-most by a Virginia Tech player. Davis was a second-round selection of the Cleveland Browns in the 2002 NFL Draft and played eight seasons in the NFL. He had

156 catches for 2,470 yards with 17 touchdowns, with most of his best work coming with the Houston Texans.

BRANDON FLOWERS
Cornerback, 2007

Flowers played only three seasons at Virginia Tech before leaving for the NFL, but he was named an All-American in two of them. He was named first-team All-America by the American Football Coaches Association as a junior in 2007, after earning third-team honors from the Associated Press as a sophomore in 2006. During his sophomore season, Flowers led the ACC with 18 passes broken up and tied for the team lead with 3½ sacks. During his junior season in 2007, Flowers had a career-high 86 tackles. Opponents rarely threw to Flowers' side of the field during his junior season, but he still managed to produce nine pass breakups, 14 passes defended, and a career-high five interceptions. A second-round draft choice of the Kansas City Chiefs in 2008, Flowers had nine interceptions in his first three NFL seasons.

Hokies in Their Own Words

BRANDON FLOWERS
CORNERBACK, 2004–2007

When I was trying to decide where to go to college, I had visits lined up to places like Tennessee and Oregon, as well as Virginia Tech. I took the Virginia Tech visit first and then never took the others. I knew where I wanted to go.

It felt like my high school environment. Everybody was one. It was not just about football for me there. The fans wrapped their arms around you and made you feel at home. We were with the student body. I felt that atmosphere and fell in love with it.

I went to the Miami–Virginia Tech game in 2007, and everything had me locked up for Tech, from the pregame walk and how the fans appreciated the recruits who were brought in to the game. They all knew my stats, everything. A lot of schools called and promised I would love it if I would just come visit, but I couldn't do it.

When I came to Virginia Tech as a freshman, Eric Green took me in and showed me the ropes, and I was expecting to play a lot as a freshman. He helped me get ready to play. The coverages were down on the board, and I learned them and was ready to go. I didn't feel like a freshman.

The first series I took an interception back, and this was the way it was going to be. I was going to play. Then, the next series, it all went away, just like that. I had a season-ending injury, a broken leg against Western Michigan.

I had to take a redshirt, and it was like starting all over again.

We had coaches at Atlantic High School in Delray Beach [Florida] who had experience in college football and broke down everything for me. We had very good coaches, so I had good foundation going to college.

The other thing that helped me was there were not any sophomores at Virginia Tech, or juniors, or seniors that were so worried about me taking their position that they wouldn't help me. They all helped me. They were teaching me everything I needed to know. Once everybody was on board trying to help me out, I was able to make it.

When we got into the film room with Bud Foster, you had to have your thinking cap on like it was another class. It was complicated, it was intense. You might come from two-hour lecture class into Bud's film room, and it's another academic class; Bud teaches on the fly, teaches with precision.

You can make a lot of plays in his scheme if you play it right. One of the things that helped us at Virginia Tech was you never knew what coverage we were in. We'd go into the game with one play with four coverages. Whatever formation the offense showed, we'd have a design to attack that formation and the plays they will run out of that formation.

When a team went to a certain formation, everybody knew to check into a particular defense. It was like an audible for us. Everybody has to get it; if not, there was a breakdown. We practiced it so much during the week that we had it.

Studying in the film room helped me be a good player and contribute, but it was also because of the work of Coach Torrian Gray. Lorenzo Ward was there the first year and taught me a lot of fundamentals. Then Coach Gray came in and built on that.

I have to give a lot of credit for being in the NFL to Coach Gray. He was a Florida guy like me, and we worked well together. He was the guy who took me to an All-America level my sophomore and junior years.

One thing he taught was the shuffle technique. If you are playing man off, and you run this technique, there is almost no way the receiver can beat you. He just trains your eyes to see how the receiver is trying to get up on you, make a move, and take off. He trains you how to flip your hips and run with him.

You have to take some film of him coaching just to see his different coaching techniques and how effective he is. He was always

Brandon Flowers (18) runs back a blocked extra point against Boston College in the ACC championship game, December 1, 2007. Virginia Tech won 30–16. *Photo courtesy of AP Images*

energetic with me because I was a laid-back guy off the field. If somebody is energetic around me, that's going to rile me up.

We could be on a regular Tuesday practice, and he would get me going, and then Macho Harris would get into it, and we would be going full speed, live tackling. He knows how to fire his guys up.

I was a boundary corner and played a lot of man-to-man, which means you could use other players to give the quarterback different looks. You could play games with those other players.

What you wanted to do was take away half the field, narrow the space the offense could attack. I was on the short side. That is what the boundary corner is all about. You also have to be good in run support. You can't play boundary corner at Virginia Tech if you can't tackle. A lot of times you are going to be in the box like a safety.

Virginia Tech cornerbacks know how to tackle. That's why Macho Harris was moved to [strong] safety with the Eagles. They label us Tech guys as tough corners. You have to come up and hit.

Macho and I were like brothers at Virginia Tech. We played on the field together almost my whole career. We competed, and each of us wanted to be the No. 1 corner at Virginia Tech. There was nothing negative going on trying to top each other. If he got one interception in the game, I was trying to get two.

My favorite tradition at Virginia Tech was when we were waiting to come out of the tunnel and "Enter Sandman" would come on. People were jumping up and down. Everybody was in maroon and orange. There is no better feeling.

Here's something else we liked to do. Every Tuesday we would all get together and go to Buffalo Wild Wings. They had cheap wings there. You had to do stuff on a budget. It was like 29¢ for a wing. We would get there around 8:00 or 9:00 PM. Carlton Powell could put away the most wings. When you have Carlton Powell in there, the trays of wings are going to start coming. You don't count with him and try and match up with him in eating wings.

My most memorable game was we played Florida State at home [a 40–21 Tech win]. We did not have a very good record at Florida State, but this one game we were not going to let Florida State and Bobby Bowden come on the field and beat us.

They had Preston Parker as a receiver and Drew Weatherford as the quarterback. I had been playing football against Preston

Parker since I was in the fifth grade. We went to the same high school, and people back home couldn't wait to see us play against each other.

The defense had a lot of turnovers and scored points. We took over the field. That was the game where I knocked Drew Weatherford out of the game. I wasn't trying to hurt him, like give him a serious injury, but he took off on a scramble out there, and I went after him. He lowered his head at the last moment, and we collided. He hurt his shoulder. I got up; he didn't. It's on YouTube.

The other memorable game was at Clemson my junior year. They had C.J. Spiller, Jacoby Ford, and James Davis, and everybody said their offense couldn't be stopped.

It was a nice atmosphere at Clemson, and everybody wanted to see that game. It wasn't a game. We dominated.

We were 11–3 that season, but that was disappointing. We have become a program at Virginia Tech where three losses is too many. We now expect to compete for the national championship. We expect to win every game. We felt like we had a bad season that year.

That winning is part of the tradition. Here's another tradition: DBU. We have become known for turning out NFL style defensive backs. Look at Jimmy Williams, DeAngelo Hall, and Macho Harris. You have Rashad Carmichael coming out this year [2011] and Jayron Hosley. Look at Kam Chancellor, who plays with the Seahawks. Aaron Rouse came out of Tech.

If you want to be a lockdown corner, you come to Virginia Tech. Torrian Gray made a lot happen in a short period of time. Every year somebody is coming out.

After the game all the players turn on a little music and get wound up, and all the coaches get in the middle and start doing a little dance. Coach Beamer's dance is great; we loved it. He got a little somethin'.

This was one of the best coaching staffs in college football. You hear guys complaining about this coach and that coach. We didn't hear that at Virginia Tech.

Here's what it means to be a Hokie. You are groomed for something else besides football. You are groomed to be a good person. It means everything to be a Hokie because we're not just talking about football. We're talking about life off the field.

JAKE GROVE
Center, 2003

A native of Forest, Virginia, Grove was a lightly recruited guard coming out of high school. By the end of his senior season, he became Virginia Tech's third unanimous All-American when he was named to the first team by all five recognized All-America squads: Football Writers Association of America, American Football Coaches Association, *Sporting News*, the Walter Camp Foundation, and the Associated Press. Grove moved from guard to center before his junior season in 2002 and became a natural fit. As a senior in 2003, he was named All–Big East and won the Rimington Trophy as college football's best center. In 13 regular season games in 2003, Grove graded out at 91.8-percent blocking on over 700 offensive snaps and led the team with 48 knockdown blocks. He was drafted in the second round of the 2004 NFL Draft by the Oakland Raiders and played five seasons with the Raiders, before spending the 2009 and 2010 seasons with the Miami Dolphins. Virginia Tech retired his No. 64 jersey in 2006.

VICTOR "MACHO" HARRIS
Cornerback, 2008

Known as "Macho," Harris extended an impressive line of shut-down cornerbacks at Virginia Tech, following in the footsteps of DeAngelo Hall, Jimmy Williams, and Brandon Flowers. Harris was named first-team All-America by *Sporting News* and second-team by the Associated Press after his senior season in 2008. He tied for 11th nationally, with six interceptions, two of which he returned for touchdowns. A two-time All-ACC selection, Harris had 15 career interceptions, which ranks third all-time at Virginia Tech. His four career touchdowns on interception returns are a school record. Harris was drafted in the fifth round of the 2009 NFL Draft by the Philadelphia Eagles and played part of the 2010 season with the Washington Redskins.

Hokies in Their Own Words
VICTOR "MACHO" HARRIS
CORNERBACK, 2005–2008

The fire in my house my senior year in high school was a calling for me to go to Virginia Tech. When my house caught on fire just before Frank Beamer came to see me on a recruiting visit, I knew I had to go to Tech.

I was burned in that fire; he had been burned in a fire. A lot of schools were recruiting me, but there was no other choice to be made after that happened. That was confirmation because we had been through the same thing.

It was December 15, 2004, when my house caught on fire. I suffered third-degree burns on my arms. He told me his story when he was burned and the direction for me after that was to Blacksburg. I was offered a scholarship by 60 schools across the nation, but it was easy to pick Virginia Tech after that.

My mother was cooking for the coaches, Frank Beamer and Coach Jim Cavanaugh. She asked my sister to go get these fries at the store and she got the wrong kind, so she asked me to watch the kids while she went back out to get the right fries.

We had this gas stove, and I guess she thought she had turned it off, but it kicked over to high. I came downstairs, and there was a burning pot of oil on the stove that had kicked some flames off onto the counter and cabinets. It was a blaze.

I knew the main fire was on the stove, so I grabbed the pot and took it outside. Then I came back and had a blanket and put the fire out. As soon as I put that fire out, Coach Cavanaugh came rushing through the door.

I didn't realize it at first that I was burned, but the fire had gotten my arms. Coach Beamer went to the hospital with me, my mom, my aunt, and my brother and sister. It caused quite a scene to go into the emergency room with the head coach at Virginia Tech.

People recognized Coach Beamer and knew me because it was my hometown. It was bad that I got burned, but he was there, so that helped. It took me several months for it to heal up. I shouldn't have done it, but I played in the Army All-America game with my arms still not healed, but I didn't want to miss it. When is the next time I could play in something like that?

That night of the fire, I decided I was going to Virginia Tech. That means something to me. Coach Beamer hugged me, and I said I was going.

My dad named me Macho when I was about two years old. I was walking around the house just being a little tough guy and picking up words people were saying and being challenging. He said I was talking trash so he wanted to give me a nickname, and it was Macho.

It has been with me ever since. Even my mother calls me Macho.

I had so many great memories at Virginia Tech. The one that sticks out at first is the one right after my mother's birthday, September 23, 2006. We were playing Cincinnati. It was a tight game, and Cincinnati was coming down to score. The coaches did a great job in film study with us because on that late drive they went to this particular formation and I knew what play was coming.

Sure enough, they threw a slant coming out of that formation, and I picked it off and went 77 yards for a touchdown. On their next possession I got another interception. That was right after my mother's birthday.

The second-most memorable game for me was also against Cincinnati. It was in the Orange Bowl, a BCS game we won for Coach Beamer. I had two pass break-ups, a tackle for loss, four tackles. One of their receivers was getting to a landmark for most receiving yards and receptions, but he didn't get it that night.

My senior year I was the boundary corner. My sophomore and junior year I was the field corner because we had Brandon Flowers as the boundary corner. He could play. I tell Brandon Flowers all the time I'm faster than him, but the reality was he was the better guy to play boundary corner; he was very physical.

When he moved on to the NFL, I moved over to boundary corner. I was ready then because I had some experience after playing running back in high school. I knew how to play the run then.

I guess I could have left Virginia Tech after my junior year, but I was just loving the school. I had a great time there. They treated

Cornerback Victor "Macho" Harris takes a victory lap after the Hokies' 17–14 win over Virginia at Lane Stadium, November 29, 2008. *Photo courtesy of AP Images*

me well there, from the coaches to the fans to the professors. They did me so great.

I wanted to come back and give them another year of Macho. After our last game together, fans were asking Brandon and me to come back. I prayed upon it.

The night before I made the decision whether to leave for the NFL or stay, I prayed extremely hard for some guidance. I also wrote down on a piece of paper the reasons I should stay on one side and the reasons I should leave on the other. I threw that piece of paper on the bed and told myself, *When I wake up in the morning whatever side of that paper is facing up, that's what I am going to do.* I prayed on it some more and went to bed.

The next morning my dad came into the room and said, "What are you going to do?" I had that feeling to just stay in school and told him I was staying and he said, "Cool," and left. I looked for the paper and it was facing up with "stay in school."

When I did go to the NFL, I went up in the fifth round. I didn't perform well and slid because I didn't do well in the Combine. When it came for the Pro Day, I did extremely well with all the scouts and coaches there.

I went low, but I got in the league and I'm doing what I love.

My situation was kind of like what happened with DeAngelo Hall. He was a very good running back in high school, and the coaches saw my talent and wanted me to come in and play corner. If I would have played running back, I think it would have been something to see. I tried to get them to let me play both ways, but they needed me at corner.

I had a good career at Virginia Tech because I was coached well. Athleticism took me just so far, but I needed something else, and that's where coach Torrian Gray and Bud Foster came in. They gave me the dog mentality. Bud Foster's mentality was to keep hitting them in the mouth, and it showed.

Coach Torrian Gray played many years in the NFL and shared his knowledge. He was one of the greatest coaches I have been around. He is so legit.

We were so disciplined back there that miscellaneous plays or trick plays teams would run could not get us out of our responsibilities. We were so focused.

Brandon Flowers also taught me a lot on the mentality to have out there on the corner on an island. I never had played cornerback, but Brandon came from Florida and in high school ball that's all they do there. They play football, and if you play corner, you play man-to-man, you and the receiver, that's it.

He taught me to have that "I don't care" mentality, that dog attitude. The receiver might try and get down the field and get open, but he was going to have a fight. Once I had that confidence, it was over. I started playing at a high level.

The one thing I could do was I could run with the rock in my hands after an interception. I knew what to do with it.

Calvin Johnson of Georgia Tech was the best receiver I played against. I did pretty well against them when we got out of zone the second half and played man-to-man. He hurt us inside a zone defense the first half, but the second half I think I did pretty well. I had an interception.

A lot of people say that was my coming-out game. I played pretty well against him, and that was my statement game in my sophomore year. He is a huge guy. He did get me on a one-yard fade. He used his body on me. Then late in the game they had a third-and-four and they threw a quick slant and he caught it for a first down.

It is a very unique thing to be a Hokie. I know a lot of people take pride in their universities, but there is a special pride for me coming from Virginia Tech. To this day, a Hokie could meet a Hokie any place in this world, and I would bet you they would be together and get along.

When we had the disaster there with the shootings, the whole community picked each other up. We thought Virginia Tech might not be the same ever. We thought that would be the day the school might go sour and people would be scared to go there.

But the Hokie Nation lifted up, man, we got together. People rallied, and to see the Hokie Nation lift up was something to see. I'm proud to say I'm a Hokie.

KEVIN JONES
Running Back, 2003

After a stellar high school career at Cardinal O'Hara High School in Philadelphia, Jones was one of the most highly sought recruits to ever sign with Virginia Tech. In 2001 Jones was named the No. 1 high school prospect in the country. He surprised nearly everyone when he selected the Hokies over Penn State. In his first season in Blacksburg, Jones rushed for a freshman record 957 yards with five touchdowns on 175 carries, including an 87-yard run against Temple. He was named Big East Rookie of the Year in 2001. As a sophomore, Jones split time with Lee Suggs in a backfield that was dubbed the "Untouchables." As a junior in 2003, Jones ran for a school-record 1,647 yards with 21 touchdowns on 281 carries. He was named a consensus All-American in 2003 and left for the NFL Draft. He was a first-round selection of the Detroit Lions in 2004 and became only the third running back in franchise history to run for more than 1,000 yards as a rookie. Jones played six seasons in the NFL before injuries derailed his career.

FRANK LORIA
Safety, 1966

Loria was one of the most beloved players in Virginia Tech history. A hard-hitting safety and electrifying punt returner, Loria became the first Virginia Tech player to earn All-America honors in consecutive seasons and the first to be named a consensus All-American as a senior in 1967. As a junior in 1966, Loria helped lead the Hokies to the Liberty Bowl, contributing three interceptions and returning three punts for touchdowns. He was named first-team All-America by the Associated Press and Football Writers Association. The next season, Loria was named to six All-America teams after finishing the year with three interceptions and 420 yards on punt returns. He had a 95-yard punt return for a touchdown against Miami, which still stands as the longest in school history. Loria left Virginia Tech owning several punt return records. Tragically, Loria was killed in a 1970 plane crash that killed most of Marshall University's football team. He was 23. He was inducted into the College Football Hall of Fame in 1999, and Virginia Tech retired his No. 10 jersey in 1971.

Hokies in Their Own Words

IN MEMORIAM: FRANK LORIA

SAFETY, 1964–1967

Frank Loria Jr., who was born one month after his father died, learned of his father's being a great player, campus leader, and coach through conversations with his father's teammates and friends. Here, Frank Loria Jr. shares their memories of his father.

It is very important to our family that my father is remembered for not only being a great football player, but a scholar, family man, and a man of integrity. From all I have heard about him, he stood for everything good that we want our student-athletes of today to strive for. I like to think that if he were still alive he would be a man of great influence today, someone making a difference. It has been more than 40 years since his tragic death, but I have hope that his story can make a difference in people's lives today. He was a small-town West Virginia boy who became an All-American through hard work, intelligence, and discipline.

My mother was seven-and-a-half months pregnant with me when my father died. Growing up, I always knew who he was. There wasn't some sort of revelation or anything like that, it was always a part of my life. When I was a kid, I had one of his awards from Virginia Tech in my room, and I remember exactly what it said: "We, the students of Virginia Tech, thank you for bringing honor and recognition to our university." I remember seeing that just about every day of my life, and it inspired me to do well. It was comforting to know that, although I would never get to know my father, he was a special person. To me, he was this larger-than-life person. I saw his picture in magazines. He was inducted into various halls of fame. There is a welcome sign in Clarksburg, West Virginia, that says, "Home of Frank Loria, All-American." It was always exciting to see that sign. I'll always remember meeting people who knew my dad and how they would tell me such great stories about him. It was important to them that I knew what a good man he was.

My feelings have changed as I've gotten older, as it has become more significant to me that he accomplished all that he did with such a high level of character. His life was truly remarkable. He was a two-time All-America safety at Virginia Tech, an Academic All-American in the classroom, and an all-around good guy. He was very well liked and respected around campus at Virginia Tech. I have been told by many alumni that they were impressed by Frank Loria, not just by his ability on the football field, but mostly by how he conducted himself off the field. He was a "big man on campus," but did not act like he was. He treated everyone he met with dignity and humility.

My father grew up in a small town in West Virginia. It wasn't really a coal town, but our ancestors who came from Italy worked in the coal mines. My dad went to a small Catholic school in Clarksburg where he excelled in school and sports. Virginia Tech was the first school to offer him a scholarship. He really wanted to go to West Virginia, but they didn't show much interest in him until later on, after Virginia Tech had already offered him a scholarship. I think it lit a little fire in his belly because he felt a little snubbed by WVU. From what I've learned, every time they played West Virginia, he had a little extra motivation to play hard.

My father was small, but he was a big hitter and pretty smart. I think his intelligence helped him tremendously. He wasn't super fast, either, but he used his brains to make up for any lack of speed. One year, when Virginia Tech played West Virginia in Morgantown, the Mountaineers had a great running back named "Galaxy" Garrett Ford. He was a big, big running back in those days. Apparently, on one tackle my dad hit him so hard, Ford was almost knocked out of the game and didn't play well. Tech won 20–7.

He really wanted to play in the NFL. He was hurt that he was not drafted. He spent one summer with the Denver Broncos but was one of the last players cut before the season. I met Larry Csonka when I was stationed in Hawaii. He and my father had played in the Hula Bowl together in 1968. They became good friends playing in a lot of the senior all-star games together. Larry told me of the day that he and my dad went swimming at the beach in Waikiki and just about drowned. I don't know if the lifeguards had to come out and get them, but they somehow got

Frank Loria was Virginia Tech's first consensus All-American as a senior in 1967. A hard-hitting, tough-nosed defensive back, Loria is one of only seven former Hokies to have his jersey number retired by the school. In 1970, at age 23, Loria was among the Marshall coaches and players killed in a tragic airplane crash.

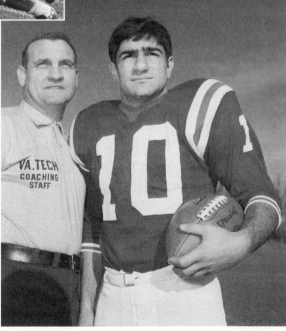

back to shore. Here they were, these big, tough football guys who almost drowned at the beach.

The day of the draft, my mom said Larry Csonka kept calling the house asking my father, "Did you get drafted yet? Did you get drafted yet?" He felt really bad because my dad hadn't been drafted. My dad spent a little bit of time in Canada, playing in the Canadian Football League, but decided to move back to West Virginia and got his master's degree from West Virginia University. Then he was hired as an assistant coach at Marshall. He was very excited about the opportunity to coach.

He worked at Marshall for two years before the plane crash. One of the players there, who didn't get on the plane, told me my dad was one of the guys on Friday nights getting all the students ready for the pep rally. He was really loved by the people at Marshall and is still remembered there.

My parents had married while my father was playing football at Virginia Tech. My oldest sister, Vickie, was born during his senior season. My sister, Julie, was born in Morgantown, West Virginia, when he was getting his master's degree in 1969. My mom said my dad wanted to have a lot of kids, and they were well on their way! He was a very good father. I have seen old movies of him playing with my sisters. He loved his girls. He would be so proud of them today.

My mom was only 22 when the plane crashed. I cannot imagine what life was like for her back then. She had my two sisters to care for and was pregnant with me. Life does not get any worse than that. Somehow she found the strength to pick up the pieces and carry on with life. She never complained about the situation. She was always positive about who Frank Loria was and what he stood for and instilled that in us.

I think she felt an obligation to him to provide a good life full of love for us kids. She's quite a strong person. I consider her a hero because of what she was dealt and how she persevered. Her story is truly remarkable, and she is a remarkable woman. We didn't have anything when my father died. My dad didn't make any money as a coach. We didn't have any insurance. We had absolutely nothing. My mom received some Social Security, which helped, but we didn't have much of anything. We moved back to Clarksburg, West Virginia, for a couple of years. All our family was there and they all helped. But my mom felt that she had to get on with life and wanted to raise us without everyone being involved in every decision, so we moved to northern Virginia. It took a lot of courage for her to do that at that time by herself, but it was the best for our little family.

I think about where my father would be today. I hear he was a very good coach, and everyone expected him to eventually be a great head coach one day. It is nice to think that, and it sure would be exciting, but it was not meant to be. I was told that Frank Beamer once was asked if Frank Loria were still alive today, did he think that my dad would be working for him. Coach Beamer said he thought he'd be working for my dad. I think that answer is Coach Beamer being the classy guy he is. I respect him a lot. He's one of the good guys. He's a selfless coach who looks out for his players and coaches. When he says things like that about my father, it just goes along with who Frank Beamer is, and I appreciate him saying that. I am sure my father would be so proud of what his former teammate has accomplished at Virginia Tech and proud of how far the program has come under his leadership.

It has been 35 years since the Marshall football team tragedy. Hokies fans should know that Rick Tolley was the head coach of that 1970 Marshall team. He was also a Virginia Tech graduate and 1960 football player at Tech. Warner Brothers made a movie about the tragedy and subsequent rise of the Marshall program [*We Are Marshall* (2006)]. This movie creates the opportunity for their story to be told, and I hope that Virginia Tech fans of today get to know about Frank Loria and all the good things he represented. Maybe someday fans will proudly wear his No. 10 jersey.

My dad realized there's a responsibility in being a student-athlete. It is not all about the glory. There is a responsibility as a role model. I think my dad lived up to that responsibility. He set the example for other athletes. It is an honor that Virginia Tech keeps his memory alive, and I am thankful to Virginia Tech for doing so. I want him to be remembered as someone who succeeded by working hard and doing things the right way. His life is worthy of being celebrated. I also hope the tragedy of his death is remembered. Not so much for the sadness of it, although it helps us to be thankful for what we have today, but in the hope the story brings. Hope that life can be very difficult, but we can overcome adversity. My mother faced tremendous adversity and persevered with life, and that should be celebrated. My father would be proud of her and thankful to her for how she carried on. She is a true hero.

Frank Loria Jr. graduated from the United States Military Academy in 1993 and served five years of active duty in the Army. He is a medical sales representative living in New Jersey with his wife and two children.

COREY MOORE
Defensive End, 1998–1999

There have been few defensive players who were as ferocious or disruptive as Moore was at Virginia Tech during the 1998 and '99 seasons. Following his senior season in 1999, in which Moore helped lead the Hokies to the national championship game, he was named a unanimous All-American by all six major All-America teams. He posted a Big East–record 17 sacks in 1999 and had 11 other tackles for loss and 60 total tackles. He also was named All-America by the Football Coaches Association as a junior in 1998, after he led the Big East with 13½ sacks. After the 1999 season, Moore won the Lombardi Award as college football's best lineman and the Nagurski Trophy as the top defensive player. He also was named Big East Defensive Player of the Year as a junior and senior.

JIM PYNE
Center, 1993

Virginia Tech's coaches didn't have to worry about Pyne carrying out his assignment. Pyne, a native of Milford, Massachusetts, allowed just one quarterback sack by the man he was assigned to block in more than 2,700 career plays in college. He became Virginia Tech's first unanimous All-American as a senior in 1993, when he helped pave the way for a Hokies offense that set school records with 444.1 yards and 36.4 points. Pyne was named first-team All-America by the Associated Press, United Press International, Walter Camp Foundation, Football Writers Association, and Football Coaches Association. He started 35 consecutive games and 41 of 42 games in which he played. Pyne was a seventh-round choice of the Tampa Bay Buccaneers in the 2004 NFL Draft and played nine seasons of pro football before becoming an assistant coach. He was the first third-generation player in NFL history, following his grandfather, George Pyne Jr., who played for the Providence Steam Roller, and his father, George Pyne III, who played for the Boston Patriots. Virginia Tech retired his No. 73 jersey.

BOB SCHWEICKERT
Quarterback, 1964

Known as "Mr. Outside" during his playing career at Virginia Tech, Schweickert was named an All-American by *Look Magazine* during his senior season in 1964. One of the finest triple-threat quarterbacks in Southern Conference history, Schweickert fought off injuries in his final college season to run for 576 yards with nine touchdowns and pass for 833 yards with nine scores. He also punted and led the team with a 37.7-yard average. Schwieckert helped engineer one of the school's biggest upsets in 1964, leading the Hokies to a 20–11 victory over undefeated Florida State. The Seminoles outgained the Hokies 333–191 in offensive yards, but Schweickert threw a 19-yard touchdown to Erick Johnson on a tackle-eligible play to author the upset. During his junior season in 1963, Schweickert ran for 839 yards to set a Southern Conference record, helping lead the Hokies to an 8–2 season and the school's only Southern Conference title.

BRUCE SMITH
Defensive End, 1983–1984

Known as the "Sack Man" throughout his brilliant college career, Smith was honored more than any other player in Virginia Tech history. He won the Outland Trophy as the country's top lineman in 1984 and was named All-America in both 1983 and '84. During his junior season in 1983, Smith recorded a whopping 22 sacks and was named a first-team All-American by the Football Coaches Association and Newspaper Enterprise Association. As a junior, he had 55 tackles, 31 of which came behind the line of scrimmage. As a senior in 1984, Smith had 16 sacks and nine other tackles for loss and was a consensus All-American by the Associated Press, Football Writers Association of America, Kodak, and Walter Camp Foundation. During his college career, Smith's 71 tackles for loss amounted to 504 yards. He was the No. 1 pick in the 1985 NFL Draft by the Buffalo Bills and was one of the greatest defensive players in NFL history. He ended his pro career in 2003 as the NFL's all-time sack leader with 200. He was inducted into the Pro Football Hall of Fame in 2009. Virginia Tech retired his No. 78 jersey.

DARRYL TAPP
Defensive End, 2005

Tapp, a native of Chesapeake, Virginia, was one of the most dominant defensive ends in Virginia Tech history. Tapp was an All-ACC defensive end at Tech, even though many Division I schools said he was too small for the position. He started four games as a sophomore and then took over as a full-time starter his junior and senior seasons. In 2004 he was the boundary defensive end and started all 13 games. He registered 60 tackles, 16.5 tackles for loss, 8.5 sacks, 23 quarterback hurries, two fumble recoveries, a forced fumble, a pass break-up, an interception, and a blocked kick. He was named first-team All-America by the American Football Coaches Association and second-team All-America by the Associated Press as a senior in 2005. In 13 games, Tapp led the Hokies with 10 sacks, 14.5 tackles for loss, and three forced fumbles. He won the Dudley Award as the best college football player in the state of Virginia and was a finalist for the Lott Trophy. During his four-year career, Tapp had 187 tackles, 23.5 sacks, and 38 tackles for loss. He was a second-round choice of the Seattle Seahawks in the 2006 NFL

Draft and played the 2010 season with the Philadelphia Eagles after he was acquired in a trade.

Hokies in Their Own Words

DARRYL TAPP

DEFENSIVE END, 2003–2006

My most memorable game? It is probably a tie.

There was my first game against UVA when Justin Hamilton blocked a punt and I recovered it and ran and dove into the end zone for a touchdown. That was my first rivalry game against UVA. We won that game [21–9] at home. That was a big day for me and the team.

Then there was my last home game, which was against North Carolina. That was my last game at Lane Stadium. I played out of my mind. I had three sacks, a blocked kick, four or five quarterback hits. It was a good game. We didn't give them a chance [a 30–3 Tech victory].

That North Carolina game I just got in a zone. It was my last game playing at Tech for the people who gave me a chance. It was my last time in maroon and orange, and I got after it.

Those last two years I was there we had a unique team because you could not pinpoint a guy who was going to make a play. We all made plays. I think the last two years I was there we had the No. 1 defense in college football.

We believed on that team that somebody was going to make a play. The biggest thing Coach [Charley] Wiles did for me was to teach me to watch the football and be aggressive. He was also one of my guys, somebody you could trust. He wanted you to attack upfield, and the more you attack up the field, the more you are going to throw off their blocking schemes.

I got some things done on special teams, and that's a credit to Coach Beamer. The pros know all about him. He is very respected. I started my NFL career in Seattle, and even way out west they know Beamer Ball. He is very respected in the NFL.

People know how he handles the program here and grooms people for the NFL. He is a father-figure who cares more for us as people than players. The stuff he told me when Tech was recruiting me came true.

One of the things he told me was I was going to have a chance to play for a No. 1 defense under Coach Bud Foster and that I was going to get my diploma. Those things happened. I graduated in three and a half years with a degree in marketing.

They put you on the right tracks, usher you down those tracks, and don't let you get off of them.

Now, if Coach Beamer was the father figure, Coach Foster was the uncle. He was the guy who could jump on your case for a mistake, but you knew you had it coming. He never talked bad to you just because he could; he always had a good reason.

Coach Foster was an aggressive coach who ran blitzes and mixed things up. I always was a hand-on-the-ground guy at Tech, a defensive end that got in a stance. They promised me I was going to play defensive end and they stuck with it.

It's funny because Tech and the University of Florida were the only schools that were going to give me a chance to play defensive end. Everybody else said I was too small. They were all going to move me to linebacker. Coach Foster said if he brought me in to Tech they were going to give me a chance to play defensive end...and he did.

Coach Spurrier was still at Florida my senior year. My in to Florida was Rick Hunley, who was from my area of Virginia. His sister was my middle school principal, so I knew I had somebody to lean on if I went to Gainesville.

My official visit at Florida was the same weekend Coach Spurrier left for the Redskins. He took his whole staff with him [Hunley played at Arizona and was on Spurrier's staff with Florida and the Redskins]. Ron Zook came in later, but I had scratched Florida off the list by then.

The final two were Virginia Tech and Maryland. I had three or four teammates who were already at Tech, so that made a difference. My older brother was in the military and stationed just 15 minutes down the road from Maryland, so I knew if I got homesick I could go down the road and see my brother.

I got recruited by a lot of people because the Tidewater area was so full of football players and college coaches knew to come down there. It was really strong around the time DeAngelo Hall played high school ball down there. I went to Deep Creek, and we were always playing against schools with players good enough to play Division I.

I took an official visit to UVA, but there was not a good feel there.

The man who recruited me to Tech was Coach Stinespring, and he saw that I was a little light for defensive end, but he told me to work out hard in the spring, get bigger, and I would have a chance to play as a freshman. I was like, "That's cool." It was a chance; that's what I wanted.

I put on 10 to 12 more pounds and then had a good off-season with building strength. I became the fifth end playing behind guys like Lamar Cobb, Cols Colas, Jim Davis, and Nathaniel Adibi. They taught me what it was like to be a Hokie. They taught me so much about what the program demanded of its players and how to apply myself.

Darryl Tapp was named first-team All-America by the American Football Coaches Association and second-team All-America by the Associated Press as a senior.

Coach Beamer asked me if I wanted to redshirt or play, and I told him I wanted to be at full-throttle and learn. Any of those players could have left early for the league, so I wanted to have my work in and be ready to start if they did leave.

Here's the thing about Virginia Tech. If you work hard, you play. You get on special teams, which are famous. I played every special teams snap my freshman year, and it was fun.

We played Texas A&M down in College Station, and I had a lot of key blocks that sprung some punt returns and kick returns. That's the first game that comes to mind. We went down there, it was loud, it was hot, and we got a victory [13–3].

The teammate I remember most was James Anderson. James and I played at Deep Creek High School and lived together my last three years. James redshirted his first year. We grew together as brothers from another mother.

James was ultra-athletic. DeAngelo Hall was ridiculously athletic, but all around James was incredible.

We had some issues living together. You have to get used to having a roommate; my brothers growing up were already out of the house. James and I, we had some issues of drinking each other's Kool-aid. There was one time I had some food and I didn't eat all of it so I put it in the refrigerator. I was thinking all the seasonings would sink into the meat and it was going to be awesome.

I got home the next day and the food was not in the refrigerator. I looked at him and said, "What did you do?" He ate it. He said he was sorry. It was a war of words after that. He bought me some dinner after that.

DeAngelo was a competitive guy. We all hate to lose, but this guy hates to lose on another level. He is really super-competitive. They always take his confidence and competitiveness as being arrogant. It was awesome playing with him in college and high school.

If it wasn't for James and DeAngelo, [the coaches] never would have come and looked at me in high school. All the big schools showed up and were there for them, and they just saw me, too.

The biggest thing that helped me at Virginia Tech was I was just excited to play the game. I didn't get a chance to play football my sophomore year at high school. My mom was afraid I was going to get hurt, so I had to play soccer and basketball, but not football. When I was a high school junior, I was still learning to play the game.

So when I got a chance to finally play football, I was so excited and, as my career progressed, I stayed excited. I wanted to practice and soak up the game.

I did the same thing going from Tech to the NFL. I maintained that work ethic I got from my parents. People said I was too small to play defensive end in the NFL, too. Heck, I played defensive tackle in the NFL. I did some for Philadelphia. It helps you pass rush when you chase Mike [Vick] around in practice all day.

It's awesome playing with Vick. He is the reason I went to Tech. He made it out of 757 [area code] and went to a big-time program. When you see that happen, it gets you thinking that maybe that can be me. When I was a junior in high school, I was thinking of places like North Carolina A&T, where one of my older brothers went. Another brother went to Norfolk State. I was thinking a smaller school, not Tech.

They were awesome programs, but then the bigger schools started coming around as I played more. I knew players out of our area could make it in big-time college football.

Being a Hokie is a way of life. Coach Beamer cultivated a spirit of family around there, and we all bought into it. When I was there, probably 70 percent of the players were from Virginia, so we knew what kind of state pride was involved with the program. We played each other in high school, so it was a brotherhood; we cared about one another. If somebody needed anything and we were down to our last dime, they got our last dime.

MICHAEL VICK
Quarterback, 1999

No Virginia Tech player is more singularly connected to its rise as a national football power than Vick, an electrifying dual-threat quarterback from Newport News, Virginia, who guided the Hokies to their first 11–0 regular season as a freshman in 1999. Behind Vick's right arm and swift legs, Virginia Tech played No. 1 Florida State for the 1999 national championship, losing to the Seminoles 46–29 in the Sugar Bowl. Vick was named All-American by the *Sporting News*, after leading Division I-A in passing efficiency with a 180.37 rating, an NCAA freshman record. Vick also completed 59.2 percent of his passes for 1,840 yards with 12 touchdowns, while running for 585 yards with eight touchdowns. He was named Big East Offensive Player of the Year and Big East Rookie of the Year.

MIKE WIDGER
Linebacker, 1968

Widger was a star linebacker at Virginia Tech from 1967 to 1969, when he was a teammate of Hokies coach Frank Beamer. Widger capped his incredible junior season in 1968 with All-America first-team honors from the Associated Press and Football Writers Association. He compiled a record 825 tackling points and was among the national leaders with seven interceptions and 203 interception return yards. Widger returned two interceptions for touchdowns and scored another touchdown against Kansas State, after pulling the football loose from a running back and returning it to the end zone.

Hokies in Their Own Words
MIKE WIDGER
LINEBACKER, 1966–1969

I grew up in Pennsville, New Jersey, a small town across the river from Delaware, and had lived there my whole life. When I first met Virginia Tech coach Jerry Claiborne, I thought he was a little different. When I went to Blacksburg for my official visit to Virginia Tech, my high school coach was with me. When we left Coach Claiborne's office on the last day of my visit, my high school coach came out and said, "You've got the scholarship." I said, "Really? That makes me happy." Then he looked at me and said, "You know how you got it? You're bow-legged. Claiborne said bow-legged people don't have knee problems."

The guy who recruited me to Virginia Tech was named Alf Satterfield, who was the offensive line coach. I went to Rutgers for a visit and I went to Maryland. Then I ended up going to Virginia Tech for a visit, and they offered me a scholarship, a full ride. I said, "Thank you very much, I'll take it." Rutgers had offered me just a grant-in-aid, and Maryland hadn't offered me a scholarship yet. So I wound up going to Virginia Tech.

I remember our first freshman game in 1966 was at Maryland, and we won that one. We had some really good freshman on that team—running back Kenny Edwards, who was from Radford, Virginia, and Bobby Slaughter, who was a really good wide receiver. They brought in 65 players my freshman year. We were down to 34 players at the end of the freshman season. Half of them quit the team, and I ended up graduating with four of them.

Coach Claiborne's practices were tough; they sure were, there's no doubt about it. I moved up to the varsity team as a sophomore in 1967 and played quite a bit. We were basically running a 4-4 alignment and had two inside linebackers. Clarence Culpepper and I played inside, and Pete Wrenn played a lot at inside linebacker, too. We won our first seven games in 1967 and were pretty hot. The third game that season was in Manhattan, Kansas, against Kansas State. I remember one play where I ripped the football out of the hands of the Kansas State quarterback and ran 40-something yards for a touchdown—they called it an interception. I don't remember exactly how I ended up with the football. I remember I was on a blitz and the quarterback was handing off to Mac Heron, and somehow or other I wound up with the football and scored. We ended up winning the game 15–3.

I'll never forget beating Villanova 3–0 the next week. There was a big fight in the second half of that game. It was a very close game and nobody scored. Villanova was trying to kick a field goal, but it bounced off the crossbar. Frank Loria picked up the football and started running down the sideline. It looked like he was going all the way for a touchdown. It was a dead ball anyway, but he was still running. Well, one of the Villanova coaches ran off the sideline and tackled him. Then it was a very big fight, and both sidelines cleared. All the players from our team and all the players from Villanova were fighting in the middle of the field. It never made a lot of sense to me when you've got a lot of football gear on and you're trying to punch somebody. It took them a while to break that fight up, and then we kicked a field goal with about 40 seconds left to win the game.

We lost our last three games in 1967 and finished the season with a 7–3 record. We lost to Miami and Florida State, two pretty good football teams, but then somehow lost to Virginia Military Institute on Thanksgiving Day to finish the season. I don't know

Mike Widger was an All-America linebacker in 1968 after compiling 825 tackling points as a junior, and was among the national leaders with seven interceptions, two of which he returned for touchdowns.

what it was. It was actually very, very strange because I don't know how we lost to VMI, but we did.

We opened the 1968 season playing Alabama in Birmingham, and it was a very tough loss. We were going in to score at the end of the game, and it was all kind of surreal because there we were, playing Alabama, one of college football's best teams, and Bear Bryant was standing on the sideline with about 75,000 fans screaming at Legion Field. But we stalled near their 20 and lost to Alabama 14–7.

We beat William and Mary the next week.

We won at Wake Forest 7–6 in the next game. It was their homecoming game, and they played us pretty tough. We should have dominated the game, but we really didn't show up. We never had much of a passing game, and that was always one of our major problems. When you needed points at the end of the game to come back, we didn't have it. We didn't have the plays and really didn't have many wide receivers with much speed. We lost to Miami that season, and once again, we were going in to score late in the game but couldn't make the plays to get it done.

That was a mark of our teams throughout my career at Virginia Tech—we played defense, but never really had an offense. We were three yards and a cloud of dust. We had a defensive back, Jim Richards, who didn't even start his senior season, but ended up getting drafted by the New York Jets and winning the Super Bowl. If I had been the coach, I would have moved Jimmy to wide receiver because he was so fast, and that probably would have cured a lot of our problems in the passing game. He had great, great speed, and we didn't have anybody out there who could run very well. Of course, we never had a quarterback who could have thrown it to him, either.

One of the highlights of the 1968 season was beating Florida State 40–22 in Tallahassee. They had Ron Sellers, and he was a really good wide receiver. I had to cover him a couple of times one-on-one. It was near the end of the game, they were going in to score, and I had to cover him man-to-man if I called a certain defense. They were on our 20-yard line, and I called the defense three plays in a row and had to cover him. Three times, he never got off the line of scrimmage because I knocked him down. But the fourth time, he put a move on me, and he was gone. I mean *gone.* I turned around and grabbed him by the back of the neck and put my legs around his legs, tackling him basically. He was upset. But nobody saw it, and I got away with it. He looked at one of the officials and said, "Didn't you see that?" The official said, "Young man, there are 22 players on this field and six of us. We can't watch everybody all the time." I got away with that one.

We ended up winning our last five games of the 1968 season and got invited to play Ole Miss in the Liberty Bowl in Memphis. Ole Miss's quarterback was Archie Manning. We were up 17–0 in the first quarter. All season long, Ole Miss had had a tendency, and we picked it up during our preparations for the bowl game. They never ran into the boundary, or hash mark. They could put a new formation into the boundary, but then they would run to the wide side of the field. In the 10 games before playing us, they never ran into the boundary, and we knew that.

So we shifted to the wide side of the field and then stunted to the wide side. I remember it was a damp, cold day in Memphis. At halftime Coach Claiborne, the defensive coordinator, and I were discussing what we were doing. I said, "Coach, they're going to figure it out." They called Ole Miss coach Johnny Vaught the "Old Fox," but he was in the hospital and watching the game on television. But he obviously called his staff at halftime and told them what we were doing on defense. I kept saying, "Coach, they're going to catch on to this pretty soon." Claiborne looked at me and said, "You're right. But we'll do it until they hurt us."

The first play of the second half, Ole Miss was on their 21-yard line. I was slanting to the right, they ran to the weak side into their sideline, and Steve Hindman ran 79 yards for a touchdown. I ran over to the sideline, looked at Coach Claiborne, and said, "Coach, I think they hurt us."

We ended up letting Ole Miss come back, and we lost 34–17. We gave them the ball three times on our 1-yard line because of turnovers. At the end of the game, they had run 11 straight plays on offense and hadn't gotten into the end zone. Well, on the 12th play, Manning was running an option to my side. I stepped across the goal line because we were lined up in the end zone, and I hit him right between the eyes and dropped him. He got up like he scored a touchdown and was celebrating. I just took my arm and pointed the other way because it was fourth down. He was going nuts, screaming, "I scored! I scored! I scored!" I looked at him and said, "No, you didn't, Archie. You didn't get in." He was upset, but he was a class act, as well.

We played Alabama again in the first game of my senior season in 1969, but this time the Crimson Tide came to Blacksburg. It was about the biggest thing that had ever happened to Virginia Tech football, I don't doubt it at all. It was my senior season in 1969, and the game took place prior to school starting. We were really looking forward to it. We were picked to go 9–1 by *Playboy* because we'd gone to the Liberty Bowl the season before and nearly all of the players from that team were back in school.

Somehow, and I still can't believe it, we lost our first five games in 1969. The Alabama game was really close, but we lost 17–13, and we never really got on track after that. We lost the next four games by a total of 15 points, including losses to Wake Forest, Richmond, and Kentucky, games we should have never lost. Our defense was still playing pretty well. During my junior season, we gave up 13 points a game and went to the Liberty Bowl. During my senior season, we gave up 11 points per game, but lost our first five games and wound up 4–5–1 at the end of the season.

We finally got our act together at the end of the 1969 season and won four of our last five games and tied Florida State. Once we finally got our heads out of our butts, we started playing like we should have played the whole year. I'm not trying to place any blame on the offense, because it wasn't the players' fault. It was just the style of offense we played. People just stacked up against us and shut us down. You just can't let them do that. You've got to make them respect your ability to potentially pass and throw. They had to respect your ability to put the ball in the air, but we never had that threat.

I finished up my last semester of school after the 1970 season, but they had a new coaching staff in there when I went back. I had a feeling there was trouble coming on after the 1969 season. When you're picked to go 9–1 and lose your first five games, you get your hats handed to you. Somebody is going to get the axe. I didn't think Claiborne would go out that quickly, but he did.

After I finished playing at Virginia Tech, the only NFL team that showed any interest in me was the Dallas Cowboys, and they had a linebacker corps of Chuck Howley, Lee Roy Jordan, and Dave Edwards. If I had gone there, I would have been on special teams the rest of my life. I was only about 200 or 205 pounds, so some teams probably thought I wasn't big enough to play in the NFL.

I started doing my student teaching in Vienna, Virginia, in 1970, and Bob Ward, who was once the head coach at Maryland, called me and we started talking. I'm glad he called me because one thing student teaching taught me was I didn't like teaching. Ward was going to be the defensive coordinator for one of the teams in the Canadian Football League and talked me into signing with them. I played nine seasons in the CFL, seven with the Montreal Alouettes and two with the Ottawa Roughriders. Marv Levy, who was later coach of the Buffalo Bills, traded me to Ottawa in 1976. I was on teams that played for the Grey Cup three times and won twice.

I loved living in Montreal. I really enjoyed living there and enjoyed Crescent Street, the section of the city that was the night-club area. They started calling me "Crescent City" Mike because I spent quite a bit of time there. I got into the construction business after retiring from football in 1978 and got into the hotel business in Canada. I ended up moving to Florida and running some night-clubs and was a business manager for a company that ran facilities for the Saudi Arabian Air Force, one of the most beautiful athletic facilities you'll ever see. Then I wound up in Egypt running a com-pound for some air force instructors. I got into the construction business after coming back to my hometown of Pennsville, New Jersey, and that's what I've been doing ever since.

JIMMY WILLIAMS
Cornerback, 2005

Williams became Virginia Tech's fourth unanimous All-American after he became one of the most feared shut-down cornerbacks during his senior season in 2005. Williams, known for his lanky frame and swift speed, was named first-team All-America by the Football Writers Association of America, American Football Coaches Association, *Sporting News*, Walter Camp Foundation, and Associated Press. He was also named All-ACC and was a final-ist for the Jim Thorpe Award as the sport's best defensive back. In 13 games, Williams had 44 tackles, including two for loss and one sack, along with 14 quarterback hurries, five pass breakups, and one interception. He was drafted in the second round of the 2006 NFL Draft by the Atlanta Falcons.

Hokies in Their Own Words
JIMMY WILLIAMS
CORNERBACK, 2001–2005

Recruiting was probably one of the most beautiful things a high school kid can go through because coaches and teams are trying to give you a shot to help their teams. It's stressful because coaches are coming into your home, but I didn't really look at it that way. It was really simple. I prayed about it. My parents didn't have any say-so in it. They didn't pressure me. They let me be my own man.

Going to Virginia Tech was just the best decision for me. They were talking about redshirting me, but in my mind, I wanted to play. I had to still pass the SAT. The coaches at the University of Virginia took their scholarship away because they didn't think I was going to pass the SAT. When I first thought about it, I wanted to go really far away, but after Christmas break during basketball season, I started to think about what it would be like being so far away.

At the time, Tech wasn't recruiting Hampton High School, so I transferred to Bethel. My friends Brenden Hill and Marcus Vick kind of helped me make my decision to go to Tech. Knowing Michael Vick went to Tech also helped. I also had my friends like Marques Hagans and Elton Brown telling me to come to the University of Virginia, but I wanted to do something different.

The choice was kind of simple once I heard that Tech wanted me to play as a backup as a freshman. Once I found out that Marcus was going there, that's what really made the transition easier. Then, Brenden decided to go to Tech. Coach Jim Cavanaugh also helped me out a whole lot. The rest is history. I still had the offers from West Virginia, Syracuse, and North Carolina State. I also had one more visit I was going to take and I thought I was going to go to Arizona State.

Everything was happening so fast and I really didn't have a lot of time to think about it. I really wanted to play more as a freshman because I thought I was better than the person in front of me [Willie Pile], but he earned his time and earned his shot. Marcus was telling me I was out there killing people, so to hear that from your peers made a big difference. I just wanted to play more, but I wouldn't have changed anything. It's done now.

Before we played Louisville in the Gator Bowl after my senior season, it felt like it did when I walked across the stage in high school. I really got sad and wanted to go back. It didn't really hit me. I wasn't really thinking about my stats.

I almost left Virginia Tech after my junior season and went to the pros. I was enjoying college so much and seeing how people were reacting to me walking around practice that I didn't want to leave after my junior year. I just love playing. Guys always talk about how it's different when you go to the pros. You're alone a lot. You have to make your own way.

When I left high school, I was the man. Then, when I was in college, I was the man. Well, other than Marcus, I was the man. People would recognize me when I went to stores. People like cashiers and everybody were noticing me. That was fun.

My dad told me what the business was like about college and playing in the NFL. When I was a kid, I was listening, but I was still trying to have fun. Now, I'm still trying to do everything I need to do, but I want to have fun doing it. There's a business side to it, but it has to be fun.

My biggest thing was that I didn't want to come back to the old neighborhood. I didn't want to be one of those kids who played in college but then couldn't cut it or couldn't get it done. When I was in college, I cut myself off some from my friends and family in Hampton because I was so focused on trying to understand the game and get on the field. I didn't want their help. I wanted to do it on my own so that they knew I was ready for the challenge. They didn't understand it, but I guess they did when they looked back at what I was doing.

In my sophomore year, I broke up with my girlfriend, who was back in Hampton. When that happened, I kind of lost the drive to come back home at all. In a lot of ways, when I came back home, people would always try to pull me back into the situations they were in. Well, they had to understand that I was headed someplace else.

I was from Hampton and the 757 [area code]. Those boys down there, there's a straight connection. Wherever we go, we get love. They know who we are and they see it.

In my freshman year I stayed in a lot and I didn't get in any trouble because I wanted to put myself in a position to be where I wanted to be. The only thing I really did wrong was get in a few confrontations with my coaches. They didn't understand me. They didn't know how to talk to me. I didn't really talk with them much in my first few years because I didn't know how to approach them.

Things got better during my junior and senior years. All I ever wanted to do was put myself in a position to help my family.

If I had to say besides my Tech family, the two people who probably drove me the most were Allen Iverson and Ronald Curry. A lot of people look up to guys like Shaquille O'Neal or Michael Jordan, but guys like Iverson and Curry, they were gods to me. That was Friday night football. People might not understand that, but when I was a little kid I used to play on some of the same courts with Iverson. Then, I played in the same recreation leagues Curry

Jimmy Williams was a lock-down cornerback at Virginia Tech and was named a consensus All-American during his senior season in 2005. After helping lead the Hokies to the 2004 ACC title, Williams returned to school instead of entering the NFL Draft as an underclassman.

played in. I used to throw the football around with that guy. They were larger than life. Those guys and my dad, there aren't three guys in the world who were more important to me.

My freshman year, I played in the Orange Bowl against Willis McGahee, Kellen Winslow, Ken Dorsey, and all them. I came in and did my thing—I got 13 or 14 tackles. I was on a high. I was watching the game on the sideline and talking to Marcus, saying, "Dog, if I get in the game, I'm going to do something big." Marcus said, "I know!" Then, when I finally got in, McGahee was running at me, but everything was going so slow. That's when I knew I could play. That's the most fun I've ever had playing in a game.

The least favorite game had to be my last collegiate football game [against Louisville in the 2006 Gator Bowl; Williams was ejected in the first quarter for grabbing the arm of an official]. Even that right there, I wouldn't change it because everybody remembers it. Everybody knew Jimmy was going to do something special going out. That's just the way it happened. Just to hear from my friends and family and fans, they said they couldn't even watch it after that. I had numerous friends watching. Guys like Tye Hill and Michael Huff said they were watching the game and they left the room for a minute. That's still my family, man.

When I first came to school, I didn't want a degree. People were trying to tell me, "Hey, Jimmy, get your degree, man." I was like, "Naw, man. I'm trying to make seven figures." But now I think about the fact that at some point, it's something that you're going to want.

It's like anything, like getting married, having children, or just being in a relationship. It's something you've just got to be ready for. When I was first there, I wasn't even thinking about getting a degree. Now I think about how it is in the business world, and well, it's something I could use. In my last year at Tech, I was learning. I was just trying to learn everything I could [about football]. That is something I want right now more than anything other than signing that contract.

To all those young people out there, things are different. You can't just make it on that high school diploma. If you want things in your life, it's getting more expensive.

chapter 6
COACHES

FRANK BEAMER, 1987–PRESENT

Other schools have hired former players as their coaches and failed. Mike Shula was never a great fit as Alabama's coach. Dave Wannstedt never found much success coaching at Pittsburgh, and Charlie Weis flopped at Notre Dame.

Few coaches have returned to their alma mater and produced as much success as Virginia Tech's Frank Beamer. A defensive back on Virginia Tech's teams from 1966 to 1968, the Hokies plucked Beamer as their coach after his successful run at Murray State. Hired to replace Bill Dooley after the 1986 season, the Hokies showed great patience during Beamer's early years. The Hokies went 2–9 in his first season in 1987 and 3–8 in his second.

After consecutive losing seasons in 1991 and '92, Virginia Tech's patience seemed to be running thin. But the Hokies went 9–3 in 1993 and 8–4 in '94, setting the stage for their rise to national prominence.

Under Beamer's direction, the Hokies played for a national championship for the first time in 1999; became only one of three Division I schools to play in bowl games for 18 consecutive seasons from 1993 to 2010; became the only school in the country to win at least 10 games in seven straight seasons from 2004 to 2010;

Coach Frank Beamer (right) and defensive coordinator Bud Foster coached together at Murray State before Beamer got the job at Virginia Tech. Beamer encouraged Foster to join him on the Hokies coaching staff, where they have stayed since 1987.

Photo courtesy of AP Images

and compiled an 84-week string of being ranked in the Associated Press top 25 poll.

During Beamer's watch, the Hokies won four ACC titles, three Big East championships, and two BCS bowl games through the 2010 season. Heading into the 2011 season, Beamer had won 240 games in three decades as a head coach, trailing only Penn State's Joe Paterno among active NCAA FBS (Football Bowl Subdivision) coaches.

Following the 1999 season, Beamer earned eight national Coach of the Year awards. He was named the Bobby Dodd Coach of the Year, the GTE Coach of the Year, the Eddie Robinson Coach of the Year, the Paul "Bear" Bryant Coach of the Year, the Associated Press Coach of the Year, the Walter Camp Football Foundation/*Street & Smith's* Coach of the Year, the Maxwell Football Club Coach of the Year, and the Woody Hayes Coach of the Year. In 2010 he was awarded the inaugural Joseph V. Paterno Coach of the Year Award, based on his school's performance on Saturdays, in the classroom, and within the community.

In 1997 Beamer was inducted into the Virginia Tech Sports Hall of Fame, and his No. 25 jersey was retired in a pregame ceremony in 2002.

Hokies in Their Own Words

BUD FOSTER

ASSISTANT COACH, 1987–PRESENT

It was 1986, and Frank [Beamer] and I were coaching together at Murray State—I was the linebackers coach and Frank was the head coach. We'd just beaten Austin Peay to win the Ohio Valley Conference championship.

We were riding back on the bus—it's not too terribly far from Clarksville, Tennessee to Murray, Kentucky—and I was sitting next to Coach. He said to me, "I'm in on this Virginia Tech job, but I haven't heard back from them. I'd like you to come with me if I get the job." I said, "I'd be honored and I'd be really excited about that."

Well, I didn't think anything about it because we went on and prepared for the playoffs and all that stuff. The next thing you know, he got the job, and it was right around Christmastime. He called all of the assistant coaches into his office. I didn't know who he was going to want to take with him to Tech, but there were a few guys on the [Murray State] staff who were really close friends of mine who didn't get offered to come.

He asked me, and I had zero hesitation. That's kind of how it got started.

I'll be honest. I didn't know a whole hell of a lot about Virginia Tech. Being an old Midwest boy, I grew up in Big Ten country and Big 8 country. At the same time, I was excited about taking the next step. That's why you get into coaching.

I coached with Frank at Murray State, but I played for him there, too. He actually came on as the defensive coordinator in my junior and senior years. Mike Gottfried was the head coach, and Ron Zook was actually my position coach. Frank came in and was a defensive guy and, obviously, a very good football coach.

He was probably at his best when things were at their worst. When an offense had some success against us, we'd come over to the sideline and he was calm and had a lot of poise. Before he got there, the coaches used to be up in your grill all the time and chewing you out and all that kind of stuff. Frank was a little more analytical as opposed to throwing out all the testosterone and all that.

That's how he is even today. We had a tough time starting out the program here at Tech, and then we had a couple of good runs.

Still, we've had a few times where we weren't quite as good, but there's none of this pointing fingers or firing people or doing this and that. In staff meetings when we thought we were about to get chewed out, that's when he has been at his best.

Now, Ron Zook was the other way around. He was the total opposite of Frank. Ron would get on you and jump around and do some of those kinds of things. That's just how he operated, and it worked for him.

I think you need to have both characteristics. Football is a violent, physical game. You've got to have that edginess or that hyped-up mentality. I played the game, so I understood that, but being on the coaching side of it, you understand your kids need to have that emotional fortitude to get ready to go out there and run into people full-speed. From a coaching standpoint, you still have to be the calm, cool guy to make adjustments and teach your guys to play that way, too.

I'm not sure I've ever reached a point where I felt comfortable with what we've had. That's just the coaching aspect of it for me. You're always trying to stay ahead of the posse, so to speak. I know when we played Nebraska in the Orange Bowl in 1996, we could field 11 on each side of the ball and a handful of other guys on each side of the ball who could compete. After that, we were very thin. In order to compete at the highest level, we really needed to create depth.

The '97 year was a tough year. We went 7–5 that year after graduating some really good players from the '95 and '96 seasons, but once we got going with the '98 and '99 seasons and got our talent back up, I really feel like maybe we started to get it going a little bit.

We went into 2000 after losing eight starters on defense, and wound up winning the Gator Bowl that year. We won 11 games that year, lost one game to Miami. That was the year, especially from a defensive standpoint, we thought maybe we're starting to create some depth. That's when we were able to start plugging some people in when we have an injury or we lose people to graduation to those types of things.

At that point, our recruiting started to change a little bit. We were starting to get the DeAngelo Halls and the Kevin Joneses and people like that. We had rarely been able to get that kind of player before then.

When we first came to Tech, I think we got our schedule changed quite a bit. We kind of used that as a deal where we started to talk about needing to get top-quality players in here and sold that based on the fact we were going to play a top-quality schedule. At the same time, we probably took some kids who were good players, but maybe had some character issues when it was all said and done.

By being placed on three years' probation and being stripped of so many scholarships when we first came in here as a staff, and really being limited on who we could take and still trying to take the best potential guy possible, we might've taken an athlete over a guy with character. Today, you've got be a good-enough athlete, but you've got to have the character aspect, too.

Sometimes that's maybe how you build a program. You've got to have some mercenaries, so to speak, to create a culture of winning. At the same time, there's some risks there involved in terms of the reputation of your program. We overcame that. That's just how it is from my point of view.

I mean, I remember when Coach let the whole defensive staff go except me, and we were pretty good on defense back then. That's what kind of shocked me a little bit. To me, that was an eye-opener and a sign that sometimes you have to do some things—including letting go of guys who are your friends—to build a program.

You know, with what we've done here and how we've built the program, I've always said people are crazy not to want to hire not just me but other people on our staff. We've done it the right way.

In my own personal head coach interviews, the interviews have been good. The Clemson deal for me, I mean, Dabo [Swinney] had a six- or seven-game interview [as an interim coach], and I had a two-hour interview. At Virginia, that job was going to go to Al Groh, and I think I was just kind of an afterthought interview.

After I was done with some of these interviews, I think they already had in mind who they wanted to hire. Maybe they heard some good things about me and wanted to meet me.

I'd love to be a head coach. I have what it takes to lead and do all the things you have to do to be in that position. At the same time, I'm not going to be one of those guys who cries myself to sleep at night and says, "What if?" I probably could've gotten some other jobs, but I've got a good job and I work for a great boss.

I'll be 52 this year, which in my mind is still young, but in some of those circles I'm looked at as an older guy instead of the 40- to 42-year-old who can be there 10 to 15 years. If I'm at a place 10 to 15 years, I'm going to wind up being 65 or 67 years old, so I think some people look at it as my window is closing.

The way I see it, I don't have to take a MAC job unless I have to. I don't have to take a Conference USA job unless I have to, unless it's the right one. I like competing and being at the highest level. That's where I want to be, whether it be as a coordinator, position coach, or a head coach. That's what still excites me and floats my boat. Plus, I know I'm in an awfully unique situation here at Tech.

To me, the Hokie Nation, the Virginia Tech alumni, the football alumni, especially in the 25-plus years I've been in Blacksburg, I think it's a unique group of people. It's a group of people who love their institution. They love the atmosphere around here. Everybody who's left here seems like they've come back here. They're genuine people. That's kind of how I was raised.

I was brought up in a caring family. Family is important to me. Virginia Tech in the big picture is just a big family. The fans love the football program like it's their family. Then, when you really start to look at it, it all starts with Coach Beamer. You know, he played here. He was my coach in college, and we had a lot of success. We had a very close family atmosphere there at Murray State. I was too young to realize that was an atmosphere fostered by the coaching staff, but I do know we had a close-knit group.

When I became a coach with Coach Beamer, we wanted to be a close-knit group, too. Your players have got to be able to trust you and know that you care about them. From a football standpoint, that's one of the things we develop at Virginia Tech—a tremendous trust and a tremendous loyalty among each other.

I think that's one thing we've been able to do here is build a culture, build a family. I think a lot of people preach family, but they don't live it. It's backed up by how you care about the kids. In the big picture, they probably know we care about them, and that's why they play so hard for us.

That's what Coach Beamer has done. I think his growing up in a small town, Virginia Tech's being a college town, and then having success and seeing how the Hokie Nation steamrolled and jumped on board and just bought into this thing helped them feel a part of what he's created.

For the most part, guys on this staff are all approachable guys, we're not ego guys. In my mind, if you ask me what it means to be a Hokie, well, a Hokie is somebody who has passion, tremendous loyalty, and who is a tremendously caring individual. Hopefully, that's reflected in our football program.

Bud Foster played for Coach Frank Beamer on the Murray State team before becoming linebackers coach there. When Beamer got the head coaching job at Virginia Tech in 1987, Foster joined him on the staff. He has been defensive coordinator since 1995, and he won the Broyles Award, given to the nation's top assistant football coach, in 2006.

Hokies in Their Own Words

Ed Wang

Offensive Tackle, 2006–2009

It was a family atmosphere at Virginia Tech, the one thing that stood out and drew me to the school and kept me there. They genuinely cared about all the players, on and off the field. It was something you could sense around the program from the time I got there. Coach Beamer stressed getting your education there, just as your parents stressed it at home when you were growing up.

The one thing that stood out for me with Coach Beamer was the attention to detail. He wanted us to do the little things, get those things right, and the big picture would take care of itself. If there was something he talked about more than anything while I was there, it was taking care of the details, which can lead to accomplishments.

The way they ran the organization over there made the players try and hold themselves to a higher standard. If things had been different and accountability not stressed, players might have gotten

Offensive tackle Ed Wang (77) blocks for Ryan Williams (34) during a 2009 game against East Carolina. Virginia Tech won 16–3. *Photo courtesy of AP Images*

into some trouble there. But we saw the standards set, and that meant staying out of trouble and bearing down on schoolwork.

When a teammate didn't adhere to what the coaches wanted from us, it was like a brother failing. That bothered the whole team because there was a standard there set by Coach Beamer and the players.

Now, we could have fun with Coach Beamer. My favorite part was watching him dance after a win. That was definitely one of my favorite things at Tech. He does a little shimmy in the locker room in front of us. He is good dancer, that's for sure.

Coach Beamer knows football, but his leadership ability was his strong point. He had a great ability to get players to buy into the program and really believe in what he was trying to instill in us and where he was trying to go with the program.

Sometimes you have players who don't really buy in and who really don't get it. I think Coach Beamer did a good job of getting most of the players to buy in to the philosophy.

Coach Newsome was my position coach. I looked up to him a lot. He cared about his players. He would invite us over to his house every Thursday night, and his wife would cook for us. We would just hang out and bond as an offensive line. It meant a lot to us, and he was a big part of our development as players.

The biggest eater? Richard Graham. He was a very impressive eater.

I just had a really good coaching staff around me; that was my biggest strength. They developed me as a player and gave me a lot of guidance for five years. I had some size and other things, but the coaches did a lot to make me a decent player.

They worked on technique and knowing your assignment and being prepared for the game. They did not want you showing up for the game unprepared. The idea was that, when it came game time you were not second-guessing yourself on your feet when you are thinking about what you have to do. They did a good job establishing a game plan for us and how we were going to approach things.

I had pretty good feet and good strength, which helped, but the coaches just got me to another level.

I enjoyed all my teammates, but if I had to pick one as my favorite it would be our tight end Andre Smith. I was pretty close to him; we were not from the same area, but he was the player I was closest to. Dre was playing a game this season while I was in the NFL, and I watched him take a guy on a sweep play and drive him into the ground. I said, "That's Dre, that's what he does."

My most memorable game was the Nebraska game where we hung in there until the last minute. They always say it is not over until it's over and the clock hits :00. That was the case in that game. We caught a break at the very end.

We completed a long pass to get us in position to score; Danny Coates got behind their secondary for this 80-yard play to their 11, or something. Then, on the play where we scored the winning points, Tyrod Taylor had to run around and around before he threw to Dyrell Roberts for the touchdown.

We did a sprint out left on that last play, and Tyrod rolled left, and the next thing I know, my guy backed off me and took off the other way. I stopped and turned around and asked, "What's going on?" That's when I saw Tyrod running the other way.

I was thinking, *Please throw the ball because my man is bearing down on you and going to hit you.* Tyrod was scrambling. I was just saying, *Please, somebody get open.* He threw the ball, Dyrell caught it, and the place went nuts.

I first went to Virginia Tech for a camp, and just from talking to the coaches and players who were over there, it seemed like the best fit for me. It seemed like I was at home. When I went back for another camp, it seemed like it was right for me.

I got recruited by a lot of schools, but I committed my second game of my junior season and asked my coach if he would shut down the recruiting. He told everybody I was not interested in going anywhere but Tech, and then it died down.

I looked a little different with my [Chinese-American] background, but everybody was pretty accepting down there. They loved football players down in southern Virginia. For the most part, everybody just saw a person, not color.

Coach Beamer got things going in the right direction, but I also think we have the best fans in America. I think our fans support us, win or lose, and you can't say that about every program in college football. You couldn't ask for anything better than Hokie Nation. Lane Stadium was a special place. We had some bad times, but they were always there cheering us on.

It means a lot to me to be Hokie. The biggest thing is that it means being a good person. You have to do things the right way, even when people are not looking. We win football games at Virginia Tech, and that instilled a good foundation in me. But the bigger picture is that you treat people with respect and do the right thing.

I wouldn't trade anything for my time at Virginia Tech.

Ed Wang began his career at Virginia Tech as a tight end, but after a redshirt year became a left tackle and a dominant run blocker and pass blocker for the Hokies. In 2009 he was second-team All-ACC. Wang was nicknamed "Godzilla" by his teammates. He was the first Chinese-American to be drafted into the NFL when he was selected in the fifth round of the 2010 draft by the Buffalo Bills. Wang's parents were athletes on the Chinese Olympic team. He grew up in northern Virginia and lives in Ashburn, Virginia. He has a degree in property management. Wang, who has become a celebrity in China, traveled to China in March 2011 to promote the NFL.

Hokies in Their Own Words

BILLY HITE

ASSISTANT COACH, 1978–2010

When I first came to Tech in 1978, I told my wife, Anne, not to get comfortable, don't get to know anybody. In a year or two, I planned to be out of there. Tech wasn't in a conference, and Anne and I had only been married for about six months at that time.

Obviously, our plans changed.

Getting my first full-time job, we were able to buy a house in Blacksburg. That was important to me. I think I paid $49,900 for it. I'd saved enough money through summer jobs and birthday money at the time to be able to put a down payment on a house.

Two years later, that's when the interest rates went up to about 18 percent, so I couldn't leave even if I wanted to go. Well, all of a sudden, we started getting guys in the program like Cyrus Lawrence and Bruce Smith and Tony Paige and Mike Johnson and Derek Carter. Things started rolling at that point in time.

We started winning, and Blacksburg was becoming a special place. Where this place was in that point in time, and where it is now, it's remarkable what Frank Beamer has done with this program. To me, it's one of the top 10 programs in the country with the facilities we have.

It's Coach Beamer, but it has also been the athletics director and the presidents of the university. I thought the neatest thing in the world was when we'd be out there practicing, and Paul Torgersen, the president of the university, would come out and watch practice three times a week.

Of course, when I was first offered the job at Tech, I turned it down. When I was an assistant coach at my alma mater at North

Carolina, Coach [Bill] Dooley offered me a job at Virginia Tech in '78, but I turned it down to stay on Dick Crum's staff at UNC through spring practice.

Virginia Tech was on the quarter system at the time, so they hadn't even started spring practice. I'd already gone through 20 days of spring practice at North Carolina. Coach Dooley told me to just come up and take a look at [Tech].

I drove up, and it was typical Blacksburg weather in the springtime. When I left Chapel Hill, it was 85 degrees and I was in an open-air Jeep. Anne and I drove up. When I left Blacksburg on Sunday, I'd already accepted the job and drove back to Chapel Hill in that open-air Jeep in 40-degree weather. We had to stop in Salem to buy gloves and a stocking hat and everything else.

I talked to Coach Crum the next morning and told him I'd accepted the job at Virginia Tech. I drove back to Blacksburg that morning and went through another 20 days of spring practice with Coach Dooley and his staff.

I started off making $13,900 [at Tech]. Anne was a special ed teacher working with emotionally disturbed children, and she started off at $12,500. Our total income was about $26,000 starting out. What Coach Beamer has done with our salaries since 2000 has been unbelievable, but I can tell you, the first 20 years I worked here, I didn't make any money.

Over all these years, I have fond memories of a lot of running backs who played for me. The most gratifying to me is to hear back from these guys today. I hear back from most of them. It's great to hear how successful they've been in their lives, and knowing that I played a small part in their success is just so gratifying.

I got a really nice letter from Andre Kendrick about two years ago. He didn't leave here on good terms [in 2000]. It was a letter thanking me for being on his side and helping him become the man he is today. That letter meant a lot to me. He was one of the guys that I didn't feel like I reached while he was here.

I tell you what, a lot of these guys helped us win a lot of big ballgames. To me, being here all these years, I still believe the first time we ever beat Miami [in '95] was the biggest game we ever won in this program. That's just my opinion. We couldn't come close to beating Miami ever before that game.

I'll never forget it. We started off that season 0–2. We had a 9:00 PM staff meeting Sunday night. We'd been working all day, grading film and trying to get ready to play Miami the next week while being 0–2. That's when all of us realized we were the luckiest coaches in the world to be working for a guy like Frank Beamer.

He walked in at 9:00. Obviously, we didn't have any team awards to go over because of the way we'd played. He looked at every one of us and said, "Our guys want to win. Put them in the best position you possibly can to win against Miami," and he got up and walked out.

We all just sat there and looked at each other. If I'd have been the head coach, I think I would've fired everybody sitting in that room. We were all in disbelief that that was all he said to us. We went out and beat Miami, and we went on to win 10 straight and beat Texas in the Sugar Bowl.

That's just one of the seasons that stands out to me, but I knew when it was time to walk away from it. Being the longest-tenured assistant coach in the nation last year, I'd just had enough.

When I met with Coach Beamer this winter, and we first started talking about these coaching moves, he said, "If this isn't what you want, then nothing is going to happen." When he told me what he was thinking about, he told me to think about it that night, come back, and we'd talk about it the next day. I took two steps out of his house, stopped, and said to myself, *What the hell do I need to think about?*

Obviously, I have all the same duties that I used to have. At the time of the decision, I was still going to remain as associate head coach, but the NCAA won't allow that [because he was no longer an active position coach on the day-to-day staff]. So we changed the title to special assistant to the head coach and advisor.

It's been 37 years that I've done this job. I've been to 26 bowl games. I've been involved in a national championship game. I've coached almost 400 games here at Virginia Tech alone. I've been to seven BCS games and won four ACC championships—and coached in five ACC championship games—and won three Big East championships. I've had enough. It's time to move on.

I'm still going to be on the sideline in the fall. I'm still going to wear a headset during the ballgame. I just can't coach or recruit. Those are the only two things out of my responsibilities that I'm not doing any longer.

There's only one person who's pissed off about this career move of mine and that's my wife, because she thinks I'm going to be home all the time now. I'm not going to be home all the time. I go to practices and I go to staff meetings and I do sit in occasionally when they're installing or watching film of practice from the day before. I'll go in there for an hour, and when I'm ready to get out of there, I get out of there.

Tony Paige is probably the last person I've talked to about this, but he turned down $1 million to come out of retirement. The Miami Dolphins offered him $1 million to come back and play one more year at the end of his career. I said to him, "How can you turn down one million dollars?" He said, "You told me a long time ago, when you lose your stinger, it's time to get out of it."

With coaching, I'm going to miss that part of it. I'm going to miss the guys like Darren Evans and David Wilson and those kinds of guys, having Ryan Williams and Tony Gregory in my meeting room. With the recruiting part of it, I lost my stinger. At one time, I was a good recruiter, but that part of the business I can't stand now. When you've done it as long as I have, and you're talking about 80 hours a week for 37 years, that's a lot of hours. Except for the players, I have not missed a thing.

With all those years and all those hours behind me, I can honestly say I know being a Hokie means being a winner and being a competitor. Those two things are inside all of us in this program.

After 34 seasons on the coaching staff, Billy Hite moved to an advisory position on the team in 2011. He joined the staff in 1978 under Bill Dooley as a recruiter and then offensive backfield coach. Having coached the running backs from 1980 through 2010, Hite was on the sideline for more Hokies games than any other coach.

BILL DOOLEY, 1978–1986

Bill Dooley is credited with helping the Hokies turn around their football program during the 1980s, but his contributions to Virginia Tech extended beyond the playing field.

Dooley was hired as Virginia Tech's football coach and athletics director in the winter of 1977 after his successful tenure at North Carolina. Under his direction, Virginia Tech's mascot went from Gobblers to Hokies, the HokieBird mascot was introduced, and a new Virginia Tech logo was unveiled.

Using a strong defense and stout running game, Dooley led the Hokies to a 9–2 record in 1983 and 8–4 mark in '84. His best season came in 1986, when the Hokies finished 10–1–1 and defeated

Bill Dooley (center) receives the 1986 Peach Bowl Trophy after his Virginia Tech team defeated N.C. State 25–24, January 2, 1986. The game was Dooley's last as the Hokies' head coach. *Photo courtesy of AP Images*

North Carolina State 25–24 in the Peach Bowl in Atlanta. It was Virginia Tech's first victory in a bowl game.

An effective recruiter, Dooley helped lure star players like running back Cyrus Lawrence, tight end Mike Shaw, defensive tackle Padro Phillips, and offensive lineman Wally Browne to Blacksburg during his tenure.

Dooley left under a cloud of controversy after the 1986 season, compiling a 64–37–1 record in nine seasons.

Hokies in Their Own Words
MICKEY FITZGERALD
FULLBACK/TIGHT END, 1976–1979

Growing up, we had pretty much lived in abject poverty, and the state took us away from my parents because we didn't have a home and were jumping from place to place. There was actually a time when we were homeless in between, so we ended up in an orphanage. When my grandmother died, we had no place to live. We sponsor an orphanage in Atlanta now because I was one of those kids. I know exactly where they're at in life. I know exactly what they're dealing with.

I remember there was a priest at the orphanage in Roanoke, Virginia, who was really good to me and my brother. He was always taking us to ballgames, taking us to the park, taking us to the lake. I'll never forget, even as a snot-nosed kid, I was really candid. We were driving around in that black Volkswagen of his one day, and I said to Father Paul, "Why do you do all these things for us? There's nothing we can do for you." He said, "Oh, there's something you can do for me. One day, you'll do it for somebody else." That made an indelible impact on me. I'll never forget that. I remember seeing the movie, *Pay It Forward*, and I thought, *Man, somebody wrote a script about my life,* because it was exactly what we had endured.

The orphanage we were in was really like an institution, with dormitory-style beds. I remember my younger brother, John, used to cry every night. I used to sneak down and comfort him. I remember having to crawl because if you walked upright, the nuns could see the silhouette. I'd get in bed with him and, golly, every night I did, he urinated on me. I told him, "If you don't quit peeing on me, I'm not going to sleep with you." Living in the orphanage made a huge impact on our lives.

That was really a devastating time for us, because kids will do anything to be with their folks. It didn't matter if we lived in a cardboard box on the side of the road. Money didn't mean anything to us. It was the love for our family. I know what that is like because I was one of those kids. But it was also, unwittingly, the best thing that ever happened to us. We just didn't know it at the time. Kids need structure, and it gave us a chance. It was something I'll never forget.

When we were living in the orphanage, high school and college athletes would come down on Saturdays and spend time with us, and I'll never forget how much that meant to me. It gave us something to look up to. I think what the orphanage did for us more than anything was give us something that we should all be entitled to as human beings, and that was hope.

When we lived in the orphanage, the nuns worked with me a lot on my speech. I was born deaf in my right ear and partially deaf in my left ear. It was a nerve deficit—I had no nerve development in my right ear and only partial development in my left. The whole time I was in grade school, I was in special education because I couldn't talk. They just thought I was slow. In the 1960s they didn't have the technology to ascertain the extent of the deafness. I knew I was deaf in my right ear, but they didn't know how deaf I was in my left ear. If anything, they thought it was better than anybody else's ear. I didn't know until I was 27 that my hearing was so bad, and it was a revelation to me.

It was tough because I was so busy trying to build self-esteem, and I didn't want to concede to my handicap. I realized early on that, in society, if you're not perceived as being someone, you can't get anywhere. No one will listen to you. It's really pretty shallow, if you think about it. I'll never forget when I got to high school. My body was so physically developed, I was a man among boys, and I was chosen one of the top 11 players in the country. I remember asking the coach at my high school, E.C. Glass in Lynchburg, Virginia, "Let me get this straight. All I have to do is knock the hell out of this guy, and everybody is going to love me? They'll read about me in the newspaper and see me on TV, and professors will work with me in the classroom?" I said, "Hey! Who's next?" I was dead serious. It meant a lot to me that I got that opportunity because it was a way out.

We were a powerhouse at E.C. Glass. If I hadn't played there, I would never have been named All-America or all-state. It means everything to play on a winning team and program. I would have gotten some notoriety and attention playing at a smaller high school, but nothing like what I got playing at E.C. Glass.

Being discarded as a youth by society, I knew football had to be a springboard for something else later in life, so I always took school very seriously. To me, in the college ranks, recruiting is the crux of it all. It all begins and ends with recruiting. I remember being recruited, and every school in the country offered me a scholarship. I was the first national recruit to ever sign with Virginia Tech. I remember Coach Jimmy Sharpe used to call me the "cowbell recruit." I didn't understand the analogy at the time. Apparently, they put a cowbell around the neck of the lead cow and want all the other cows to follow. Virginia Tech wanted to keep all the Virginia high school players in the state.

Some of the best high school football was being played in Virginia, and Jimmy Sharpe said if one school could get all those recruits in Virginia, that team could play anybody in the nation competitively. Bill Dooley had built a great program at North Carolina by robbing all the players from Virginia. It was true, because when I was being recruited there, when I saw Joe Montana's first game at quarterback for Notre Dame in Chapel Hill, more than half of North Carolina's roster, if not three-quarters, were Virginians. Maryland and Penn State were doing the same thing. There was no fence around the state of Virginia. One of the state schools needed to build that fence to keep the talent at home.

In the 1970s schools could sign as many recruits as they wanted and then weed them out. Bear Bryant was famous for doing that at Alabama. He would sign 200 or 300 guys and then weed them out. Then the NCAA established scholarship rules to create parity, and those rules are still in place today. It also made it more conducive for programs like Virginia Tech to develop.

I remember when Coach Bryant came to Lynchburg to recruit me. Usually, they sent an assistant coach to see you. But all the coaches on the East Coast came to see me—Joe Paterno at Penn State; Woody Hayes at Ohio State; Bear Bryant; Bobby Bowden at Florida State; and the Dooley brothers, Vince at Georgia, and Bill at North Carolina. I remember on the same day Woody Hayes and Bear Bryant were out there watching my high school team practice. It was wild.

By the end of my senior season of high school, I had pretty much narrowed my college choices down to Virginia Tech, Alabama, and Notre Dame. I never visited Notre Dame. I wasted a trip going to Duke. I don't know why I did that. I remember flying back to Alabama with Coach Bryant on the university's jet. I'll never forget, he drank a 16-ounce glass of Scotch, burped, then fell back in his chair and slept all the way back to Tuscaloosa. I thought, *Wow! I'm with a legend.*

I didn't sign with a college until late April. I remember the night before I signed with Virginia Tech, I remember Coach Danny Ford slept with me in the bed. He'd wake me up about every hour and say, "Where are you going to sign tomorrow? Where are you going to play football?" I had already announced I was going sign in the morning. I told him, "I don't know. I'll tell you in the morning." He'd wake me up an hour later and say, "What are you thinking now?" I told him, "You know what, if you go home and leave me alone and let me sleep, I'll sign with Virginia Tech in the morning." I was kind of leaning that way anyway. They did a great job of recruiting me.

Coach Charley Pell was on Coach Sharpe's staff, and he started recruiting me when I was a high school sophomore. I used to go up and stay with Coach Pell and his family at their house. He was the one who taught me how to water ski. Boy, that took some patience. Once he got me up, I never went down. What a great recruiter he was. To me, he was a man's man and, not having a father figure in my life, he to me was the Marlboro Man—the tough, quiet, silent, wise cowboy whom I admired as a father.

I signed with Virginia Tech and started at tight end as a freshman, which was interesting because we ran the wishbone under Coach Sharpe. Virginia Tech had gone 8–3 in 1975, the year before they signed me. We went 6–5 during my freshman season in 1976. In 1977, during my sophomore season, I was playing both ways. I think I was one of only two players in the country playing both ways at the time. My forte was blocking. Coach Sharpe, who had coached at Alabama, always said that John Hannah and I were the best blockers he had seen on the football field. I always took a lot of pride in that comparison.

The catalyst for the wishbone is that first option on the triple-option. If your first option doesn't warrant respect from the defenses, then your second and third options aren't going to work that efficiently. They needed a big fullback going up the middle who would suck in the defense. That would make it more viable

Mickey Fitzgerald was one of the most versatile and talented players to ever sign with the Hokies. He started at tight end as a freshman at Virginia Tech in 1976 and later played fullback, defensive tackle, and linebacker. Fitzgerald is the only Hokie to run for 100 yards or more in each of his first four starts.

for the second option, which, of course, is the quarterback keeping it; and the third option is when he pitches it. I had never carried the football before in my life. But in midseason, after we had lost five of our first seven games, they switched me to fullback.

I remember we were playing Florida State for homecoming, and I would stay out after practice, and they would keep working me. I wasn't even in Bobby Bowden's scouting report at fullback, so they were shocked. They asked him after the game what he thought about me. He said, "Well, we graded him as the best blocking tight end that we had ever played against. Hell, we had no idea he could carry the ball, too. Dadgum, it surprised us." I ran for 100 yards in each of the last four games that season. The offensive line started calling me the "Incredible Hulk," because they said, "If we don't block and get out of the way, the Hulk is going to run over us, too."

We really struggled during our sophomore season and finished 3–7–1. They fired Coach Sharpe, and it took a long time for them to hire the next coach. I had already told the press I was going to transfer to the University of Alabama and had talked to Coach Bryant. Coach Bryant said, "Come on down here, boy, we've got a place for you." But I ended up staying at Virginia Tech for two reasons: Dr. William Lavery, who was the president at Virginia Tech at the time, and Jimmy Sharpe. Coach Sharpe asked me to stay there, and I could never figure that out. He told me, "Stay here and prove to them that they were wrong about me."

One night during the coaching search, I heard a light knock on my door around midnight. I knew it wasn't a player, and hoped it was a girl, but Dr. Lavery was at my door when I opened it. So I went for a walk with Dr. Lavery, and it was about 19 degrees outside. He told me, "If you leave, whatever we've done to build this program crumbles, and it would set us back light-years." He asked me to allow him the chance to find the new coach who could take the program to where it needed to be. He said, "Will you give me that chance and not leave until then?" I was a very impressionable college kid, and the president of the university was asking me to stay, so I couldn't say no to him. He told me if I went to Alabama, I'd be just another player. But at Virginia Tech, I really had a chance to be the anchor. He told me I needed to do it for him, Virginia Tech, the state of Virginia, my family, and myself.

I loved my grandmother, Nellie Sweeney, and I used to take her out to the parties with me after games. You want to talk about a way to meet women. Granny would always sit on the bench with me during games. When I would score a touchdown, she would come out on the field and give me a high-five. I remember one time Coach Sharpe was lecturing us about discipline on the sideline. He said, "I looked over at the bench one time and Fitzgerald was sitting over there with his entire damn family!"

So I stayed at Virginia Tech, and they ended up hiring Bill Dooley from North Carolina. During the first spring under Dooley, Eddie Ferrel, our assistant team chaplain at the time, told me that Coach Dooley wanted me to report to his office immediately. I thought, *Oh, God,* because "immediately" just didn't sound good. When I walked into Coach Dooley's office, they told me to close the door, which didn't sound good, either. Coach Pat Watson, the offensive line coach, then asked me, "Mickey, how would you like to make $1 million?" In my sophomoric sense of humor, I replied, "Do you guys know of an easy bank?" Their response certainly seemed to be of genuine laughter. But then Coach Watson got real serious and told me that three of his guards had been drafted in the first round of the NFL Draft, and as a result, he had the attention of the pro scouts. He said he guaranteed me I'd go in the first round if I would make the move to guard and give him my remaining two years of eligibility.

I had already played tight end, defensive tackle, linebacker, and finally fullback, and now I was being asked to move to guard after becoming the first running back in Tech history to run for 100 yards in each of his first four starts. Now, the carrot had been changed to being drafted in the first round. Undoubtedly, it was tough for a 20-year-old kid to understand enough to give up the headlines that come with being a running back. I'll tell you, the last person who felt that kind of pressure was buried under the Alamo.

I stayed at fullback and became a blocker in Coach Dooley's I formation offense and didn't carry the ball that much. The last game of my college career, I had a catastrophic knee injury. We were playing at West Virginia on that old turf. I tore every ligament in my right knee. My foot came up and touched my thigh. It tore my meniscus, my PCL, ACL, MCL. You name it, I tore it. My brother, John, carried me off the field. It certainly seems easy to say it now, but I wish I had made the switch to guard, a position where a knee injury of that magnitude is much less likely to happen. I will never forget that tragic and painful moment as my career went down the drain. There were more drugs running through my body than Mick Jagger's to help me deal with the pain. Doctors, trainers, and my own brother said I would never play football again.

In the 1970s, when you tore knee ligaments, you were done. Dr. Rippley, who did my surgery, said it was the worst knee injury he had operated on in 45 years as a surgeon. I said, "Well, what did you do?" He said, "Quite honestly, when I opened your knee up, I sat down and said a prayer because I didn't know what to do." Basically, what he did was cut muscles out of my thigh and threaded my knee with them. My thigh is all cut down the side and looks as though someone actually filleted me. It was the only thing we had. Even today, with surgeries being light-years ahead of where they were then, you still don't come back from that.

It took me two solid years to rehab the knee to the extent to which I could take a handoff. After two years, NFL teams forget about you. After lying out two years, I had to beg for a tryout. I got a tryout with the Atlanta Falcons and led the team in rushing, receiving, and scoring for three preseason games and hadn't played in two years. How determined was I to come back from that kind of surgery? Just a few years before that, I couldn't even walk. I made the Falcons team and played in three games and hurt my knee again. The reason I should have never played football again—and I came back on sheer determination—was that the knee was so loose that it just made it conducive for it to happen again and again and again. I kept getting up off the canvas and getting that thing fixed and doing it all over again. I ended up with seven knee injuries. There was no reason I should have kept playing, but I was doing what I wanted to do at the time.

After I hurt my knee with the Falcons, I went to Europe and bounced around there for about nine months. Every time I went to a city with an English newspaper, I read about this new league in America called the USFL. I went to Europe to get football out of my system. But I kept reading about this new league. I decided football wasn't out of my system and thought the new league would be perfect for me. I had signed with the New York Giants, so the New Jersey Generals had the rights to me. I went to training camp in Orlando and couldn't pass the physical. The Denver franchise of the USFL wanted to pick me up, so I flew to Arizona for training camp. I got cut during training camp there, and Jimmy Sharpe had been hired as an assistant coach with the Memphis Showboats. He called me and said, "I've been waiting for you to become available." I played with the Showboats for two years until the league folded.

George Klein, who was Elvis Presley's best friend, became a good friend of mine while I was playing for the Showboats. We hung out and did a lot of things together. He kept asking me to go see this doctor, John Shea. He would say, "Come on, Mickey, he's the best doctor in the world for this." Every town I'd lived in, everybody always said they had the best doctors, so I was used to it. So I said, "Okay, George." Every now and then, two and three months would go by, and he'd say, "Did you see Shea yet?" So one day he asked me, "Mickey, will you do me a favor?" I said, "Yeah, whatever you want. What do you want me to do?" George said, "No, no, just tell me you will do it." I agreed and he said, "Go see Shea."

I was 27 years old at the time, and I hadn't had my hearing checked since grade school. I had always been told I had an ear infection when I was young and had gone deaf during grade school. It really affected my equilibrium, and I had a hard time walking when I was young. When I played fullback growing up, I couldn't hear the plays or the cadence, I would just watch the ball get snapped and then move. It's the reason I couldn't play tight end in the pros, which was probably my best position for professional longevity, because I couldn't hear the count, nor see the ball from that position. If I was totally deaf, then I would have just played defense.

Well, I was really impressed with Dr. Shea, who had graduated from Harvard Medical School when he was 20. They did some tests on my ears and he told me, "You're deaf." I said, "Boy, doctor, I'm really glad I came here." He told me I'd never been able to hear out of my right ear, and that there was no nerve in the ear. He told me the hearing in my left ear wasn't very good because the nerve in my left ear wasn't fully developed and I had only about 35 percent hearing. I said, "Wow, if that's true doctor, how can I can annunciate the way I do?" He said, "That's a damn good question, but I'm going to give you a better answer. It's because you were never told that you couldn't."

Dr. Shea was dead-on, and I started remembering all the times I was in grade school and special education. I knew I didn't belong there. You just know what you know, and my instincts have been darn good through the years because I had to compensate for so many other things. But I remember having trouble speaking, and I just had to learn how to say words over and over and over. Even today, with our clinic, if I don't say the medical terms over and over and over, I botch them and it's pretty embarrassing professionally. I do it quite a bit because these are words I don't say very often.

After the USFL closed its doors, I went into business in Arizona and was flipping land sometimes two and three times. My partner and I decided I would go to Japan to try and raise money for our venture. While over there, I met Jesse Takamiyama, who was an American from Hawaii and the first foreigner to win a sumo wrestling tournament there. I started training under him and became a sumo wrestler. I met several members of the Japanese mafia, and you could always identify them because they cut off their pinky fingers to show their allegiance. If you messed up, they'd cut off another one of your fingers. So if you ever shook hands with a guy who was missing two or more fingers, you knew you were dealing with a real screw-up!

When I look back on my career at Virginia Tech and everything that has happened since, I've almost had a Forrest Gump–like existence. But I think everything I've done is the result of my being that scared, insecure little boy who was afraid the nuns were going to smack his hands with a ruler. I've always wanted to prove that I belonged, and I wanted to exceed everyone's expectations for me.

Mickey Fitzgerald was named one of the country's best 11 high school football players during his senior season at E.C. Glass High School in Lynchburg, Virginia, in 1975. He started at tight end as a freshman at Virginia Tech in 1976 and later played fullback, defensive tackle, and linebacker. Fitzgerald is the only Virginia Tech player to run for 100 yards or more in each of his first four starts. He suffered a catastrophic knee injury in his last game for the Hokies in 1979 and played parts of four seasons in the NFL and USFL, and was briefly a sumo wrestler in Japan. Fitzgerald is president of Clinical Support Services, a neuro-monitoring firm in Atlanta, and is president of the NFL Alumni, Atlanta Chapter, and founder of Mickey's Rascals Foundation, which provides financial help to underprivileged children in rural areas.

JERRY CLAIBORNE, 1961–1970

When athletics director Frank Moseley went searching for his own replacement as the Hokies' football coach in 1961, he didn't stray from the family tree. Moseley was a disciple of legendary Alabama coach Paul "Bear" Bryant, and he hired one of Bryant's other assistants as his new head coach.

Jerry Claiborne, who worked as Bryant's defensive coordinator and played for him at the University of Kentucky, was hired as Virginia Tech's new coach after the 1960 season. In his third season in 1963, Claiborne guided the Hokies to an 8–2 record and their first Southern Conference championship. He was named Southern Conference Coach of the Year. He also directed Virginia Tech to the Liberty Bowl in 1966 and 1968.

Claiborne left Virginia Tech after the 1970 season with a 61–39–2 record in 10 seasons. He was inducted into the College Football Hall of Fame as a coach in 1999.

Hokies in Their Own Words
TERRY STROCK
WIDE RECEIVER/DEFENSIVE BACK, 1957–1961

I grew up in Hagerstown, Maryland, and my coach there, Mel Henry, had been an outstanding football player at Virginia Tech. He directed me and two of my high school teammates—his son, Pat, and Bloice Davison—to Virginia Tech, and the three of us went to Blacksburg in the fall of 1957.

I played on the freshman team in 1957 and was redshirted in 1958. I'd say there were probably in the neighborhood of 35 to 40 freshman who came in with us in 1957, and I'm not sure if all of them were on scholarship. I played running back and defensive back on the freshman team, and we went 3–2.

I moved up to the varsity in 1959. I started the season against North Carolina State as a starter, but didn't have a good game and was beat out. I probably played in about six or seven of the 10 games that season, mostly as a receiver. I think I caught nine passes that season and had three touchdown catches. We didn't have any spread receivers at the time; everything was just about three backs in the backfield at the same time. So all the catches I had were coming out of the backfield or out of a wing set. Late that season, in a game at West Texas State, I caught the game-winning touchdown with 11 seconds left in our 26–21 victory. It was right at the end of the game.

Terry Strock was a star receiver and defensive back for the Hokies and led the team in scoring as a junior and senior. He was a team captain as a senior in 1961. Strock twice served as an assistant coach at Virginia Tech and became one of the athletic department's lead fund-raisers.

I started all 10 games as a junior in 1960 and had a kickoff return for a touchdown against Virginia as a junior and again as a senior in 1961. The touchdown against Virginia in 1960 was the opening kickoff, and the one in 1961 was the second-half opening kickoff. It was just a matter of picking a hole and then running. I don't think I was touched at all on either one of those runs and got some great blocking. During my junior season, we lost to Clemson 13–7 right at the end of the game when we thought we had the game won.

We lost to Davidson 9–7 near the end of the 1960 season, and I guess that was one of the sore spots in Virginia Tech football history. They were just a partial scholarship type of team and came into Blacksburg and beat us. We actually scored on a screen pass late in the game to go ahead, but it was called back for a holding penalty. That was a bad spot in Virginia Tech history, I guess, as far as getting beat by a team that we should have never been beaten by.

I think that probably cost Coach Frank Moseley his job. He gave up the head coaching position and stayed as athletics director after that season. Coach Moseley was very demanding, kind of a hard-nosed, tough guy, and I understand he was that way as a player. He was a Bear Bryant disciple and coached under Coach Bryant at Maryland and Kentucky before becoming the coach at Virginia Tech.

But I got to know Coach Moseley in a different light when I came back to Virginia Tech as an assistant coach in 1966. When he was a coach, he was very demanding and tough on his players. We practiced hard, and hell, I think sometimes we probably scrimmaged on Thursdays. We did a lot of running. But he was a fair man and was just coaching the way he was brought up as both a player and by the people he coached under.

I played one season of baseball after spring football practice was over in 1959. I played nine baseball games after spring practice was over. The next year, in the spring of 1960, I was allowed to miss spring practice and played the whole season of baseball. After my senior season of football in 1961, I went back out for baseball the following spring, but I had hurt my knee playing football. I tore the knee up again playing baseball and had to have an operation and missed the rest of the season.

After graduating from Virginia Tech in 1962, I taught one year of elementary school in Clifton, Maryland. The next year, I got into high school football coaching in Colonial Heights, Virginia, near Richmond. I was an assistant coach under Bobby Ross in 1963 at Colonial Heights High School. [Ross later was head coach at Maryland and Georgia Tech; was head coach of the San Diego Chargers and Detroit Lions in the NFL; and is currently head coach at Army.] I stayed with Coach Ross for only one year at Colonial Heights and became the head coach at Culpeper High School in Virginia and spent two years there.

In 1966 I went back to Virginia Tech as an assistant coach. Jerry Claiborne had been my head coach during my senior season in 1961, and he brought me back as an assistant coach in the summer of 1966. I worked there for five years until 1970. Coach Claiborne played under Coach Bryant and was kind of the same way as Coach Moseley, but I think he was closer to his players. Coach Moseley was kind of standoffish, I guess, or maybe we put him up on a pedestal. A lot of the guys I've talked to over the years have said they were afraid to go talk to him, as far as going in and sitting down in his office.

Coach Claiborne was more of a guy who was interested in you as a person, not to say that Moseley wasn't, but you were much more receptive to going into his office and sitting down and having a conversation with him about subjects other than football. He was just a very fair man, but still very demanding, not only on the football field but also in getting your degree, your social life, and everything else.

While I spent 23 years with Coach Claiborne as an assistant coach, I got to see the other side of him. We left Virginia Tech after the 1970 season. It was a situation where some of the alumni wanted to make changes. We had two bad years in 1969 and 1970, losing the first five games each season, after we had gone to bowl games in 1966 and 1968. Other than a Sun Bowl appearance in 1947, Virginia Tech had never been to a bowl game. But we had bad starts in two seasons, and the alumni were up in arms. So they called Coach Claiborne in and said if things didn't improve, they were going to make a change.

As I understand it, Coach Claiborne wasn't even under contract, and at one point they told him he could coach at Virginia Tech as long as he wanted to. But he told them right then that they could start looking for a new coach because he would not be back after the 1970 season. We knew by mid-year that we would not be back, and we ended up winning five of the last six games that season and finished 5–6.

After that, I got out of coaching for one year and worked at a bank in Lynchburg, Virginia. I was probably on the job for 10 months and decided that it was not what I wanted to do with my career and got back into coaching. Coach Claiborne became the head coach at the University of Maryland in 1972, and I rejoined him there. We were there for 10 years, through the 1981 season, and then I followed him to Kentucky and spent eight years with him there until he retired after the 1989 season.

In 1990 I went to Georgia Tech and worked with Coach Ross again. In 1990 we shared the UPI national championship with

Colorado, which was one of the thrills of my coaching career. I came back to Virginia Tech with Coach Frank Beamer in 1992 and coached through the 1997 season.

I'd coached Frank when he was a senior at Virginia Tech in 1968, and I remember he was a very hard-nosed, aggressive, tough player. He didn't have great speed but was very smart. He wasn't very talkative. He did more of his leading in the way he played the game, rather than any type of "rah-rah" talking. We had a great secondary that season with Frank Loria, who was an All-American that year, and Ron Davidson, who is in the Virginia Tech Hall of Fame.

I coached six years with Coach Beamer at Virginia Tech until the spring of 1998, when they created a position for me as director of the Monogram Club, or letterman's club. I did that for 18 months until I retired.

Looking at Virginia Tech's growth, I think the toughest part was not being associated with a conference for so long. Virginia Tech left the old Southern Conference after the 1964 season, and from 1965 until 1991, when they joined the Big East conference, you had to have a pretty good football team, a good record, and play a good schedule in order to be ranked and considered for bowl games. Through the late 1970s and 1980s, there weren't as many bowl games as there are now.

I think the biggest change came when we joined the Big East. We had an opportunity to play for conference championships, and when Miami came into the conference, that helped. Since then, the program has really just grown and we've played in bowl games every season since 1993. The quality of the players, the opportunity to play for a conference championship, and the recognition the school has gotten has just grown over and over again throughout the years.

What does it mean to be a Hokie? The name "Hokie," of course, is derived from what used to be known as "the Fighting Gobblers" to the Hokies, which has created an interest in people wanting to know what a Hokie really is. I think it's just a pride in the school, the location, the quality of education, and how we've developed that pride in the athletics program, not just in football, but in all athletics.

Terry Strock was a star receiver and defensive back for the Hokies and led the team in scoring as a junior and senior. He was a team captain as a senior in 1961 and is the only Virginia Tech player since 1950 to return two kickoffs for touchdowns—both came against rival Virginia—including a 96-yarder in a 20–0 victory on October 21, 1961, which was then the longest kickoff return in school history. Following graduation, Strock coached college football for nearly 30 years, including two stints at Virginia Tech, under Coach Jerry Claiborne from 1966 to 1970 and with Frank Beamer, whom Strock coached as a player, from 1992 until 1998. Strock is retired and lives in Blacksburg.

Hokies in Their Own Words

BOB GRIFFITH

LINEMAN, 1963–1967

I GREW UP IN LOUISVILLE, KENTUCKY, and Moon Conde, one of the Virginia Tech assistant coaches, recruited five of us from the Louisville area. Virginia Tech was really the biggest school recruiting me at the time. Some local schools, such as Western Kentucky and Louisville, were recruiting me, but I ended up signing with Virginia Tech. Milt Miller and I ended up making it through five years, but three other guys from Louisville flunked out during our freshman seasons.

I really liked Blacksburg. Even though I'm from a big city, I really liked the mountains, and it was a beautiful area. I liked the coaches and really thought the world of Coach Jerry Claiborne. I came to Virginia Tech in the fall of 1963 and played on the freshman team. We were able to play freshman games, so we weren't really blocking dummies like we were the next season as redshirts. I can remember being fourth-string on the freshman team, and that was a little depressing. I think they signed 69 freshmen that season.

I redshirted in 1964, and spring practice was tough. Football was a lot different then than it is now. Football was tough. Coach Claiborne played under Coach Bear Bryant, and that was his philosophy. He signed a lot of players and ran the weak ones off—the guys left were going to be pretty good players. That's what happened to us. They signed 69 players, and I think 11 of us ended up finishing.

During my redshirt season in 1964, we weren't playing well and had lost two of the first three games. We had a linebacker named Burt Mack Rodgers, who was all-conference and a really good player. He was about 6'3" and 250 pounds. We were practicing one day, and Coach Claiborne was in the tower. Burt Mack was standing around not doing anything. Coach Claiborne came out of the tower, went over, and forearmed him in the mouth. Burt Mack took his helmet off, threw it to the ground, walked off the field, and quit.

We didn't lose another game until Syracuse near the end of the season. We all played well after that incident. He really was just a hard-nosed, great coach who really cared about us off the field. But football wasn't like it is now. Football was tough. Practice was brutal. I talked about quitting a lot of times. Of course, we did have a lot of guys who quit. If you slept on the bottom bunk, you risked getting trampled by guys leaving in the middle of the night.

I started every game in the 1965 season and ended up starting 31 consecutive games at guard. They moved me to center before my senior season. I played defense during the spring of 1965 and was a starting defensive guard. But when fall practice started, they moved me to offense about two weeks before the first game. I was second-team offense and was really disappointed because I had been a starting defensive player. But before the Wake Forest game at the start of the 1965 season, I ended up being a starter. Wake Forest had a really good defense, and I lined up against a really fast defensive lineman. But it was hot that day and he ended up getting tired, so I had a pretty good game. I kept my job and kept it for three more years. We beat Wake Forest 12–3 in the Harvest Bowl in Roanoke and then beat Richmond, William & Mary, and George Washington.

We were 4–0 going into the Vanderbilt game, and I really remember that game well because I didn't play very well at all. It was my worst game as a college football player. Coach Claiborne singled me out during film session, and it really embarrassed me. I swore to myself that that would never happen to me again, and luckily it didn't. I really didn't play well at all at Vanderbilt. We lost 21–10.

They dedicated the new stadium at Virginia Tech when we played Virginia, and we won 22–14. Then we went down to Florida State and lost 7–6 after we missed an extra point. We ended up losing two of our last four games and finished 7–3.

We opened the 1966 season at Tulane, and we practiced hard. But we were practicing up in Blacksburg where it was cool. When we got to New Orleans, we took our first drive, and after that, everybody was gone and couldn't get it going because of the heat and humidity. We just never got anything going and lost 13–0. We blew out George Washington and then tied West Virginia at home, 13–13. West Virginia had a defensive back named John Mallory, who ended up playing for the Atlanta Falcons. I remember we were driving on our last drive to kick a field goal to win the game. Back then, they taught you to block downfield and roll at their ankles and all of that stuff. He ended up spitting in my face. I wanted to jump up and punch him, but I knew if I did, that it would take us out of field goal range, so I didn't do anything. We missed the field goal and ended up in a tie.

A year later, we played at West Virginia, and I still haven't forgotten it. Mallory was returning punts, and I was covering punts. He gave one of those fake fair-catch signals, like they do at the 10-yard line, and then kind of jogged off. I came from about 50 yards away and hit him right under the chin. The whistle hadn't blown; it was a clean hit. The funny thing about that was about three years later, I was at a party in Atlanta and ran into Wayne McDuffie and a bunch of guys from Florida State. They started talking about the "No. 61 punt return." Florida State had watched our film from the West Virginia game and saw that lick and thought it was really a cheap shot. So they had a punt return just for me, where everybody on their team hit me. They thought it was really funny. They were laughing, and I said, "Yeah, I was No. 61."

I remember that play because I had moved to tackle when our tackle had gotten hurt. When we covered the punt, I moved out to tackle. I got hit a bunch of times, and they were still hitting me out of bounds. I went back to the sideline and said, "Man, these tackles catch hell on punt returns. I'm going back to guard."

Bob Griffith started 31 consecutive games on the offensive line for the Hokies from 1965 to 1967, and was cocaptain with defensive back Frank Loria of the 1967 team that finished 7–3.

We played at Kentucky in the fourth game of the 1966 season, and I remember it was really special. We were ahead late in the game. I was standing on the sideline, and they were driving. We stopped them and won 7–0. Those of us on the team who were from Kentucky really wanted to beat them because they had never recruited us, or we probably would have gone to our home university. It was really nice to beat them. As freshmen, we played Tennessee and got beat something like 60–0. The same season, Kentucky beat Tennessee 76–0. So to come back and beat Kentucky was really big.

We beat Vanderbilt 21–6 in the Tobacco Bowl in Richmond and then won at Virginia 24–7. We were 4-1-1 when we played Florida State at home. I remember late in the game, it was fourth-and-four inches to go, and they ended up getting three. We had a couple of really big goal-line stands in that game. I remember our punter, Gene Fisher, punted the ball back over his head. He had fooled around in practice kicking it back over his head. We kicked off to them one time and our kicker missed the ball, but it popped up about 10 yards down the field and we recovered it for an onside kick. We ended up beating Florida State 23–21 in a really good game.

We beat Wake Forest and William & Mary in two really tough games and then finished the season against VMI. We were just killing them, and most of the starters were out of the game by the second quarter. But we only had one extra-point team, so we had to keep going back in for the extra points. On the 70th point of the game, I got thrown out of the game. They had a linebacker who jumped early and jumped on our center's hands with his cleats. I was playing guard and punched him. Coach Claiborne was a little upset about that. We ended up winning 70–12.

We played Miami in the Liberty Bowl after the 1966 season. It was a cold day in Memphis. I'll never forget playing against Ted Hendricks. Right before halftime, the official came up and had a face mask in about 15 pieces in his hands. He said, "Who does this belong to?" It was our quarterback's face mask after Hendricks had just killed him. I remember we had a penalty on a blocked punt for roughing the kicker, and they got the ball back and scored and scored again. We ended up losing 14–7. But it was a great year, and we had a really good team. We got a bowl bid against a really good Miami team.

I was cocaptain with Frank Loria during my senior season in 1967. We started 7–0 that season and beat Tampa and William & Mary in the first two games. Then we played at Kansas State in the third game, and I never really knew why we went all the way out to Manhattan, Kansas, to play a game. It was a tough game, but we ended up winning in the end 15–3. It was a long trip. We came back home and beat Villanova 3–0, and I'll never forget the end of that game. We were winning 3–0, and they were driving for a field goal to tie the game. The field-goal attempt hit off the crossbar, and Loria caught it and started running down the sideline. A Villanova coach came off the sideline and tackled him, and a big brawl ensued.

We came back and got another satisfying win at Kentucky and beat Richmond the following week. Then we went back to West Virginia, and along with getting even with the guy who spit in my face, there was another funny story from that game. I was on the kickoff receiving team, and they had a one-armed guy who covered kickoffs. He weighed about 240 pounds, but he didn't play because he only had one arm, and I guess he couldn't tackle very well. He was sort of a wedge buster. On the first kickoff, he was my man. Usually on kickoffs, you just hoped you got a piece of the guy. They came down fast and put a move on you, and you just tried to scrape them off. But this guy just lowered his head and ran right over me. He didn't make the tackle, but, man, he clocked me. The next kickoff, we were turned the other way, and I didn't have the guy. But he came from across the field and hit me again. I said, "Man, this guy is after me for some reason." So on the third kickoff, Damon Dedo was lined up on the guy, and I said, "You better watch out for the guy." Sure enough, he hit him and turned Dedo's helmet around, and he was looking out the ear hole, saying, "Who is that guy?" But we played really well and won 20–7.

We went back to Blacksburg and were undefeated and getting ready to play a really big game against Miami. We couldn't move the ball at all against Miami. We didn't have a chance. We hardly even scratched. Loria returned a punt to keep us in the ballgame, but we ended up losing 14–7. We had to go to Florida State the next week and really weren't mentally prepared to play. Florida State was really good and had Ron Sellers, and he caught a bunch of balls. I was on the kickoff return team, and they line-drived one at me, and it hit me right in the stomach. I was playing center at the time, and it felt like I ran for 50 yards, but it was only four. So I averaged four yards during my college career.

My last college football game still haunts me to this day. Being a senior captain and not getting the team ready to play VMI just still haunts me. It was basically the same VMI team we beat 70–12 the season before. It was just one of those games that wasn't meant to be, I guess. I remember watching film of the game—I was covering punts and just fell down. Coach Claiborne asked me why I fell down, and I said, "I don't know." It just wasn't meant to be. We just weren't ready to play. You've got to give them all the credit in the world. One of their linebackers broke his neck making a tackle. That's kind of the way they played—if it takes breaking my neck to stop you, so be it. It cost us another bowl bid. I think we were going to go back to the Liberty Bowl if we had beaten VMI.

If you played for Coach Claiborne, you loved him. If you didn't, you hated him. I ended up loving him. Being a football player, I got a college degree because of him. He stayed on my butt for five years. I finally realized during my fifth year that football was over, and I figured out I better start doing something in the classroom.

He stayed on me and stayed on me. The only reason I got a degree was because of him.

During two-a-days before my senior season, I got my "Greetings from the President" letter and got drafted into the Army. I said, "Well, I'm not even going to practice because I got drafted." Word got back to Coach Claiborne. He made a phone call and I was out of the draft. The same thing happened during my junior season. I got a letter from the school saying I'd flunked out. Coach Claiborne picked up the phone, and they put me on probation and gave me one more chance.

I ended up getting drafted two weeks after my senior season and went into the Army and spent one year in Vietnam. Coach Claiborne and Moon Conde wrote to me when I was in Vietnam, and I still remember their letters. After coming back from Vietnam in 1970, I moved to Georgia and got a high school coaching job. I coached high school football for more than 25 years.

What does it mean to be a Hokie? It's something I'm very proud of because of the era in which we played college football. Being a Hokie encompasses a lot of things, as far as being a Virginia Tech student. But when I think of being a Hokie, I think of the football we played. It was just so tough and demanding. When you survived, you were really proud of it. I think it was just the significance of surviving the years there. Even though I had a chance to get killed in Vietnam, it wasn't as physically tough as playing college football back then.

Bob Griffith started 31 consecutive games on the offensive line for the Hokies from 1965 to 1967. He was cocaptain with defensive back Frank Loria of the 1967 team that finished 7–3. After Griffith was drafted into the Army and served one tour in Vietnam in 1970, he moved to Georgia and became a successful high school football coach. Griffith retired in

April after working as the Georgia Tech football program's director of high school relations. He lives in Statesboro, Georgia.

Hokies in Their Own Words
MILT MILLER
Offensive Lineman, 1963–1967

I kind of fell in love with the guy who was recruiting me for Virginia Tech. Coach Moon Conde had played for Bear Bryant at the University of Kentucky, as did Coach Jerry Claiborne, and I was playing at Seneca High School in Louisville. Seneca High was a relatively new program, and we didn't even have a winning record until my senior season. But Virginia Tech was going into Kentucky and getting some players who were willing to leave the state. It wasn't any type of high-profile recruiting in my case. I wasn't a highly recruited athlete, but I just loved to play football. I was getting some interest from schools such as Eastern Kentucky and Western Kentucky, but I signed the scholarship with Virginia Tech before I even visited the campus in Blacksburg.

I was on the freshman team at Virginia Tech in 1963, and we played about four games and went 3–1. The varsity team was 8–2 in 1963 and won the Southern Conference championship, the only time the school won the league title outright. Then they decided to redshirt a bunch of us in 1964, and all we did was practice. We just practiced a lot and played the extra Monday "bowl" games, which was what we called them. We played wherever they needed a body in practice that season.

There wasn't limited recruiting back then, so they signed about 65 of us as freshmen in 1963. Coach Claiborne had been at the now-famous Junction, Texas, camp with Coach Bear Bryant in 1954. Well, in 1964 things weren't a whole lot different at Virginia Tech. Coach Claiborne learned a lot of things from Coach Bryant, and he knew how to use them. At the end, by our senior seasons, only 14 of us were still on the team: Bob Griffith, Tommy Groom, Rusty Fife, Tommy Francisco, Jud Bigelow, Dave Farmer, Andy Bowling, Pete Wrenn, Tommy Stafford, Richard Mollo, Sal Garcia, Donnie Bruce, and Sands Woody.

I didn't play much as a sophomore in 1965, which was the first year they really went to two platoons with an offense and defense. The guys who could run went to the defensive side; the guys who couldn't run that fast went to the offensive line. I went to the offensive line. I alternated on the offensive line as a redshirt junior in 1966, playing center and guard. Scott Dawson was playing center, and Dave Farmer and Bob Griffith, my roommate from Louisville, were the guards. I played guard and center and even played some tackle.

The first game of the 1966 season, we played at Tulane, and I'll never forget that Dickie Longerbeam, one of our running backs, broke his neck and missed the rest of the season. He came back and had two good seasons. I remember that Tulane had a good quarterback named Bobby Duhon, who hurt us really, really badly in that game, and we lost 13–0 in New Orleans. We beat George Washington 49–0 the following week, and Frankie Loria had an 80-yard punt return. Then we played at West Virginia, and I'll never forget Loria having some big licks on Garrett Ford, their big running back, and knocking him out of the ballgame.

We went home to play at the University of Kentucky early that season, and that was really a thrill for the guys who had come to Virginia Tech from Kentucky. I remember we were fourth-and-1 late in the game, and Tommy Francisco stuck it, and we won 7–0.

Milt Miller was a starting offensive lineman for the Hokies in 1966 and 1967 and later became one of the most successful high school coaches in Georgia, winning state championships at two schools.

That was a special game for the Kentucky guys because we all had friends playing at Kentucky, and a couple of Virginia Tech coaches had left from Coach Claiborne's staff to go back there. It was just a special night for us.

That Kentucky game really seemed to get us on a roll, winning at the end like that. We ended up winning our last seven games that season, beating Virginia in Charlottesville 24–7, and then beating Florida State 23–21 in Blacksburg. Florida State had Ron Sellers, who was just a great player and gave us all kinds of problems. [Sellers caught 13 passes in that game, which still ranks as the second-most in a game by a Virginia Tech opponent.] It was one of the first games we played on television, and it was just a great ballgame.

We ended up beating Virginia Military Institute 70–12 in the last game, which would later come back to haunt us, and then played Miami in the Liberty Bowl at the end of the 1966 season. It was Virginia Tech's first bowl game in a while. I remember it was an awfully cold day in Memphis. Of course, Miami had the "Mad Stork," Ted Hendricks, out there playing at end, and he was very tough to handle. We were moving the football really well and had the lead early in the game, 7–0, after Jimmy Richards blocked a punt to set up a touchdown. We blocked another punt in the third quarter, but they called us for roughing the punter, and Miami scored a touchdown to tie the game. I remember that was the turning point of the game. [The Hurricanes won the game 14–7 when fullback Doug McGee scored on a one-yard run on fourth down with about eight minutes to play.]

We won our first seven games in the 1967 season, and I think we started looking ahead to a bowl game. We had gone over to West Virginia and beat them 20–7, and then had Miami coming to Blacksburg. After we played them so close in the Liberty Bowl the previous season, we just knew there was no way they were going to beat us in Blacksburg. It was a revenge game for us from the Liberty Bowl, but then they beat us on a flea flicker late in the game. We lost to Miami, and the score again was 14–7. That loss really just deflated the whole team. We had to go back down to Tallahassee and play Florida State, and they were looking for revenge after we'd beaten them in Blacksburg the season before. Sellers just ran wild down there and had a record-setting night. They blew us out 38–15.

Well, then we had an open week before playing Virginia Military Institute, and we'd beaten them so badly the year before that we just didn't get ready to play. They beat our tails down there in Roanoke, 12–10. I'll never forget that feeling at the end. I know that one game made me a better coach for the rest of my life. I always knew that no matter who you were playing, if you weren't ready to play, you were going to get your rears beat. That's something I'll never forget about that game.

I graduated from Virginia Tech in December 1967, which was my fifth year, and I went into the Army the following February for an ROTC commitment. I only spent six months in the Army and was discharged that August because of an elbow problem. So I went right into coaching football back in Louisville. I coached five seasons in Kentucky and then moved to Georgia. I was an assistant for Bob Griffith, my teammate and roommate at Virginia Tech, and worked with him for three years. I got the head coaching job at Worth County High School in Sylvester, Georgia, in 1977 and stayed there 15 years. I went to Lowndes County High in Valdosta, Georgia, in 1992 and coached for 10 seasons until I retired.

I took a lot of what I learned from Coach Claiborne and used it in coaching. There wasn't a finer, more straight-as-an-arrow individual. He practiced what he preached more than anybody I've ever been around in my life. He really had a genuine care for his players. You've got to be yourself when you're a coach, you can't copy anybody, but you can take things from others you've been associated with and incorporate them into your own style. I know whenever I had a tough decision to make about how to handle a player, I always thought, *Well, what would Coach Claiborne do?* I always knew he would be hard but fair.

What does it mean to be a Hokie? I think Coach Moon Conde might have put it best in a letter he wrote to me in August 1989. He probably exemplified the Hokies spirit more than anyone else I knew.

In the letter, Coach Conde kind of exemplified our whole group when he wrote, "You young men are family with each other and always will be because of what you accomplished while you were together. The hours, the days, the months, and the years that you all put in together in school and football practice produced winners at Virginia Tech. Look around you, all your teammates are doing okay. That's because down deep inside they wanted to play, they wanted to graduate, and they had an intangible quality of togetherness. You young men helped and looked after each other, and the results of brotherhood were winning and graduating. Hell, you had the finest club and fraternity on campus, and it didn't even have a name."

Milt Miller was an offensive lineman for the Hokies in 1966 and 1967. He was one of the most successful high school coaches in Georgia history, winning a state title at Worth County High in 1987 and Lowndes County High in 1999. Miller lives with his wife in Lake Park, Georgia, and is a salesman for an athletic equipment manufacturer.

FRANK MOSELEY, 1951–1960

Frank Moseley inherited Virginia Tech football at one of its lowest points—after the Hokies went 1–25–3 from 1948 to 1950 under former coach Robert McNeish.

A former teammate and assistant coach of legendary University of Alabama coach Paul "Bear" Bryant, it didn't take Moseley long to transform the Hokies into winners. Moseley preached toughness and conditioning, and many of his players could not handle his rigorous program.

After consecutive losing seasons in 1951 and '52, the Hokies finished 5–5 in 1953. In 1954 Moseley led the Hokies to an 8–0–1 record. Moseley retired from coaching after the 1960 season, turning over the program to another Bryant assistant, Jerry Claiborne. Moseley had a 54–42–4 record in 10 seasons as Tech's coach. He remained Virginia Tech's athletics director until his retirement in 1977.

Moseley's most significant contribution was establishing the Virginia Tech Student Aid Foundation, which helped modernize the school's athletics department and facilities. He also spearheaded the school's drive to build Lane Stadium.

Hokies in Their Own Words

BUZZ NUTTER

OFFENSIVE LINEMAN, 1949–1952

I was recruited by West Virginia and I made one visit to the University of Kentucky, but Coach Bear Bryant wasn't interested in a guy my size playing center. I was supposed to go to Marshall University because I was from Huntington, West Virginia, and of course, the Marshall campus was right there. I had practiced with Marshall its whole spring practice season when I was in high school during my senior year. My high school, Vinson High School, had won the first Class B state championship in West Virginia history my senior season in 1948, and Marshall was recruiting a few of the players off that team.

But then I visited Virginia Tech. I liked the place and I wanted to get away from home, so I decided right after I played in the high school all-star games that I didn't want to stay at home. The coach at Marshall, Cam Henderson, had told me he was going to coach about one more year and then retire. He was the coach for football, basketball, and baseball at Marshall and was about 65 years old. So I decided to go to Virginia Tech, and that's where I went.

Robert McNeish was the coach at Virginia Tech at the time, and he was from West Point. I had to play on the freshman team my first year because that was the NCAA rule. Allan Learned was the freshman team coach my first season in 1949, and we had about 26 players, I guess, on scholarship. The next year in 1950, we all went to the varsity as sophomores. We stunk. We were terrible.

McNeish just didn't have the players to compete with the teams on our schedule. We were in the Southern Conference and Virginia, George Washington, William & Mary, Richmond, and Washington & Lee all had good football programs back then.

We went to William & Mary during my sophomore season in 1950, and we got beat 54–0. We didn't win a single game, and McNeish quit or was fired after about the fourth game. Learned took over as coach and finished the season, but we weren't any better after he took over. We went to Maryland for our last game in 1950, and it was a complete disaster. We got beat 63–7. Maryland had about five All-Americans. We had no business playing Maryland, but they were on the schedule.

After the season, Virginia Tech brought in Frank Moseley as coach, and he had coached for Bear Bryant at Kentucky. Moseley did everything just like Bear Bryant did. I'm sure you've seen the movie, *Junction Boys*, when Bryant took his teams to Texas A&M and all that stuff. It was just like that at Virginia Tech when Moseley took over as coach. By the time Moseley got to Virginia Tech, there were probably only 16 of the players from my freshman class left on the team, and to get right down to the honest truth, Moseley started to run everybody off the team.

Moseley only wanted the players that he recruited there, so he started running off all the people who were already there before him. He wanted his recruits to be players, and the rest of us, well, we were just on the team. Moseley didn't take our scholarships away. Instead, when we'd come out for practice, he'd be standing there and he'd say, "Start running." When practice was over, we'd still be running. Guys would do that for about three days and then would disappear.

Back then, you were allowed about 40 days of spring practice. Before Moseley's first season at Virginia Tech in 1951, when I was a junior, we had practiced for about two weeks in the spring. Then Moseley told the local newspaper that we were going to start spring practice the following Monday. It was pretty rough.

Moseley catered to the guys he recruited, so we didn't get along too well. One time, during the spring of his first year, we ended spring practice with an intrasquad game. He put all of his recruits on one team and all of the returning players on the other team. He gave his No. 1 assistant the team with his recruits, and our team ended up beating the hell out of them. It was no contest. After the game, Moseley got on me, and I told him, "Well, you can't run me off. You can kick me out, if that's your intent, and take my scholarship. But don't try to run me off. I can stay on that field much longer than you can." That's the way it ended up.

I was in the ROTC at Virginia Tech, but I didn't like it at all. In the ROTC, you had demerits, and anytime you got demerits you had to march them off. I probably set a record in one quarter for demerits, so I think the military was glad to get rid of me. I was glad to get out of it. I didn't like the way things were going in football, either.

There were only about 3,500 students at Virginia Tech when I went to school there. Most of the male students were either returning veterans or in the cadet corps. Probably about 2,000 students were in the cadet corps, so the only civilian students were a few football players. If you were not a veteran or a member of the cadet corps, you could not live on campus. Well, when I got out of the ROTC, I didn't have the money to pay for off-campus housing, so they gave me a room in the gymnasium. It was a small room in the basement of the old War Memorial Gymnasium. It was nice. I had my own room and my own swimming pool and all of that stuff. It was adequate.

Well, after the first quarter of my junior year in 1951, Cam Henderson, the coach at Marshall, retired from football and stayed on as the basketball and baseball coach. The guy who was supposed to get the Marshall football job, Roy Short, who was the only assistant coach they had and had been there for about 15 years, had recruited me and a couple of other guys from Huntington. If I had gone to Marshall from the beginning, I probably would have been the starting center as a freshman because Marshall was in a different NCAA class, and freshmen could play on the varsity team.

Well, Short came to our houses during the winter break and talked to all of us about coming to Marshall when he got the job.

I told him I would think about it, but went back to Virginia Tech and re-enrolled for second semester. So Short said, "When I get the job, I'll be down at Virginia Tech to pick you up." I came down from my dorm room one morning that spring, and Short was sitting outside. One kid went with him, but I told him I would stay at Virginia Tech for the rest of the year, anyway. In the end, Short did not get that job. So I guess it was a good thing I decided to stay at Virginia Tech.

By my senior year at Virginia Tech, relations between Moseley and me weren't as bad as they had been. Before my senior year, he asked me what I wanted. I said, "Well, I'm not going to finish school in four years. I need an extra quarter, and all I ask is that you let me keep my scholarship until I finish." He said, "Yes, if you do what you're supposed to do and all of that, you're welcome to come back to school."

I was drafted in the 12th round by the Washington Redskins in 1953, and I was very surprised to get drafted because we never had a winning record when I was at Virginia Tech. I remember they sent me a contract for $3,500 to play 12 games and six exhibition games. You had to buy your own shoes, but, of course, the colleges back then let you keep your own shoes when you left. Anyway, I told Moseley about the contract, and he said, "Geez, since you're a draft choice, I would think you could get at least $4,000." I told the Redskins I couldn't sign for $3,500, and they gave me $4,000.

I went to training camp with the Redskins in the summer of 1953. Alex Webster and I were the last players cut. We were 34 and 35 on a 33-man roster. George Marshall owned the team, and if you weren't an All-American, you didn't get to play anyway. You got to run under kickoffs and things like that. In six exhibition games, I probably got in the game for five plays as a linebacker.

Buzz Nutter, a center and linebacker at Virginia Tech from 1949 to 1952, was the first Hokies player drafted by an NFL team when he was selected in the 12th round by the Washington Redskins in 1953. Nutter was cut by the Redskins as a rookie but signed with the Baltimore Colts two years later and was their starting center on NFL championship teams in 1958 and 1959.

When we got cut, we had to go down and meet with Mr. Marshall to sign a contract. If you signed the contract, they owned you. I told Mr. Marshall that I was going to play somewhere, but I was not going to play in Washington because I felt that I should have made the team.

I went back to school for one semester and finished, got married, and went to work. Then Weeb Eubank, who had been an assistant under Paul Brown in Cleveland, got the Baltimore job in 1954. Eubank had been in charge of Cleveland's draft, and he brought in every free agent in the country who had been on Cleveland's draft board, and I was one of them.

I just got lucky with the Baltimore Colts. Tom Cosgrove, who had been an All-American at Maryland, was supposed to be the starting center. I went as a linebacker. During the first exhibition game, Cosgrove hurt his ankle, and I was the only other center we had. So I went in as center and stayed there for the next eight years. George Preas, who had played with me at Virginia Tech, was our right tackle, and he was a very good football player. He never got much publicity or anything like that, but he was a very good player.

My first year with the Colts, we won three games. But four years later, we won the NFL championship game. [The Colts beat the New York Giants 23–17 for the 1958 NFL championship, in a game that is still called "The Greatest Game Ever Played" by football historians. Nutter, the team's center, had a key block on fullback Alan Ameche's winning one-yard touchdown dive in overtime, the first sudden-death victory in NFL history.]

People still ask me about the 1958 game and have for almost 50 years now. I tell them, "That's the game that made the NFL," and there's no doubt that it was. Back then, television wasn't that great, and baseball was the sport of America. But after that 1958 game, the NFL took over and has been in control ever since. We were much better than the Giants and should have beaten them in regulation. They still call it the greatest game ever played, and it was.

Looking back on my days at Virginia Tech, as hard as it was to play for him, I believe Frank Moseley was the coach who really turned Virginia Tech around. I think Moseley is the reason Virginia Tech is where it is today. For a long time, Virginia Tech had been pretty bad in terms of football. Moseley coached for about 10 years and then brought in Jerry Claiborne, another one of Bear Bryant's assistants. Between the two of them, they really turned Virginia Tech into a good football team. Moseley got the new stadium built, and he got the fieldhouse built. Before that, the facilities weren't that good. But it's a great school and a beautiful campus, and it was beautiful back then.

> *Buzz Nutter, a center and linebacker at Virginia Tech from 1949 to 1952, was the first Hokies player drafted by an NFL team when he was selected in the 12th round by the Washington Redskins in 1953. Nutter was cut by the Redskins as a rookie, but signed with the Baltimore Colts two years later and was their starting center on NFL championship teams in 1958 and 1959. Nutter still owns a beverage distributing company with his two sons and lives in La Plata, Maryland.*

Hokies in Their Own Words

HILMER OLSON

Lineman, 1950, 1954–1956

I actually started classes at Virginia Tech in 1950, was on the football team for one season as a freshman, and then went into the military service. Once I got out of the service in 1954, I went back to school. My teammates always called me "Swede" because my grandparents were immigrants from Sweden. I grew up in a tiny

Hilmer "Swede" Olson's Virginia Tech career was interrupted when he was drafted by the military. He came back to school and was a member of Virginia Tech's 1954 team that finished 8–0–1 and ranked No. 16 in the country.

mountain town in Pennsylvania, and my father was an electrician and a bus driver, and my mother was a homemaker.

One of the Virginia Tech coaches, George Tebow, was from a town about five miles from my hometown of Lansford, Pennsylvania. I guess that was one of the ways Virginia Tech first found out about me. I was being recruited by Syracuse, Penn State, Virginia, Rutgers, George Washington, and North Carolina State. Somewhere in the neighborhood of 20 schools were recruiting me. But I visited Virginia Tech and just fell in love with the campus. I was about ready to go and play football at George Washington, but then I went and visited Virginia Tech and changed my mind when I saw it. Virginia Tech had the curriculum I was interested in; I wanted to study education and become a shop teacher.

When I got to Virginia Tech in 1950, we had a really, really good freshman team. We went undefeated that first season, winning five or six games. But the varsity team didn't win a game that season and, to be honest, we seemed to get the best of them in practices, so I thought we had the chance to turn things around once my freshman class got to the varsity.

I really thought things would turn around once Coach Frank Moseley got there in the spring of 1951. It was pretty clear very early that you either wanted to play his way, or that was it. Put it this way: he separated the men from the boys. You could sure tell that he had coached for Bear Bryant at Kentucky. He was tough and expected nothing but dedication and discipline from his players. It was his way or the highway.

Well, after the third quarter of my freshman season, I got drafted into the military. The government sent a letter to my mother's home in Pennsylvania right after I got out of school in June 1951. I got the letter and figured it was my time to go. My grades during the first year weren't that good, and the Korean War was going on at the time. My grades weren't good enough to where I could stay deferred from serving in the military. If your grades were up, you could stay in school.

I was a pretty good athlete in high school, and it was pretty easy when you were an athlete as far as going to classes and getting grades. I got to Virginia Tech and figured things would be the same way, but they weren't the same in college, especially at Virginia Tech back then. No matter what sport you played or how good you were, you made your grades or you weren't going to stay there.

Going to class was one thing Mr. Moseley made sure you did. If you didn't go to class, he wasn't going to put up with it. So once I found out I wasn't going back to school, I called Coach Moseley and told him I was going into the service. He told me to do the best I could and to stay safe. I got drafted and made my mind up that I wasn't going to join the Army because I had two good friends from high school who got drafted and they had been killed over in Korea while they were in the Army. So I wasn't going to do that and entered the Air Force instead.

I went to a weather school and was supposed to be a weather observer, but when I got overseas, I was put on temporary duty at the gymnasium in Germany. I liked basketball and played football in the service, so they let me run the gymnasium while I was overseas. I got to Germany in June 1951 and stayed there for about 14 or 15 months.

I only spent two years in the Air Force and got out when my father died in 1953. My mother had three small children still living at home, so I got out of the service in September 1953 and worked for General Electric for a while. But I thought that job wasn't for me, so I put a call into Coach Moseley and asked him if he thought it was possible for me to come back to school.

Coach Moseley told me to come on back to Virginia Tech, and I made it down there in time for spring practice in 1954. When I got back to Blacksburg, there was another player, Jim Randall, who had started school with me in 1950 and had gone to the service and come back. Coach Moseley always treated us like old men and wanted us to take care of the younger boys. We had a few years on them in age, and he thought we could look out for them. All of us were pretty close, and there weren't any players whom I can remember not getting along with.

When I first got to Virginia Tech in 1950, I had played running back. But while I was in the Air Force, I put on a great deal of weight, so Moseley put me on the offensive line and at linebacker. I played guard and center both that first season, but we had Billy Kerfoot at guard, Jack Prater at center, and Jim Locke and George Preas at tackle, so it was a pretty tough first team to break into. I didn't play at all in any games that first season. I had come back to school as a sophomore, and we were 8–0–1 my first season back in 1954. I remember we tied William & Mary 7–7 on a cold, blowy, snowy day in Blacksburg.

As a junior in 1955, I played guard and linebacker and got into some games and played both ways. We went 6–3–1 and played the first four games on the road. We lost at Wake Forest in the first game, but then won at Pennsylvania, William & Mary, and Florida State. We tied Richmond at home in the fifth game, and our quarterback, Johnny Dean, broke his leg in the ballgame. Billy Cranwell took over and alternated with Jimmy Lugar. We still beat Virginia 17–13 in Victory Stadium in Roanoke the following game.

We always played Virginia and VMI in Roanoke. I think Victory Stadium was a little bigger than our stadium in Blacksburg at the time, and there was a little more pageantry involved when you played a game in Roanoke, rather than on campus. Of course, it's not that way anymore. We beat Virginia all three seasons I was at Virginia Tech, so I've still got bragging rights today.

After Dean got hurt in 1955, we lost two of our next three games but then beat North Carolina State and Virginia Military

Institute in the last two games. During the Florida State game, somebody came running from about 10 yards away and knocked me on my butt pretty good while I was centering the football. That 1955 Florida State team had a halfback named Burt Reynolds, but I don't remember much about him playing in the game.

In 1956, which ended up being my senior season, we beat East Carolina pretty good and then lost at Tulane. We won our next five games, beating N.C. State, Florida State, William & Mary, Richmond, and Virginia all pretty good, but then we had to go down and play Clemson in Death Valley. I remember how hot it was down there, and we ended up losing 21–6. We played Wake Forest at home the next week, and I blocked an extra point kick late in the game to preserve a 13–13 tie. We blew out VMI 45–0 in Roanoke in the last game and finished 7–2–1 during my senior season.

After leaving Virginia Tech, I got drafted by the Detroit Lions in the 16th round in 1957, but I tore up my knee during training camp and never played again. So I started teaching school and coached football in Buena Vista, Virginia, for two years and then got married. I went into business with my wife's father.

I'll always remember my time at Virginia Tech. It reminded me a lot of my hometown in the mountains. I just enjoyed the people who were there with me. They were all very congenial. After I had to leave and join the military, I came back and my grades were much better. I even made the dean's list one quarter. The military service really straightened me out. If it wasn't for the military, I probably would have never played football at Virginia Tech and finished school.

Hilmer "Swede" Olson was a member of Virginia Tech's 1954 team that finished 8–0–1 and ranked No. 16 in the country, and was a starting lineman and linebacker on the 1955 and 1956 teams. Olson

and his family operated a crab processing plant in Hampton, Virginia,
for more than 35 years, and he still lives in the southeast Virginia city.

Hokies in Their Own Words
BILLY HOLSCLAW
QUARTERBACK, 1954–1958

I was raised in Charleston, West Virginia, and my uncle, Duncan Holsclaw, had played at Virginia Tech in the early 1930s. I never really visited Virginia Tech before I went to school there. The first day I stepped foot on the Virginia Tech campus was the day I went to play football. I had visited some other schools before, but my uncle had always talked about Virginia Tech while I was growing up. I don't know why, but I always said, "Well, that's where I'm going to go." I just made up my mind that I was going to go to Virginia Tech.

I visited Vanderbilt, West Virginia, Virginia Military Institute, and a few others. But I never really wanted to visit anywhere else. I just knew I was going to go to Virginia Tech. One of the Virginia Tech coaches came over with the scholarship papers, and I signed them and showed up in the fall.

Luke Lindon was the equipment manager back in those days, and he had been with coach Frank Moseley for a long time. Luke was a big old guy. He was a wrestler, really. When I went to Virginia Tech before my freshman season, I was standing outside the gymnasium where they gave out equipment in the basement. I was listening to the veterans talking about going to get their equipment, and I didn't say much because I was a freshman. But I heard them talking about how they didn't want to go down to see Luke.

It kind of got me uneasy when I was called to go down and get my equipment. So I went down, and there Luke was sitting behind some of those Dutch doors with his arms crossed, sitting on the counter. I walked up to him, and he said, "What do you want?" I was kind of scared and said, "I'd like to get my football equipment." He said, "What? Football equipment? You're no football player. You're not big enough to play football, son. You better turn around and go back out that door."

Luke was serious, too. I said, "No, I'm supposed to get my football equipment." He looked at me and said, "Okay, but you'll probably be back in here to turn the equipment back in after two or three days." After that, I kind of ended up loving him, really. He was kind of a folklore person in Virginia Tech football all through the 1950s and was something else.

I was scared to death of Coach Moseley until I got through school. I kind of get choked up when I talk about him. If it wasn't for him, I would have never gotten through school. I would have never had the family that I have. And I would have never ended up coaching football. When I came out of West Virginia, I was kind of wild. But Coach Moseley helped me a lot, and I got out of school and graduated with my teaching degree. All of that happened because of him and the coaching staff that was there. All those coaches there at the time really helped me get through school.

When I went to school at Virginia Tech, all of the athletes were in H Company and the ROTC. It was tough on me. Even though I ended up going into the National Guard and Army after college, it was hard. We had to march and all of that and had the ROTC classes and so forth. At the end of my sophomore year, they gave us the option of staying in the ROTC program or getting out. I decided to get out, and a lot of other guys got out as well.

Billy Holsclaw played football for four seasons at Virginia Tech and was the first Hokies quarterback to throw for 1,000 yards in a season when he had 1,013 yards and nine touchdown passes as a senior starter in 1958. He became a very successful high school football coach in Virginia.

Before my freshman season in 1954, they brought in a lot of freshman players. The freshman team went undefeated, and the varsity team went undefeated, too. It kind of scared me when I went over there because there were about five quarterbacks who came into Virginia Tech that fall. I had been a tailback in a single-wing offense in high school in Charleston and had never played quarterback before. When I came in at Virginia Tech, I was starting fresh under the center. I had never gotten up under the center before.

The adjustment to playing quarterback took me a little while. It didn't take me long to get used to getting under center. I played on the freshman team in 1954, and they redshirted me in 1955. My inexperience at playing quarterback was maybe one of the reasons they decided to redshirt me.

They had a lot of quarterbacks on the team: Jimmy Lugar, Bobby McCoy, and Billy Cranwell, who was a sophomore who had taken over the varsity team when Johnny Dean got hurt. That team went undefeated in 1954, and Cranwell started again in 1955. Bobby McCoy had gotten hurt, too, and everybody was fighting for the quarterback job during each of those first three seasons.

In 1956 Lugar had taken over at quarterback, and I played defense, because you played both ways, and Coach Moseley played me a little bit at running back. The following season in the fall of 1957, Cranwell came back from an injury and started at quarterback. I played enough to letter those two years, playing defense and tailback. I played a little bit at quarterback, but I wasn't playing much. I didn't play a whole lot of it.

Finally, before my senior season in 1958, Coach Moseley decided to give me a chance at quarterback, and I made the most of it, I guess. I think Coach Moseley thought during those first couple of years that I was a little erratic and a little inconsistent. But that last year, he gave me a chance to go. He told me during the spring that it was my job to lose and said, "I'm going to let you go with it." Thank goodness I was able to hold onto the job and played the season out.

I made my first start at quarterback in the 1958 season opener against West Texas State in a game we played at Victory Stadium in Roanoke. I had a fairly decent game starting out. Back in those days, we didn't throw the football very much. But starting in 1958, Coach Moseley was going to open the offense up a little bit. We had been a running team all those years. During that era, teams ran all the time and didn't throw much. But he was going to open it up a little bit. So in that first game, I completed six of 12 passes for 150 yards and two touchdowns and rushed for 53 yards. We won the game 28 12, and that game got me started off pretty good.

We played Wake Forest the next week in Norfolk, Virginia, and lost 13–6. We won our next two games, over William & Mary and Virginia, but then lost two in a row and then tied North Carolina State. The receiver who caught the game-winning conversion pass in one of the games we lost, 21–20 at West Virginia, played fullback with me at Charleston High School in West Virginia. He had lined up over the tackle, making him ineligible, but the officials didn't see it, and we lost the game. Florida State just annihilated us and beat us bad.

We only had five seniors on that 1958 team and finished with a 5–4–1 record. After the season, Coach Moseley said he was satisfied with the way the season came out. When I go back and think about the games, my fondest memories are that we weren't supposed to be very competitive or very good that year. We ended up with a winning record but easily could have won seven games with the way the West Virginia game ended and tying North Carolina State.

Everybody hung together and played hard, and despite only having five seniors and a bunch of new players, we had a pretty good season. I thought it was a good year and got a chance to play, which made me happy. It was also special because my cousin, Duncan Holsclaw, was on the team with me.

After I finished playing football at Virginia Tech, I came back and helped coach during the spring of my senior year. I helped with the freshman football team and helped with the quarterbacks. Moseley let me do that and started letting me learn how to coach. Of course, I think that put me into 40 years of high school coaching. When I was in school, I really didn't know if I would go into coaching or not. But when he let me help out that one spring, I guess I got the coaching bug. He was a great influence on my life, really. I probably took it all from Coach Moseley and copied him. I was hard and aggressive. Coach Moseley used to run us a lot after practice and things, and so did I with my teams. I probably copied him step by step. I just came up through that Bear Bryant and Coach Moseley style of coaching and did it for 40 years.

I think all of the guys who came into the Virginia Tech program in 1954 are all still very close and talk to each other and go on golf trips together. We go up to the Monogram Club spring game each year and see each other up there. We're all still very close. When you live with a bunch of guys for five years in a dorm, you're all very close. You're almost like brothers.

Even though Virginia Tech has become so prominent in football in the last 15 years, even back then, I swear to Gus, I always felt during those years that someday we would be where we are right now. When I was coaching high school football and would go back and watch them practice, I always felt we were just on the tip of being really successful. And now it has grown to what it is today.

Billy Holsclaw played football for four seasons at Virginia Tech and was the first Hokies quarterback to throw for 1,000 yards in a season when he had 1,013 yards and nine touchdown passes as a senior starter in 1958. Holsclaw, whose uncle and cousin also played football for the Hokies, later became one of the most successful high school coaches in Virginia, spending 25 seasons as a head coach at Spotsylvania High School, Osbourn Senior High, and Woodbridge High. He retired from coaching in 1987 and lives in Manassas, Virginia.